The Rough Guide to
The Lord
Of The Rings

The Credits

Text editors Paul Simpson, Helen Rodiss, Michaela Bushell
Writer Angie Errigo
Contributors Richard Pendleton, Shaun Campbell, Jess McAree,
Sue Weekes, Dave Burton, Rachel Heels
Production Ian Cranna, Caroline Hunt, Lesley Turner, Kath Stathers
Picture editor Jenny Quiggin
Thanks to Cathrine Keen, Julia Bovis, Mark Ellingham, Simon Kanter, Richard Green,
Martin Tullett, David Brawn, Chris Smith, Marianne Dugan, Amy Handkammer
Cover design Frank Foster
Design Sharon O'Connor
Printed in Spain by Graphy Cems
Dedicated to Jack Simpson, Gavin, Howard, Dominic, IWG

Publishing information

This edition published October 2003 was prepared by Haymarket Customer Publishing
for Rough Guides Ltd, 80 Strand, London WC2R 0RL.
TOLKIEN® is a registered trademark of The JRR Tolkien Estate Limited.
The Rough Guide to The Lord Of The Rings is published with the permission,
but not the approval, of The JRR Tolkien Estate Limited.
The Lord Of The Rings and its constituent volumes, The Fellowship Of The Ring,
The Two Towers and The Return Of The King, and The Hobbit and The Silmarillion are published
by HarperCollins Publishers Limited under licence from the Estate of the late JRR Tolkien.

Acknowledgment

Rough Guides and Haymarket Customer Publishing acknowledge that all opinions
expressed in this work are their own and that they are solely
responsible for any errors or inaccuracies of fact which it may contain.

Distributed by the Penguin Group
Penguin Books Ltd, 80 Strand, London WC2R 0RL.

◁ Gandalf welcomes you to Middle-earth in general and Bag End in Hobbiton in particular

Contents

1. Introduction 37-42

A rough guide to exactly why The Lord Of The Rings
has become the best-read novel of the last century

2. The Origins 43-66

The life and times of JRR Tolkien, and how they led
to the creation of his masterpiece

3. The Books 67-108

The making of The Lord Of The Rings, plus the myths,
themes, subplot interpretations and reviews...

4. The Motion Picture Trilogy 109-148

From printed page to movie screen – how Hollywood finally
turned Tolkien's trilogy into a blockbuster movie

5. The Characters 149-184

Meet the good (most of the hobbits, Aragorn), the bad (Sauron)
and the ugly (the orcs, the uruk-hai) inhabitants of Middle-earth

6. Middle-earth 185-208

A sightseeer's guide to the culture, geography
and language of Tolkien's Middle-earth

7. The Locations 209-240

From South Africa to New Zealand via Birmingham: the
locations which helped inspire and enrich The Lord Of The Rings

8. Ephemera 241-272

The world of The Lord Of The Rings and Tolkien memorabilia,
from first editions to duvet covers and hobbit costumes

9. The Context 273-303

How Greenpeace, 1970s progressive rock, computers and
Russian politics were touched by The Lord Of The Rings

Isildur could resist anything but temptation, so he wasn't the ideal candidate to find the Ring

Gollum springs to life: Tolkien once recorded a passage about Gollum from The Hobbit

A lone wizard riding into town usually meant adventure, and danger, for Bilbo Baggins

Thanks to the Ring, Bilbo Baggins vanished from his own eleventy-first birthday party

Bilbo Baggins lived in Bag End; Tolkien's Aunt Jane's house was known as Bag End to locals

For once, in literature, a night river crossing signifies escape from death, not death itself

Gandalf the Grey traps the Ring in a classic pincer movement

Saruman's genetic experiment with the uruk-hai seems an early precursor of cloning

Aragorn, the hooded hero, strikes a light at the Prancing Pony Inn while waiting for Frodo

Frodo, Sam, Merry and Pippin never knew from where danger would come next

A dark beauty escaping from the ringwraiths: Arwen rides to Frodo's rescue

The ringwraiths ride blithely into the river and into Arwen's windy, watery trap

The Council of Elrond possessed much more gravitas than your average local council

Nephew and uncle were both destined to care for the Ring; Frodo's custody was more painful

The Company embark on a journey that will last nine months but will feel like a lifetime

Gandalf's spells can't open the way to Moria, but Frodo knows a thing or two about puns

The Fellowship enter heroic, and unequal, combat with an enraged cave troll

The sight of Aragorn and his arrows was enough to make even big, stupid monsters quiver

Beautiful and virtuous (she turns down the Ring), Galadriel can see into the future

Knowing Frodo has a painful road ahead, Galadriel gives the hobbit a soothing kiss

The uruk-hai prepare to battle the Fellowship at Amon Hen

Aragorn tells Frodo he has no interest in the Ring. Unlike almost everyone else, he means it

Gandalf the White stages the kind of comeback seldom seen since the Gospels

For Frodo and Sam, the journey gets tougher, the risks greater and the pain harder to bear

Gollum and Sam Gamgee in the Middle-earth equivalent of hand-to-hand combat

Heroes and horses, a pose straight out of a Western

Scrumptious Éowyn isn't just decorative: disguised as a man she slays the Lord of the Nazgûl

The beautiful Éowyn is tormented by hopeless love and Black Breath, the Nazgûl disease

Gríma, aka Wormtongue, and the old king Théoden have a quiet, poisonous chinwag

Aragorn and Éowyn: Two-thirds of what the tabloids might call a Middle-earth love triangle

Théoden, king of Rohan, healed by Gandalf, shakes off the decay that almost killed him

The conflict with Saruman was messy, unpredictable and savage, just like a real war

For Aragorn and Théoden conflict is almost perpetual, the need for vigilance is constant

Legolas and his comrades lead a charge against the forces of Saruman

Wormtongue and Saruman: two sharply contrasting hairstyles, one nefarious purpose

Helm's Deep: a battle so intensely imagined and filmed, it could have been real

Elendil, father of Isildur, mariner and warrior extraordinaire

Wicked! Tricksy! False! These kind of creatures simply abound in Tolkien's Middle-earth

Super hero: Orlando Bloom, alias Legolas, says Superman inspired him to become an actor

Tolkien being such a fine linguist, British fans assume 'Legolas' is a pun on 'legless'

One critic called The Two Towers "one of the greatest swashbucklers ever"; you can see why

From the east, famed for bravery, the Easterlings are Mongols by any other name

For a studious Oxford don, Tolkien had a surprising ability to imagine all kinds of monsters

The first scene for Karl Urban (Éomer) involved 300 orcs and 500 men on horseback

The Rohan are Vikings with medieval armour and a genetic bent towards fine horsemanship

Literary gent: Orlando Bloom (Legolas) is named after a character in a Virginia Woolf novel

Elrond realises that having Aragorn as a son-in-law means Arwen won't live forever

Éowyn was hopelessly devoted to Aragorn – but eventually finds solace with Faramir

Stout Fellows: Legolas, Gandalf and Aragorn keep Sauron distracted from Frodo

Merry, as played by Dominic Monaghan, is the tallest hobbit – standing 5ft 7in tall

Legolas and Aragorn: both parts might have been played by other actors

Wormtongue's loss is Faramir's gain: he wins Éowyn's hand in marriage

Frodo Baggins is a different Hollywood hero: thoughtful, self-sacrificing and not a braggart

For such a thoroughly nice Fellow, Sam Gamgee could be very useful when it came to a fight

Peter Jackson is a method director: to direct hobbits he needs to become a hobbit

Picture Credits

INTRODUCTION

THE LORD OF THE RINGS:
A MASTERPIECE AGAINST THE ODDS

Gandalf the wizard changes hue – from grey to white – but never changes sides

"I HAD GIVEN A GREAT DEAL MORE THOUGHT TO THE MATTER
BEFORE BEGINNING THE COMPOSITION TO THE LORD OF THE RINGS;
AND THAT WORK WAS NOT SPECIALLY ADDRESSED TO CHILDREN OR ANY
OTHER CLASS OF PEOPLE. BUT TO ANYONE WHO ENJOYED A LONG
EXCITING STORY, OF THE SORT THAT I MYSELF NATURALLY ENJOY"

Tolkien, in a letter to the New Statesman

"This is not a work which many adults will read through more than once," the *Times Literary Supplement* noted snootily in 1954 in its review of The Fellowship Of The Ring, the first instalment of JRR Tolkien's trilogy. In 1961 the critic Philip Toynbee went even further, gleefully predicting that the whole Rings craze was passing into "merciful oblivion".

It's easy to laugh in hindsight but neither they, nor Tolkien, could have foreseen that, as the 1960s came into their own, the work of a proudly old-fashioned, deeply religious, pipe-smoking specialist in obscure and ancient languages and dialects would connect with half-stoned 19-year-olds on campuses throughout Britain and America. Stranger still, the pop cultural moment that proved the *Times Literary Supplement* and Toynbee so spectacularly wrong took place in a TV series starring the manufactured teenybop idols The Monkees. Drummer and singer Mickey Dolenz, for reasons that even he cannot now quite remember, pinned a button to his poncho which said: 'Frodo Lives!'. "I do remember people reading the books, comparing notes, so I had the buttons made and handed them out," Dolenz recalled. "It was a cult thing."

Yet even though the first two movies based on the trilogy have taken nearly $1.8 billion at the box office, making them the seventh- and fifth-biggest grossing movies of all time, it still is a cult thing. While Tolkien is hobbit-forming, as the graffiti on campus walls used to proclaim in the 1960s, the trilogy's popularity has continued to irritate, dismay and infuriate some serious literary critics, the heirs of the *TLS* and Toynbee. Although you can study Tolkien at sundry American campuses, the books are still not regarded as academically respectable. It's exactly the same kind of snobbishness which, 50 years ago, dictated that Charles Dickens wasn't fit to be studied as part of an English degree. As **Terry Pratchett**, author of the acclaimed **Discworld** series of fantasy novels, puts it: "The Lord Of The Rings is a cult classic. I know that's true because I read it in the newspapers, saw it on TV and heard it on the radio. We know what 'cult' means. It's a put-down word. It means 'inexplicably popular but unworthy'. It's a word used by the guardians of the true flame to dismiss anything that is liked by the wrong kind of people."

The most obvious evidence that many people, especially those who like to think of themselves as opinion-formers, just don't get **Tolkien** is the derision heaped on his fans. They have been variously dismissed as nerds, geeks or, as the satirical magazine *Private Eye* once put it: "Those with the mental age of a child, computer programmers, hippies and most Americans." The regularity with which the books top various polls as the greatest novel of all time – or at the very least of the 20th century – has only served to wind up the snipers even more.

The obvious explanation for such hostility is the work itself. The Lord Of The Rings trilogy isn't avant-garde or brilliantly witty. It doesn't – as many Penguin Modern Classics would routinely boast on their jacket – "offer a devastating critique of contemporary society." It is not written in pursuit of a fashionable intellectual theory, nor is it superficially clever. But it is intelligent – fabulously so in its detailed creation of an alternative world –

> IF TOLKIEN DIDN'T ACTUALLY INVENT THE FANTASY GENRE, HE CERTAINLY DEFINED IT

though even his defenders concede that **Tolkien** is not a great prose stylist (although the books are far, far more readable than critics usually allow).

Then there's the fact that the problems with which the books (and **Tolkien**) seem to grapple aren't that intellectually fashionable. *The Lord Of The Rings* isn't modernist, let alone post-modernist. For some, as **Michael Stanton** (author of Hobbits, Elves And Wizards) says, "There's something comforting about being able to inhabit a world where the rules are a little clearer and the struggle between good and evil is sharply delineated." For others, brought up in the less absolute ways of secular humanism, such simplicity seems threatening.

Yet think what the world would be like without the trilogy. If **Tolkien** didn't actually invent the fantasy genre, he certainly defined it. His influence can be found in the works of novelists as diverse as Ursula Le Guin, Margaret Atwood, Alan Garner, Stephen King, Stephen

Peter Jackson and Viggo Mortensen pick their favourite Lord Of The Rings trading cards

Donaldson and JK Rowling. There is a vast sub-cultural continent called Dungeons & Dragons – not to mention the role-playing games which have followed from it – and such Japanimated children's sagas as Pokémon and Dragon Ball Z, which would not exist in the same way without *The Lord Of The Rings*. The trilogy inspired many rock acts – from Marc Bolan to Led Zeppelin to Marillion – and the founder of Greenpeace.

Six of the ten greatest box-office hits of all time are Tolkien influenced. As well as Peter Jackson's definitive *The Fellowship Of The Ring* and *The Two Towers*, there are the first two Harry Potter films, plus two Tolkienesque space operas: Star Wars and Star Wars: The Phantom Menace.

You don't have to agree with Tolkien politically, religiously or even philosophically to enjoy the Rings trilogy, because at the heart of the books is a very powerful story, a tale which has all the authority of myth. Many others have tried to dress up their fiction with mythic touches, but most of them have failed because, chiefly, they didn't understand or love mythology as much as Tolkien did. But Tolkien's mythology – and this is another point of difference which may have led to his work being misunderstood – isn't the usual Greco-Roman tradition you find in most Western literature. It's the old myths of the North. When Tolkien pored over languages he was fascinated by Finnish, an academically neglected language outside the European mainstream.

The photographs of the genial, pipe-smoking, bufferish don in his study can be misleading. Tolkien dared to be different, and the product of that daring (and his originality of mind) continues to enthral millions today. He might not have worried about his popularity but, being an essentially kind bloke, he might secretly have been chuffed to hear that some readers had found personal solace in his books in hard times.

That, again, is deeply unfashionable, but in a world full of novels whose main aim seems to be to achieve a certain notoriety or impress you with the writer's knowledge – as if the novel were just an excuse for the author to do his Michael Caine "not a lot of people know that" routine – it's not such a bad thing to have a work that sometimes changes people's lives. Even if, as Pratchett has pointed out, we should remember, with sympathy, all the children called Galadriel or Bilbo whose parents lived on a commune in Wales or in a camper van in Cornwall in the 1960s.

THE ORIGINS

THE LIFE, TIMES AND INSPIRATIONS
OF JRR TOLKIEN

"One Ring to rule them all"

"EALA EARENDEL ENGLA BEORHTAST OFER
MIDDANGEARD MONNUM SENDED"
["HAIL EARENDEL BRIGHTEST OF ANGELS ABOVE
THE MIDDLE-EARTH SENT UNTO MEN"]
from Crist, by the Anglo-Saxon poet Cynewulf

✦ The Creator Of Middle-earth ✦

JRR Tolkien was a 45-year-old professor of **Anglo-Saxon** at Oxford University when The Hobbit was published. The erudite philologist and sometime poet was pleasantly surprised by the success of what had begun as an amusement for his children, but he was in his sixties when The Lord Of The Rings – his 'sequel' that evolved into an awe-inspiring epic – finally appeared. And he was well into retirement by the time the work had grown from cult reading to cultural phenomenon.

Although he was gratified by the appreciation, **Tolkien** was bemused to find himself the object of obsessive fan worship. In his later years the demands of his enthusiastic correspondents and unlooked-for visitors made him more anxious than ever to complete what he regarded as his true literary life's work, The Silmarillion. But it is for *The Lord Of The Rings* that he will be remembered, and the story of its creation is interwoven with his own quietly remarkable life story.

John Ronald Reuel Tolkien – Ronald to his family, John Ronald to school chums – was born in Bloemfontein, capital of the Orange Free State, in South Africa on 3 January 1892. His father, Arthur Reuel Tolkien, was descended from an 18th-century Saxon immigrant to England (Tolkien is a corruption of *Tollkühn*, which means **foolhardy**), and the Tolkien family had prospered as piano-makers. But the family business had been lost and by the late 19th century their circumstances were severely reduced. Having gone into banking, Arthur moved to South Africa hoping for speedier advancement and, with things going well, sent for his fiancée, **Mabel Suffield**, the well-educated daughter of an old Midland family also fallen into impoverished gentility. As soon as she arrived, Mabel, only 21, and Arthur, 34, married in Cape Town cathedral. They set up home 700 miles away in Bloemfontein and nine months later Ronald arrived, his brother **Hilary** following two years later.

Arthur flourished in Bloemfontein but the oppressive climate did not agree with Mabel or young Ronald, so when Ronald was three Mabel took the children to England for an extended visit. The plan was for Arthur to join them, but by the time Ronald had regained his health, his father had become stricken with rheumatic fever and died shortly afterwards. The child was left with just a single memory of his father – a moustachioed man painting his name on a piece of family luggage.

At first the family stayed with Mabel's parents, the Suffields. Ronald developed a deep affection for them and their middle-class Englishness, and also for their pride in their origins in Evesham, Worcestershire. (An aunt had a farm called Bag End there, and his brother Hilary would settle there as a fruit farmer.) As a result, Tolkien saw himself as a true West Midlander both by blood and in spirit. This identification was to play an important part in his specialised academic interests and in his writing.

When **Tolkien** was just four, Mabel rented a cottage in Sarehole, a quiet hamlet south of Birmingham. This was to make a huge, lasting impact on the boy. "I loved it with an intensity that was a kind of nostalgia reversed," he once said. "It was a kind of double coming home, the effect on me of all these meadows."

IN BIRMINGHAM, TOLKIEN ACQUIRED SOME LOCAL VOCABULARY, INCLUDING THE WORD 'GAMGEE' FOR COTTON WOOL

That summer the boys ran freely in the English countryside. They were enchanted by the meadow, an old mill on a stream and Moseley Bog, and by some deliciously scary locals, whom they dubbed **The Black Ogre** (a farmer) and **The White Ogre** (a dust-coated miller), who chased them. "The two of them were perishing little nuisances," the miller recalled to one local shortly before his death. No coincidence, then, that hostile millers appear in several Tolkien stories.

Ronald, now learning botanical drawing, became interested in nature, embracing his surroundings. The boys also acquired some local vocabulary, including the word 'gamgee' for cotton wool (named after the Birmingham doctor who'd invented a dressing made from it). All these memories would resurface decades later in *The Lord Of The Rings*.

It was also in Sarehole that Mabel began schooling Ronald at home. At four he could read and write. Not much later he showed a startling

The Tolkien name is derived from a word meaning foolhardy, but JRR was no fool

The Tolkien Family
THE KEY PEOPLE IN JOHN RONALD REUEL'S LIFE

EDITH TOLKIEN (wife)

Edith Bratt was born on 21 January 1889 in Gloucester. She was 19 when she first met JRR Tolkien, in 1908. A fellow boarder (and fellow orphan) at the lodgings arranged for Tolkien and his brother Hilary by their guardian, Father Francis Xavier Morgan, her "engaging manners and artistic charms" (playing the piano and dancing were particular talents) made a deep impression on Tolkien, who was three years her junior.

Edith and JRR were engaged in 1914 and were married in March 1916. She bore him four children.

Edith died on 22 November 1971 after a short illness and was buried in a grave (where she was joined by her husband two years later) in Wolvercote cemetery in Oxford.

The headstone reads "Edith Mary Tolkien, Lúthien, 1889-1971. John Ronald Reuel Tolkien, Beren, 1892-1973", a reference to Tolkien's tale of Beren and Lúthien for which Edith had been the inspiration; she had danced for Tolkien in the woods at Roos, near Hull, when he was stationed there, and he had always regarded her as "his Lúthien".

JOHN FRANCIS REUEL TOLKIEN (son)

JRR Tolkien's eldest son was born in Cheltenham in November 1917 and named after both his father and the priest who had been his father's guardian, Father Francis Xavier Morgan.

Following in the footsteps of both his namesakes, John ardently practised the Catholic faith. He entered the seminary, studied in Rome and then returned to England to serve as a parish priest. He died in January 2003, aged 85.

MICHAEL HILARY REUEL TOLKIEN (son)

The second son of JRR Tolkien was born in October 1920 and, like his father, he embarked upon an academic path. He attended Trinity College and, after serving in the Royal Air Force, became a schoolmaster.

Michael's teaching career included a spell at Stonyhurst College and St Mary's Hall at Hurst Green in the Ribble Valley, where he taught Classics from the late 1960s to the early 1970s. This renewed a family link with the college; JRR Tolkien had stayed there with his eldest son, John, during World War II –

Tolkien was a man of many parts: novelist, poet, philologist, pipe smoker, rugby player

a period when he penned much of The Lord Of The Rings. John had been evacuated from the English College in Rome to the Jesuit seminary at St Mary's Hall, now the preparatory school for Stonyhurst College (whose Jesuit roots date from 1593). Michael died in 1984.

CHRISTOPHER REUEL TOLKIEN (son)

Born in November 1924, Christopher went to Trinity College and became a college lecturer. He ultimately completed and published many of the works begun by his father before his death. He completed The Silmarillion,

published in 1977, as well as Unfinished Tales and the History Of Middle-earth series.

During World War II he was a pilot in the Royal Air Force and was consulted by JRR on various aspects of his writing. He also drew many of the Middle-earth maps.

PRISCILLA MARY REUEL TOLKIEN (daughter)

The last of the Tolkien's four children, Priscilla was born in 1929. After completing her degree at Lady Margaret Hall, she became a probation officer and social worker in Oxford.

Tolkien at an age where he was beset by "Snoopers, Goopers and transatlantic lion hunters"

aptitude for Latin and an extraordinary ear for language – although he was less inclined to study French. He did later learn Spanish, Italian and Russian, but more because he thought he ought to than from any real enthusiasm for modern tongues. He was also greatly taken with fairy tales, such as those compiled by George MacDonald and Andrew Lang. He especially liked ones with dragons, and in particular Lang's adaptation for children of the Icelandic *Volsunga Saga*, **The Story Of Sigurd** in the *Red Fairy Book*. At seven, he tried writing his own first story, about "a green great dragon".

But eventually Tolkien had to join his peers at school and his mother decided on King Edward's Grammar School in Birmingham, his father's old school and the city's best. The downside was that it meant leaving Sarehole after four formative years, the family moving into a succession of dreary accommodations. The situation was not helped by Mabel's decision to convert to **Catholicism** – a decision which extended to the two boys. This caused a rift with outraged Protestant Tolkien and Suffield families, who promptly withdrew all their financial support.

> AT SEVEN, TOLKIEN TRIED WRITING
> HIS OWN FIRST STORY, ABOUT
> "A GREEN GREAT DRAGON"

By 1904 Mabel had become careworn and exhausted. Diagnosed with diabetes, she was hospitalised for months. To aid her convalescence, her confessor and friend Father Francis Xavier Morgan arranged pleasant country lodgings and care for her and the boys, but in November that year she died. Ronald was 12 years old.

Mabel had made **Father Francis** her sons' guardian, and he boarded the boys with an apparently dreary relative near Birmingham Oratory. There, every morning before school, they came to assist him at Mass, have breakfast and plague the rectory cat. They joined the parish's new Boy Scout troops, and during holidays the priest took them to the Oratory's country retreat at Rednal, where they roamed the woods and the Lickey Hills, and to the Dorset seaside town of Lyme Regis in summer.

Immersed in classical studies, Tolkien was happy at school. He was for a time captivated by "the surface glitter" of Greek and was mightily impressed by his form master George Brewerton, who read Chaucer's Canterbury Tales aloud in the original **Middle English**. Later he was inspired by headmaster Robert Cary Gilson to pursue philology – the science of languages, their development and their relationships – while

·v·

Stræt wæs stan fah stig wisode gumum
æt gædere guð byrne scan heard
hond locen hring iren scir song in searwum
þa hie to sele furðum in hyra gry
re geat wum gangan cwomon setton
sæmeþe side scyldas rondas regn heard[e]
wið þæs recedes weal · bugon þa to bence
byrnan hring don guð searo gumena
geatwas stodon sæman na searo samod
æt gædere æsc holt ufan græg · wæs
iren þreat wæpnum ge þur þad þa þær
þa on hæleð oret mecgas æfter hæle
þum frægn · hwanon ferigeað ge fæt
te scyldas græge syrcan 7 grim helmas
here sceafta heap ic eom hroð gares
ar 7 ombiht · ne seah ic el þeodige þus
manige men modiglicran · wenic þ ge foro

Ancient script from one of Tolkien's favourite Anglo-Saxon poems, Beowulf

Brewerton introduced him to Anglo-Saxon (or Old English), the language in which the dragon-slaying warrior-hero Beowulf is immortalised. Tolkien marvelled at Sir Gawain And The Green Knight in Middle English, thrilled to discover that it preserved the West Midland dialect spoken by his ancestors. (His translation, in collaboration with EV Gordon, was first published in 1925, and has since become a classic edition of this poem.)

Tolkien then began to teach himself Old Norse so he could read the original text of Sigurd, the story that he had so loved in childhood, and demonstrated an extraordinarily precocious linguistic facility and knowledge. From this he moved on to a serious lifelong preoccupation, inventing his own languages and alphabets. As children, he and his cousin Mary had already evolved a private language called Nevbosh (New Nonsense). In adolescence he conceived Naffarin, influenced by Father Francis's Spanish books (the priest was part Spanish and spoke the language fluently). After discovering the remnants of the dead Gothic language – in a primer by Joseph Wright, who would later, as his Comparative Philology lecturer at Oxford, prove to be one of his biggest inspirations – he began systematically creating words to fill in the gaps.

When he was 16, Tolkien and his brother were relocated by Father Francis, who hoped they would enjoy more congenial company and the musical evenings at lodgings run by a Mrs Faulkner. He would soon rue the day he made that decision however, after Ronald became friendly with the pretty 19-year-old in the room below.

Edith Bratt was also an orphan, whose training and aspirations as a pianist had been cut short by her situation. Though Ronald was three years younger than her, he looked more mature and had gentlemanly manners. The pair shared a premature experience of suffering, spent whole nights leaning out of their windows talking, and subsequently fell in love.

After belatedly discovering the infatuation, Father Francis took drastic action – primarily because Ronald was supposed to be concentrating on winning a scholarship to Oxford. If the good Father had had more experience in affairs of the heart, he might not have reacted as he did, and the youthful romance might not have continued. But he immediately moved the boys to other lodgings and, after Ronald failed his scholarship exam and had been seen with Edith, his unhappy guardian forbade him to see her again before he turned 21. To defuse the situation, Edith left Birmingham to stay with elderly friends in

Cheltenham, adding the glamour of banishment to their separation.

Ronald now threw himself into the male company of his school, devoting his time to rugby, the debating society and the informal gatherings of his small clique: best-friend Christopher Wiseman, Robert Quilter Gilson (the headmaster's son) and later Geoffrey Bache Smith. Calling themselves first the Tea Club, then the Barrovian Society and finally TCBS (a combined acronym of these names), the clever and literary youths met for high-spirited teas with poetry recitations (including their own juvenile verse) and amusements, including Tolkien's dramatic re-tellings of Norse and Finnish mythology.

In December 1910 Tolkien won an Open Classical Exhibition award to Exeter College, Oxford. A bursary from his school and continued help from Father Francis enabled him to take his place in November 1911. But before going up to Oxford he and Hilary found time to fit in a walking tour of Switzerland. There Tolkien was nearly killed in a rock fall on a glacier, but was dazzled by the adventure and the spectacular scenery. Among the souvenir postcards that he bought was Joseph Madlener's painting *Der Berggeist* (The Mountain Spirit), depicting an old, bearded man in a cloak. Many years later he wrote on the paper in which he had carefully kept it wrapped: "Origin of Gandalf."

Oxford was wonderful to Tolkien – he fell in love with the place as soon as he arrived, driven there by a kind schoolmaster. Diverted by his insatiable taste for Northern and Germanic literature, he neglected his required Classics work (by then he had already become bored with Latin and Greek). But he made many friends, played rugby, joined several societies and formed the Apolausticks (much like the TCBS but with alcohol and pipes of tobacco, for "those devoted to self-indulgence"). He savoured the sound of Welsh, studying its medieval form, and was "intoxicated" by Finnish – he wrote a paper in which he envied the Finns their ancient myths and ballads of the Kalevala: "I would that we had... something of the same sort that belonged to the English." Putting Gothic aside, he began inventing a Finnish-inspired language that evolved into Quenya, now known to us as High Elvish. More seeds had been sown.

On the day he turned 21, Tolkien lost no time in writing to Edith, eager to marry after three years spent idolising her. She wrote back – but only to

> TOLKIEN SAVOURED THE SOUND OF WELSH, STUDYING ITS MEDIEVAL FORM, AND WAS "INTOXICATED" BY FINNISH

Frontline action at the Battle of the Somme, where Tolkien served in the Lancashire Fusiliers

deliver the shattering news that she had become engaged to another man. Tolkien refused to accept that he had lost her and promptly took a train to Cheltenham to persuade her to change her mind. But personal happiness interfered with his work and, having tried to cram a year's work into six weeks, he achieved only a Second Class in the crucial Honour Moderations (examinations which counted towards his final degree). However, his Comparative Philology paper was so remarkable, and his particular gifts so apparent, that Exeter College recommended he switch from Classics to the English School and Linguistics.

Tolkien could now pursue the intense connection that he felt to the West Midland dialect in Middle English, the speech of his ancestors. The treasury of Icelandic myth and lore of the Elder Edda in Old Norse became another speciality for him. Old English, too, still had a host of revelations for him, such as those two lines from the religious poem Crist by Cynewulf: "Eala Earendel engla beorhtast/ofer middangeard monnum sended."

"I felt a curious thrill," Tolkien recalled. "There was something very remote and strange and beautiful behind those words, if I could grasp it,

JRR, CS Lewis & The Inklings
THE WRITERS' SUPPORT NETWORK THAT KEPT JRR GOING

Friends, rivals and fellow fantasists, JRR Tolkien and CS Lewis had a deep and complex relationship for nearly 40 years. While parallels in their lives and work often link them in readers' minds, there were sharp differences between Tolkien and the author of the popular Chronicles Of Narnia.

On his return to Oxford as a professor, Tolkien longed to recapture the fellowship of the TCBS, and so he formed the Kolbitars (Coalbiters), a reading group for several Oxford dons with whom he could share his pleasure in Icelandic literature (in the original language, naturally) and a good whisky.

In 1926 he met another brilliant scholar and medievalist, Clive Staples Lewis (universally known as Jack), then 27 and a Fellow of Magdalen College in English Language and Literature. Lewis joined the Coalbiters, and he and Tolkien became great chums.

They shared intellectual insights and religious debate; cheerfully argued the merits of fantasy writers William Morris, Lord Dunsany and George MacDonald; and were equally indifferent when it came to dress and passionate about Norse mythology.

For years the two met up on Mondays after lectures and headed for the pub; in between, late-night sessions in Lewis's rooms saw the friends smoking their pipes, discussing college politics and assessing each other's writing.

Lewis urged Tolkien to keep going on The Silmarillion and Tolkien would say of him, "The unpayable debt that I owe to him was not 'influence' as it is ordinarily understood, but sheer encouragement. He was for long my only audience. Only from him did I ever get the idea that my 'stuff' could be more than a private hobby." Lewis joked that he had been taught never to trust a papist or a philologist, but Tolkien was both.

Like Tolkien, Lewis lost his mother when he was very young. He also had a brother, Warren, to whom he remained close (indeed, the inseparable Lewis brothers share the same grave). Lewis, too, fought in the trenches of World War I.

Unlike Tolkien, however, Lewis's experiences had made him an agnostic. It was Tolkien's arguments that brought him to a belief in God. Another devoutly Christian friend, Hugo Dyson (a lecturer at Reading University), often joined them, and it was after one particular long night deep in conversation with these two men that Lewis experienced a complete conversion.

The Inklings were an informal literary circle of male friends who congregated around the jovial Lewis from the early 1930s, meeting to read each other their work in progress.

The most famous Inklings are Lewis, Tolkien and poet, playwright and novelist Charles Williams, but Dyson, WH 'Warnie' Lewis, Chaucer expert Nevill Coghill and Tolkien's Catholic neighbour and doctor RH Havard were also regulars.

Lewis's epiphany had been profoundly influenced by Tolkien, but his choice of the Anglican Church rather than Roman Catholicism disappointed Tolkien, who became increasingly uncomfortable with Lewis writing religious allegories and with his second, high-profile career as a moralist.

Tolkien also liked Williams very much, but not his Celtic-flavoured, romantic, Christian quest fantasies (notably War In Heaven and

Descent Into Hell) or his influence on Lewis. He also thought Williams's 'Arthurian' notions ruined That Hideous Strength, the third in Lewis's sci-fi fantasy trilogy whose hero Ransom, the questing interplanetary philologist, was based on Tolkien.

Still, Lewis championed The Hobbit and through the 1940s put the pressure on Tolkien whenever he was distracted from writing The Lord Of The Rings. It was chiefly the Lewis brothers and Williams to whom Tolkien read new chapters in a pub as he progressed, heartened by their praise. When Williams died suddenly in 1945 it was a terrible blow and the small, precious circle of intimates began to shrink.

After Lewis accepted a professorship at Cambridge in 1954 and married Joy Davidman (the love affair dramatised in Shadowlands), Tolkien found himself more solitary than he had ever been – or than he liked.

When Lewis died in 1963 Tolkien, writing to his daughter, likened himself to an old tree that had suffered "an axe-blow near the roots". On Tolkien's death in 1973 The Times published an affectionate and penetrating appreciation with an obituary prepared long before... by Lewis.

Fellow Inkling, fantasy novelist and moralist CS Lewis

far beyond ancient English." In 1914 he wrote a poem inspired by the lines, **The Voyage Of Earendel The Evening Star**. His old TCBS pal GB Smith asked what the original lines were about. "I don't know," Tolkien replied. "I'll try to find out." It was this simple request which marked the beginning of his most impassioned labours.

But by then World War I had begun. After getting his degree – with First Class Honours – Tolkien joined the Lancashire Fusiliers as a second lieutenant with the 13th Battalion (not, as he had hoped, the 19th Battalion in which his friend GB Smith was already serving). He married Edith in March 1916 but his embarkation orders to France were not long in coming and he arrived in Calais on 6 June, in time to take his place in the horror of the **Battle of the Somme**.

Rob Gilson was the first of his youthful fellowship to die, followed by GB Smith, who succumbed to gas-gangrene after being injured by an exploding shell. "The immortal four" had become two – Tolkien and Christopher Wiseman (after whom Tolkien's youngest son would be named), who was serving in the Royal Navy. Most of his other friends

Tolkien's Religion
THE BELIEFS UNDERPINNING THE WRITING

Reconciling Tolkien's devout Catholicism with his work can be tricky, since God is never mentioned in the pre-Christian world of his mythology. But he was surprised, and a little disappointed, that the Roman Catholic press largely ignored his monumental work. ("One of my most charming notices, however, was in The Tablet of New Zealand," he noted with pleasure.)

From serving as an altar boy to his final Sundays spent attending church and visiting his wife's grave, Tolkien found consolation and contentment in his religion, and deep joy in receiving the sacrament of the Eucharist.

Whenever he was unable to go to confession he denied himself the Eucharist – and he was hard on himself in the insecurities he suffered following the death of his mother.

He felt she had suffered and died for their religion since it had estranged her from her immediate family; failure to observe that religion would be to discredit her. He never outgrew that ardent, youthful piety.

Tolkien wrote not to moralise but to entertain. He was critical about the religious aspects of CS Lewis's novels. But the quests and battles of his elves, men, wizards, dwarves and hobbits are in keeping with his belief that God gives men, via imagination, glimpses of an underlying cosmic truth: "Always I had the sense of recording what was already 'there': not of 'inventing'."

In The Silmarillion the great angelic powers, the Valar, are subject to the One, unseen but omnipotent. The mythology is built on Tolkien's understanding of morality and a true universal order. The legends that spring from there all deal implicitly with the relationship between nature and supernature, with the conflict between heaven and hell and with the doctrine of free will, classically expressed in The Lord Of The Rings in the choice of embracing or rejecting the power of the Ring.

The mercy Bilbo and Frodo show Gollum is their salvation; their suffering earns them passage to the next world. That is, presumably, what Tolkien hoped for himself. For a different interpretation of the book's possible religious meaning, turn to page 296.

Thoughts On Tolkien
UP CLOSE AND PERSONAL WITH TOLKIEN

"I was lucky enough to meet Tolkien, you know. He was a charming man and always laughing. For me, he was the greatest author of his time. I was speechless in his presence."
Christopher Lee, actor

"My main impression of him was how incredibly nice he was. I never remember him being angry or upset in any way."
Simon Tolkien, grandson

"He is a great enough magician to tap our most common nightmares, daydreams and twilight fancies... Let us at last praise the colonisers of dreams."
Peter S Beagle, author

"He is slightly smaller than I expected. Disconcertingly, he seems to think I know The Lord Of The Rings as well as he does. I cannot hear everything that he is saying... whole phrases are elided in the haste of emphasis."
Humphrey Carpenter, biographer, on his first meeting with JRR Tolkien

"Tolkien was a most genial man with a steady twinkle in his eyes and a great curiosity – the sort of person one instinctively likes... While he talked he stood up and walked about or sat on his cot. [He] continually fiddled with his pipe but actually smoked little. As his talk grew in enthusiasm, he would sometimes put his face almost against mine, as though to make sure he was completely understood. One had the feeling that he had thought considerably about whatever opinion he was expressing and simply wanted to state it accurately. He told me that he had many times been given a story as an answer to prayer."
Clyde S Kilby, professor at Wheaton College, Illinois, USA

"He had a hatred of all things Hollywood and did not believe in the idea of imitation being the best form of flattery."
Michael White, biographer

"I knew and liked Tolkien, who in a bufferish sort of way was very kind to me and encouraging."
Michael Moorcock, critic

"Professor Tolkien lectured to the floor, had a speech impediment

and was all too often given to wandering off into Welsh cognates. I met a classmate of Tolkien's who told me good old Ronald ('whatever became of him?') was deeply inquisitive about backwoods Kentuckians who grew pipeweed and had names like Baggins and Barefoot."
Professor Guy Davenport, author

"Tolkien was a good man, moral and upright, trustworthy and very intelligent, but he was not in line for canonisation."
Michael White, biographer

"Tolkien was a very loyal man and he trusted you completely. We got on fine because in a sense, I think, he felt I understood him from way back when I was ten years old."
Rayner Unwin, 'responsible' for The Hobbit's publication

"The greatest inventor of language and legend in my lifetime."
Christopher Lee

"At Magdalen College it became apparent that, for me, the guide of guides was going to be a plain-looking, waistcoated man with a quicksilver mind, Professor Tolkien. I saw Tollers at weekly intervals. He puffed at his pipe while I told him of my work. He made acute

observations. He beamed when I made some discoveries. Now and then he mentioned the hobbits, but he didn't press them on me."
Robert Burchfield, author, lexicographer and former editor of the Oxford English Dictionary

"Tolkien set out with a good heart to write a good story. The goodness of the former shines forth in the latter."
Joseph Pearce, author of Tolkien: Man And Myth

"[His Catholicism] was so important. He was practically raised by a Catholic priest. It was so important to him – a major part of his life, really."
Michael Coren, journalist

"The greatest living poet."
George Sayer, English Master at Malvern College, Oxford

"The author was very attached to his childhood memories, and his view of 'Englishness'. He was fond of 'plain food', and disliked continental cuisine and its impact on English tastes. He mourned the loss of a simpler, agrarian society and regretted the noise and fume of industrialisation."
Jim Layman, regional director, Campus Crusade for Christ

Tolkien at Merton College, Oxford, where he served as a Fellow until his retirement in 1959

and comrades were also killed. In what proved ultimately to be a blessing, Tolkien came down with pyrexia (**trench fever**) on 27 October, and having been taken from the trenches to hospital in Le Touquet, on 8 November he found himself on a boat back to England and a reunion with Edith. A return to the trenches was a lingering possibility, but his convalescence was slow and recurring relapses of illness – possibly stress-related – ruled out any further participation in combat.

By this time, he recalled, "I had in mind to make a body of more or less connected legend... which I could dedicate simply: 'To England, to my country'." Wiseman had encouraged him to start his epic and, during his convalescence in 1917, he wrote **The Fall Of Gondolin**, the first story for his *Book Of Lost Tales* that would become *The Silmarillion*. He refined Quenya and developed a second, 'everyday', elven language, Sindarin, modelled on Welsh. His first child, **John Francis**, was born in November 1917. It was around this time that Edith inspired the most romantic of all Tolkien's legends, the passionate love story of the mortal man Beren and the elven beauty Lúthien, the ancestors of Aragorn and Arwen.

EDITH INSPIRED TOLKIEN'S MOST ROMANTIC LEGEND, THE LOVE STORY OF THE MORTAL BEREN AND THE ELVEN BEAUTY LÚTHIEN

At the end of the war Tolkien returned to Oxford, where he and Edith made their first real home, supported by his work compiling entries for the monumental **New English Dictionary**. Their second son, **Michael Hilary**, was born shortly after Tolkien was appointed as Reader in English Language at the University of Leeds in 1920; the post of Professor of the English Language was then created for him when he was still only 32. His third son (and future map maker, collaborator and literary executor), **Christopher**, had just been born in November 1924 when Tolkien's academic dream came true: he was offered the **Professorship of Anglo-Saxon** at Oxford University.

It's a lasting source of regret to Tolkien's fans that he didn't publish more. But for much of his life his storytelling had to take a back seat to his work as a conscientious professor, and he established himself as a widely influential expert in his field of philology. The evidence is that Tolkien was a **great teacher**, a tutor unusually generous with his time and insights (many of his students became world-class scholars and writers),and a fascinating lecturer who attracted unusually high attendances for arcane linguistic topics. After achieving his own fame as a poet, **WH Auden** wrote to Tolkien: "I don't think I have ever told you what an unforgettable experience it was for me as an undergraduate, hearing you recite. The voice was the voice of Gandalf."

Tolkien marked exam papers to supplement his academic salary. He and Edith raised four children (a daughter, **Priscilla Mary**, was born in 1929) in their modest suburban home; he also enjoyed gardening, attended church faithfully and socialised frequently. That he wrote as much as he did was partly because he was able to work late at night, and partly because of the enormous pleasure and encouragement he found in a group of writer friends among the Oxford dons. This group, **The Inklings** (see page 56), earned their own place in literary history.

The Hobbit was published in September 1937, and by Christmas the first edition had sold out. Its success brought urgent appeals for a sequel, but **Tolkien** wanted to complete The Silmarillion first and was miffed that no one seemed too eager to publish it. Yet he often found himself contemplating how much the ancient world of *The Silmarillion* related to his hobbit characters and their adventures (in effect, *The Lord Of The Rings* can be seen as a sequel to *The Silmarillion*), and gradually the story of the **War of the Ring** took hold of him.

TOLKIEN WANTED TO COMPLETE THE SILMARILLION, BUT THE STORY OF THE WAR OF THE RING TOOK HOLD OF HIM

In his foreword to the second edition of *The Lord Of The Rings* Tolkien charmingly explained, with modest understatement, that it took him until 1949 to finish the book because he had "many other interests as a learner and teacher that often absorbed me." The Inklings cheered him on, listening to each chapter as Tolkien produced it. Finally the phenomenal book appeared. It was **split into three parts** by the publishers (something Tolkien was not keen on) for economic and logistical considerations: the first two volumes were published in 1954 and the third in 1955. Tolkien, as was his wont, practically had to have the work ripped out of his hands, so fretful was he about improvements. He sighed over its imperfections but yielded it up with: "It is written in my lifeblood, such as that is, thick or thin; and I can no other."

There were great reviews (including a glowing one from **CS Lewis**) and carping reviews. There was an immediate readership, but it took more than a decade, a pirated all-in-one volume in America and the counter-culture of the flower children to make Tolkien the author of the age.

The Father Figure
THE FORCE BEHIND TOLKIEN'S FORMATIVE YEARS

When, guided by Mabel's preference for worship at the Birmingham Oratory, the Tolkiens moved to the Birmingham suburb of Edgbaston in 1902, her new parish priest soon came to welcome them. He was 43-year-old Father Francis Xavier Morgan, a boisterous and sympathetic character who owed his fun-loving, loud and generous personality to his mother's Spanish blood rather than to his non-Catholic Welsh father's. He was not academic or intellectual, but he was an old boy of the Oratory School, inspired by its eminent founder Cardinal John Henry Newman (1801-90), under whom he'd served. Father Francis became a kind friend to the Tolkiens, and on Mabel's death he acted as the boys' guardian, a moral compass and benevolent protector.

The Oratory is a community of secular priests with the principle "charity alone to bind them together" but without the rule of a religious order, such as the vow of poverty. So Father Francis had his own private income from a share in his Spanish family's vineyards, from which he supplemented the Tolkien boys' meagre inheritance.

He also had sufficient wisdom to keep Ronald at King Edward's School, rather than at the less scholarly Oratory School.

These financial ties may have influenced Ronald's unhappy compliance in the separation from his sweetheart Edith until he was of age, but he also had genuine respect and regard for the priest, who, amid his parish work and teaching, was a source of jollity, sympathy and encouragement.

Summer holiday reunions at Lyme Regis – chosen initially as Father Francis had friends there – were still a mutual pleasure in the 1930s, with the elderly priest an exuberant surrogate grandfather to the Tolkien children. Ronald's eldest son was named John Francis in his honour, was baptised by Father Francis and was eventually ordained himself.

Father Francis died in 1935, in his Oratory room, aged 76, bequeathing £1,000 each to Ronald and Hilary Tolkien. More importantly, he had given Ronald the constancy of his friendship and a lifelong, old-fashioned respect for the Church, its doctrine, its clergy, and the obligations of a pious, practising Catholic.

It turned his conservative, ordered life upside down, fans inundating him with queries and bizarre gifts, telephoning from the other side of the world, or as Tolkien himself bemoaned "Hoopers, Snoopers, Goopers, press-gangs, phone-bugs, and transatlantic lion hunters and gargoyle-fanciers." Arguably he was lucky to pass away before the interest in the fantasy genre that he inspired peaked in a craze for 'other world' trilogies or series that veer from wonderful to cringe-making.

When it became too much, the Tolkiens retired quietly to **Bournemouth**, more for the increasingly infirm Edith's sake than for her husband's. When she died at 82, Tolkien had her gravestone inscribed with her elven name Lúthien. Although his family and friends rallied round, he was lonely. He was glad to return to Oxford, where the rare honour of a **resident honorary fellowship** was bestowed on him by Merton College, with rooms in a college house. In the next two years he was showered with honours and honorary doctorates, and received a CBE from the Queen.

Tolkien expected to live to a great age, but nevertheless he attempted to re-order his endless rewrites of *The Silmarillion* for completion by his son Christopher. Visiting friends in Bournemouth at the end of August 1973, he was suddenly taken ill. He died a few days later, aged 81, on 2 September, and was mourned the world over. Buried with Edith in the cemetery at Wolvercote on the outskirts of Oxford, **JRR Tolkien**'s own elven name, Beren, was added to their gravestone.

THE BOOKS

THE CREATION, THE PLOTS, THE INSPIRATION,
THE CRITIQUES, THE MYTHOLOGY

Bilbo Baggins: the little hobbit whose adventures started something big

"IN A HOLE IN THE GROUND THERE LIVED A HOBBIT"

The opening line of The Hobbit

✦ How It All Began ✦

Neither **JRR Tolkien** nor his children could remember when it was that he started telling them the adventures of a little hairy-footed fellow called Bilbo Baggins. But the writer felt sure that he had spontaneously scrawled what became the first line of The Hobbit on a piece of scrap paper without knowing why he had written it or what to do with it. He was wading through some exam papers when he came across a blank sheet of paper, on which he scrawled the now famous line about a hobbit.

There is, as you would expect, quite some debate over the etymology of the word hobbit. Robert Burchfield, former editor of the *Oxford English Dictionary*, found the term mentioned in a list of 197 supernatural creatures in a series of pamphlets called **The Denham Tracts**, collected by a Yorkshire tradesman in the 1840s. It's just as possible that Tolkien never read these and instead created hobbit as a play on rabbit.

But he did not, until a very long time after he had written Bilbo's tale, realise the connections to be made between the hobbits' world and the mythology of The Silmarillion, which was still a growing collection of legends, poems, rewrites of rewrites and incomplete thoughts.

Tolkien had published a number of poems, *A Middle English Vocabulary*, scholarly linguistic and literary essays, some humorous verse and an eminent edition of *Sir Gawain And The Green Knight* when, probably early in the 1930s, he began to write the children's story that became a popular classic. Ultimately it was also to become the bridge between his long-nurtured lore and his masterpiece, The Lord Of The Rings.

The Critics' Views

"Some who have read the book, or at any rate have reviewed it, have found it boring, absurd and contemptible; and I have no cause to complain, since I have similar opinions of their work"

JRR Tolkien

"Here are beauties which pierce like swords or burn like cold iron."
and
"Like lightning from a clear sky... heroic romance, gorgeous, eloquent and unashamed."
and
"No imaginary world has been projected which is at once so multifarious and so true to its own inner laws; none so seemingly objective, so relevant to the actual human situation yet so free from allegory."
CS Lewis
on The Lord Of The Rings

"A combination of Wagner and Winnie the Pooh."
John Heath-Stubbs
on The Lord Of The Rings

"A unique, wholly realised other world, evoked from deep in the well of time, massively detailed, absorbingly entertaining, profound in meaning."
The New York Times
on The Fellowship Of The Ring

"It has been my nightmare that Tolkien would turn out to be the most influential writer of the 20th century. The bad dream has materialised."
Germaine Greer on JRR Tolkien

"The first thing one asks is that the adventure should be various and exciting... Tolkien's invention is unflagging."
and
"If someone dislikes it, I will never trust their literary judgement about anything again."
and
"For anyone who likes the genre to which it belongs, the Heroic Quest, I cannot imagine a more wonderful Christmas present."
and
"A masterpiece of its genre."
WH Auden
on The Lord Of The Rings

"An astonishing, imaginative tour de force."
Daily Telegraph
on The Return Of The King

"A work of immense narrative power that can sweep the reader up and hold him enthralled for days and weeks."
The Nation
on The Lord Of The Rings

"The wars are never dynamic; the ordeals give no sense of strain; the fair ladies would not stir a heartbeat; the horrors would not hurt a fly."
and
"A children's book which has somehow gotten out of hand."
and
"...juvenile balderdash."
Edmund Wilson
on The Lord Of The Rings

"An extraordinary work – pure excitement, unencumbered narrative, moral warmth, bare-faced rejoicing in beauty, but excitement most of all."
New York Times Book Review
on The Two Towers

"Among the greatest imaginative fiction of the 20th century."
Sunday Telegraph
on The Lord Of The Rings

One of the most remarkable works in our, or any, time."
Bernard Levin
on The Fellowship Of The Ring

"These books have passed into a merciful oblivion."
and
"...dull, ill-written and whimsical."
Philip Toynbee
on The Lord Of The Rings

"Tolkien's stories take place against a background of measureless depth. That background is ever-present in the creator's mind and it gives Frodo and company a three-dimensional reality that is seldom found in this kind of writing."
Washington Post Book World
on The Lord Of The Rings

"This is escapist fiction at its finest, yet at the same time it has profound relevance to our troubled age."
Arthur C Clarke
on The Return Of The King

"No fiction I have read in the last five years has given me more joy."
WH Auden
on The Fellowship Of The Ring

"John Buchan for teenagers."
Michael Moorcock
on The Lord Of The Rings

"One of the great fairy-tale quests in modern literature."
Time magazine
on The Lord Of The Rings

> "I HAVE CHOSEN MR BAGGINS...
> THERE IS A LOT MORE IN HIM THAN YOU GUESS,
> AND A DEAL MORE THAN HE HAS ANY IDEA OF HIMSELF"
>
> **Gandalf silences the dwarves' concerns about Bilbo**

The Hobbit:
✦ Or There And Back Again ✦

The Hobbit is a children's book. It can stand entirely alone without its far darker, adult 'sequel' and without any understanding of Tolkien's mythology – although he does give young readers a simple introduction to runes and the key to translating Thrór's Map (the guide to the book's journey, which he drew before the tale had taken shape in his mind). It isn't strictly essential to read *The Hobbit* before The Lord Of The Rings, either; in fact it has put some people off ever reading the great work because they erroneously imagine it, with dread, to be another thousand pages of the same. The prologue of *The Lord Of The Rings* summarises the parts of *The Hobbit*'s story most pertinent to later events: how Bilbo Baggins acquired the Ring.

For grown-ups The Hobbit's chief interest – apart from the appeal it may claim as a charming, chattily styled, peril-packed 'story of long ago' – is that it introduces, lightly and with simplicity, for his own pleasure, characters and themes Tolkien would explore deeply in *The Lord Of The Rings*. The Hobbit, the bulk of which was written down quickly by Tolkien's standards, grew out of 'the leaf mould' of his memories (of Sarehole and stories of dragons, of respectable rustic forebears and courageous wartime comrades, of a walking tour in the Alps).

In *The Hobbit* we are introduced to Mr Bilbo Baggins, 50 years old, well-to-do, enjoying a cosy little life in his homely hobbit hole in The Hill "long ago in the quiet of the world, when there was less noise and more green." Tolkien was not in the least embarrassed to acknowledge humorously, "I am, in fact, a hobbit in all but size," citing his love of gardens, trees, pipe-smoking, good plain food, mushrooms and

Bilbo Baggins was having a nice quiet life until Gandalf came along…

ornamental waistcoats. Bilbo and Tolkien also share an absorption in their genealogy, their roots, in maps, runes and letters.

Bilbo is placidly smoking his pipe on his doorstep one day in spring when a peculiar, big, old man with "long bushy eyebrows that stuck out further than the brim of his shady hat" introduces himself as the celebrated wandering wizard Gandalf. To Bilbo's dismay, terror and wonder, Gandalf sends a party of 13 dwarves, led by Thorin Oakenshield, descended from kings, to partake of Bilbo's hospitality and enlist him in their dangerous quest: to reclaim their ancestral treasure from the lair of the dreadful dragon Smaug under the Lonely Mountain. Gandalf mischievously claims bourgeois Bilbo has been chosen because he is an expert burglar; it is hinted, however, that he knows it is important for Bilbo to play his part in an adventure with far-reaching consequences.

> BAGGINS AND TOLKIEN SHARE AN ABSORPTION IN THEIR GENEALOGY, THEIR ROOTS, IN MAPS, RUNES AND LETTERS

On their journey Bilbo and the dwarves are captured by trolls and rescued by Gandalf; from the trolls' loot, Gandalf takes the elven sword Glamdring (Foe-hammer) and Bilbo acquires an elven dagger he will name Sting. The Company have a rest in Rivendell as guests of the kind, fair and noble Elrond – chief of a house "who had both elves and heroes of the North for ancestors" – who helpfully translates the ancient runes on their treasure map. Next they are captured by goblins in the Misty Mountains. They are rescued by Gandalf but they lose Bilbo who, in the dark depths of the goblins' realm, finds a ring and meets the nasty Gollum whose "preciousss" it is. They engage in a riddle game until, accidentally discovering the ring makes its wearer invisible, Bilbo effects his escape, leaving the despairing Gollum shrieking: "Thief, thief, thief! Baggins! We hates it, we hates it, we hates it forever!"

Next the Company are cornered by goblins and wolves. They are rescued by the Lord of the Eagles and recover with Beorn, a skin-changer who is sometimes a fierce man and sometimes a great bear. Gandalf departs on mysterious business concerning a malevolent character referred to as the Necromancer. The dwarves are captured in Mirkwood by great spiders and rescued by the invisible, Sting-wielding Bilbo, only to be taken prisoner by wood elves. Again they are rescued by Bilbo, who is growing in the dwarves' estimation for his bravery and usefulness.

After they reach their destination, Bilbo's invisibility enables him to discover Smaug's weak spot, although the dragon-slaying falls to a man named Bard. Bilbo's most important reward from the treasure is a small coat of mail, made, for a young elven prince, of mithril (silver steel) with a belt of pearls and crystal. Gandalf reappears in time for the climactic Battle of Five Armies, in which elves, men and dwarves unite to defeat goblins and wild wolves. The Elvenking utters a prophetic farewell to Gandalf: "May you ever appear where you are most needed and least expected." Bilbo finally arrives back home, a year after he left, to find his cousins, the Sackville-Bagginses, helping themselves to his property, after which they will never be on good terms. His reputation for respectability is ruined but he happily settles down to write his memoirs.

Tolkien showed his unfinished typescript of *The Hobbit* – abandoned for several years after he smote Smaug – to a former student who was doing some work for the publishers George Allen & Unwin in 1936. She told a colleague about it, the work-in-progress went to London, and soon he had a request to finish it. When he had, Rayner Unwin, the ten-year-old son of the publishers' chairman Stanley Unwin, was paid a shilling to write a report on it. He wrote that Bilbo "had a very exciting time" and "it is good and should appeal to all children between the ages of five and nine." Thus *The Hobbit*, with Tolkien's own illustrations, was published in September 1937. A rave review in *The Times* stated: "All who love that kind of children's book which can be read and re-read by adults should take note that a new star has appeared in this constellation." The review was written by CS Lewis.

Before Christmas a second printing was already necessary. In America *The Hobbit* won best new children's book honours from the *New York Herald Tribune* and became a perennial seller. (In 1951 a second, revised, edition was published with Tolkien's rewritten Chapter V, Riddles In The Dark, in which Bilbo encounters Gollum and makes off with the Ring, altered to tally with the account of Gollum in The Lord Of The Rings.)

Within weeks of its publication Stanley Unwin asked for a sequel. Doubtless what he had in mind was a brand new hobbit adventure, which he probably assumed an author as clever as Tolkien could knock out within a year.

Bilbo Baggins's adventures meant storytime in the Shire was not to be missed

"THANK YOU FOR YOUR MOST KIND LETTER AND FOR
YOUR GENERAL INTEREST IN MY WORK. I AM HOWEVER
NOW AN OLD MAN STRUGGLING TO FINISH SOME OF HIS
WORK. EVERY EXTRA TASK HOWEVER SMALL DIMINISHES MY
CHANCE OF EVER PUBLISHING THE SILMARILLION"
JRR Tolkien in a letter to Michael Salmon

✦ The Silmarillion ✦

Tolkien did, in fact, write a first chapter, 'A Long-expected Party', for the proposed *Hobbit* sequel within days. But his priorities lay elsewhere. He was hopeful now of publishing The Silmarillion and wrote to Stanley Unwin – who was trying politely to deflect those hopes – "I am sure you will sympathise when I say that the construction of elaborate and consistent mythology (and two languages) rather occupies the mind, and the Simarils are in my heart... And what more can hobbits do? They can be comic, but their comedy is suburban unless it is set against things more elemental."

The Silmarillion was eventually published in 1977, four years after Tolkien's death. In it we learn of the beginnings of Middle-earth and are introduced to characters who will later feature in *The Lord Of The Rings*. The novel tells of the creation of the world by Ilúvatar (God) and the 'sub-gods' known as the Valar who have considerable powers themselves – they can, for example, raise mountains. In the land of Valinor live seven Valar and seven Valier, their queens. There is also another member of the Valar called Melkor, who turns to evil and takes on a role similar to that played by Lucifer. His evil servants include dragons, balrogs (one of whom reappears in *The Lord Of The Rings*) and the disgusting spider Ungoliant. Shelob is described in *The Lord Of The Rings* as "the last child of Ungoliant to trouble the unhappy world."

The book contains a series of discrete stories and legends that mostly revolve around the Silmarils, three radiant jewels wrought by the master craftsman Fëanor, that are coveted and fought over in much the same way as the One Ring. A number of the great elves who appear in *The Lord Of The Rings* also oppose Melkor's will (later Morgoth) in these battles: Galadriel, Glorfindel, Elrond and Círdan. One important story, the love of the elf princess Lúthien for the mortal man Beren, is later echoed in the love of Arwen and Aragorn. It is Beren who eventually steals a Silmaril from **Morgoth**, who has captured them, and while dying, returns it to Lúthien's father, thus fulfilling his Quest for the right to marry her. The story is important because it explores one aspect of the ambivalent and wary relationship between men and elves that is seen more clearly in *The Lord Of The Rings*.

The Silmarillion also introduces us to Sauron, Morgoth's servant and the **Dark Lord of The Lord Of The Rings**. Sauron is responsible for corrupting the men of Númenor, who take up arms against the Valar and whose island, west of Middle-earth, is consequently drowned in punishment. Sauron attempts to corrupt elves, posing as their friend and helping their smiths in Eregion to forge 16 of the 20 rings of power.

The elves intend to use these rings to preserve and heal the beauties of Middle-earth, but Sauron seduces them into thinking this will enable them to create a land as beautiful as Valinor, where they can rule instead of the Valar. In secret, he forges his own ring which reveals to him the thoughts of those who wear the others, and allows him to enslave and control them. The elves, perceiving his intention, stop using their own three rings and hide them – but Sauron captures **their creator Celebrimbor** and tortures him into revealing the whereabouts of the others. Nine of these he gives to kings of men, who are enslaved to his will and become the ringwraiths. Seven go to dwarves, but Sauron is unable to bend these creatures to his will. Of the seven he recovers some, while the rest are consumed by dragons. The three elven-rings he never finds: they are too well hidden, and when Sauron loses the One Ring the elves are able again to use the three.

The Silmarillion ends with the Final Alliance of Men and Elves against Sauron, where he is cast down and the One Ring cut from his hand by Isildur. Later ambushed by orcs, Isildur loses the Ring in the river Anduin... where it is eventually picked up by Sméagol (Gollum) to begin the events of *The Lord Of The Rings*.

"THE ROAD GOES EVER ON AND ON
DOWN FROM THE DOOR WHERE IT BEGAN.
NOW FAR AHEAD THE ROAD HAS GONE,
AND I MUST FOLLOW, IF I CAN"

Gandalf's song in The Fellowship Of The Ring

The Long Road To
✦ The Lord Of The Rings ✦

When Tolkien did have a crack at a sequel to *The Hobbit*, he soon decided a younger hobbit (initially Bingo Baggins, son of Bilbo) would undertake a journey with his cousins (then Odo and Frodo). He had it in mind to discover that Bilbo's ring has magical properties other than invisibility, and wrote down "make return of ring a motive". Then he wrote to Unwin, making what may well be the greatest understatement in publishing history: "Stories tend to get out of hand and this has taken an unpremeditated turn."

The Black Riders, the dark realm of Mordor, the unmasking of the Necromancer as the ancient and terrible Sauron rising back to power, the revelation that Bilbo's ring is the ruling Ring that will make Sauron invincible, the idea that it had to be thrown into the Crack of Doom to be unmade, and the title The Lord Of The Rings (who is Sauron) were among the many turns the story began to take before 1938 was over. It was no longer a children's book, and it was only a sequel in that it inherited the hobbits, setting them against things more elemental and more profound, rooted in the lore and legend of the Elder Days of his imaginary world. Tolkien had entered into a personal challenge to combine his mythology, theology, philosophy and poetry into a cohesive narrative. It would be 16 years before the public "clamouring… to hear more from you about hobbits" (as an optimistic Unwin wrote to Tolkien) would be satisfied.

Tolkien made good early progress, but he had the demands of his Oxford University workload, domestic crises and awful bouts of writer's block to contend with. There were months when he had to let

He Also Wrote...

THE FRUITS OF TOLKIEN'S LITERARY LABOURS

"I had great difficulty to get my story published,
and it is not easy to say who is most surprised at the result:
myself or the publishers! But it remains an unfailing delight...
that the 'fairy story' is really an adult genre, and one
for which a starving audience exists"

JRR Tolkien

The interest in Tolkien's long-awaited trilogy failed to persuade him to increase productivity in the genre, but Tolkien could still be described as a prolific literary scholar (for a complete list, go to www.tolkiensociety.org). He had a fervent desire to create a new world for his audience, while his unbridled love of languages meant that much time was taken up with translations...

A Middle English Vocabulary The Clarendon Press, Oxford, 1922

Sir Gawain & The Green Knight Ed. JRR Tolkien and EV Gordon; The Clarendon Press, Oxford, 1925

Songs For The Philologists Department Of English, University College, London, 1936

The Hobbit: Or There And Back Again George Allen & Unwin, London, 1937

The Reeve's Tale Ed. "J.R.R.T."; Oxford, 1939

Sir Orfeo The Academic Copying Office, Oxford, 1944

Farmer Giles Of Ham George Allen & Unwin, London, 1949

The Adventures Of Tom Bombadil And Other Verses From The Red Book George Allen & Unwin, London, 1962

Ancrene Wisse: The English Text Of The Ancrene Riwle Early English Text Society, Original Series No. 249, Oxford University Press, London, 1962

Tree And Leaf George Allen & Unwin, London, 1964

The Tolkien Reader Ballantine, New York, 1966

Smith Of Wootton Major George Allen & Unwin, London, 1967

The Road Goes Ever On: A Song Cycle Houghton Mifflin, Boston, 1967

Bilbo's Last Song George Allen & Unwin, London, 1974

Sir Gawain & The Green Knight, Pearl And Sir Orfeo

Ed. Christopher Tolkien, George Allen & Unwin, London, 1975
The Father Christmas Letters Ed. Baillie Tolkien, George Allen & Unwin, London, 1976. Reprinted (with minor omissions) in three mini-volumes, HarperCollins, London, 1994; as Letters From Father Christmas, Houghton Mifflin, Boston and HarperCollins, London, 1995
The Silmarillion Ed. Christopher Tolkien, George Allen & Unwin, London, 1977
Pictures By JRR Tolkien Ed. Christopher Tolkien, George Allen & Unwin, London, 1979
Unfinished Tales Of Númenor And Middle-earth Ed. Christopher Tolkien, George Allen & Unwin, London, 1980
Letters Of JRR Tolkien Ed. Humphrey Carpenter with Christopher Tolkien, George Allen & Unwin, London, 1981
The Old English Exodus Ed. Joan Turville-Petre, The Clarendon Press, Oxford, 1981
Mr Bliss George Allen & Unwin, London, 1982
Finn And Hengest: The Fragment And The Episode Ed. Alan Bliss, George Allen & Unwin, London, 1982
The Monsters And The Critics And Other Essays Ed. Christopher Tolkien, George Allen & Unwin, London, 1983

The History Of Middle-earth series:
The Book Of Lost Tales, Part I Christopher Tolkien, George Allen & Unwin, London, 1983
The Book Of Lost Tales, Part II Christopher Tolkien, George Allen & Unwin, London, 1984
The Lays Of Beleriand Christopher Tolkien, George Allen & Unwin, London, 1985
The Shaping Of Middle-earth Christopher Tolkien, George Allen & Unwin, London, 1986
The Lost Road And Other Writings Christopher Tolkien, Unwin Hyman, London, 1987
The Return Of The Shadow Christopher Tolkien, Unwin Hyman, London, 1988
The Treason Of Isengard Christopher Tolkien, Unwin Hyman, London, 1989
The War Of The Ring Christopher Tolkien, Unwin Hyman, London, 1990
Sauron Defeated Christopher Tolkien, HarperCollins, London, 1992
Morgoth's Ring Christopher Tolkien, HarperCollins, London, 1993
The War Of The Jewels Christopher Tolkien, HarperCollins, London, 1994
The Peoples Of Middle-earth Christopher Tolkien, HarperCollins, London, 1996

his teeming ideas and multiple plot strands percolate before he could proceed. His friends **CS Lewis** and **the Inklings** encouraged him, voicing suggestions and criticisms (which he typically ignored, particularly Lewis's frank opinions of the poems). His son Christopher was similarly supportive, and contributed by drawing the map of Middle-earth for his father. And then Britain went to war with **Nazi Germany**.

Two of Tolkien's sons served (Christopher joining the RAF much to his father's deep distress, not only because it was so dangerous but because he deplored aerial war as morally indefensible) and Tolkien did his turn as an air-raid warden. He wrote bitterly: "I have in this war a burning, private grudge against that ruddy little ignoramus Adolf Hitler for ruining, perverting, misapplying and making forever accursed that noble northern spirit, a supreme contribution to Europe, which I have ever loved and tried to present in its true light."

It had been Tolkien's lifelong love of **Norse mythology** that informed much of *The Lord Of The Rings*; he absolutely loathed what he saw as the counterfeit Germanic-Scandinavian mythology that was presented in Wagner's *Der Ring Des Nibelungen* opera cycle and grotesquely misappropriated into Hitler's Aryan master-race claptrap.

Just naming characters, places and things in what he called his act of "sub-creation" took careful thought, since Tolkien constructed them from his invented Elvish languages **Quenya** and **Sindarin**. He also had to invent additional languages, or at least their basics, such as **Westron** (the common speech of men and hobbits), **Adûnaic** (the speech of the Dúnedain of Númenor, Aragorn's ancestors), **Khuzdul** (the secret language of the dwarves) and the **Black Speech** of Sauron and his servants. As a result, it was 1947 before Tolkien thought he was nearly done.

Rayner Unwin, who'd given his approval to *The Hobbit* as a ten-year-old, was by this time studying at Oxford and was shown the unfinished manuscript. His assessment was cautiously positive: viewing it "weird" but "brilliant", though he added "I don't know who is expected to read it."

Tolkien finished it, revised it, added an epilogue and revised it again. In 1949 he gave the manuscript to Lewis, who wrote a letter of affectionate and effusive congratulations: "The steady upward slope of grandeur and terror (not unrelieved by green dells, without which it would indeed be intolerable) is almost unequalled in the whole range of narrative art known to me... **All the long years you have spent on it are justified.**"

The Lord Of The Rings is driven by the plain, powerful narrative device of a great journey

But the long years were to stretch still longer. Tolkien was disenchanted with Allen & Unwin because they had shown no enthusiasm for *The Silmarillion*, which he wanted published alongside The Lord Of The Rings. He subsequently entered into a lengthy discussion with another publisher, Collins, where he was encouraged to believe both books would be welcome. Stanley Unwin again turned to his son, now at Harvard University, for his opinion of the matter; Rayner saw no necessity for *The Silmarillion*, a view which disappointed Tolkien.

After a heated exchange of ultimatums, Tolkien pinned his hopes on Collins. But his champions there went abroad, an international paper crisis impacted on publishing costs, and Tolkien was left dangling. In the middle of 1952 the dispirited 60-year-old wrote a humbled appeal to Rayner Unwin, at last a member of the family firm: "Better something than nothing! Years are becoming precious."

Hedging their bets, Allen & Unwin offered Tolkien a profit-sharing contract rather than royalties. Any profits the book made after its production costs were covered would be split equally between Tolkien

The Quest For Meaning

COULD SAURON AND FRODO REALLY BE HITLER AND JESUS?

"Tolkien's The Lord Of The Rings is undoubtedly the most influential fantasy book ever written. It is the paradigm for cod-epic, conservative secondary world fantasies." So said sci-fi writer China Miéville, quoted in 2000, in the International Socialism Journal.

Any time a critic reaches for the word paradigm, you know you're in trouble. But Miéville, like the rest of us, is struggling with the endlessly debated issue: what exactly is The Lord Of The Rings really about?

It's an easy question to ask, but a hard one to answer. For John Yatt, writing in The Guardian, the trilogy is a work of racism "soaked in the logic that race determines behaviour." For David McTaggart, one of the founders of Greenpeace, the key to the books is the author's warning about the destruction of the environment. For Elisabeth Carey, writing for the New England Science-Fiction Association, The Lord Of The Rings is "permeated with Catholic moral theology... [and] about moral choices." For Julian Dibbell in the Village Voice, it is the "sine qua non of

geek culture." For professional controversialist Germaine Greer the book is "Nazi tosh", although opinion remains divided on whether she has actually read the books or merely been appalled, when she studied at Cambridge in the 1960s, by the sight of so many of her contemporaries reading them.

For other critics, the high elves' retreat from Middle-earth to return "west across the sea" is Tolkien's allusion to the end of the British Empire and the independence of India. Others have seen the books as a reaction to World Wars – although opinion differs on whether it was memories of the First or anticipation of the Second which drove Tolkien.

The recent release of the films has even prompted some American liberals to suggest that the Rings trilogy is pro-war – a position tenable only if you ignore the suffering that Tolkien witnessed at first hand in World War I.

Meanwhile sci-fi novelist Michael Moorcock, one of Tolkien's fiercest critics, sees the menace of Sauron and his henchmen as a conservative's fear of the communist mob.

For WH Auden and Tom Shippey (the latter is the author of JRR Tolkien: Author Of The Century), the meanings are more abstract: Frodo is Everyman, his quest the quest we all share for self-knowledge, while the Ring's sinister charm is society's struggle to handle power.

If nothing else, the sheer variety of interpretations suggests that The Lord Of The Rings is a subtler, richer experience than many of its critics allow. If it were really a book of annoying verse, dreadful songs, unfunny humour and a suffocating earnestness, would we all still be arguing over what it means?

The author himself would have shivered at all this debate. He could get quite cross with those who pointed to certain myths, and would not have had much time for those who equated Sauron with Hitler and the Ring with the atomic bomb – or for those, like the Greenpeace founder McTaggart, who might see the Ring as industrial technology.

This isn't to say that Tolkien's masterpiece is entirely imaginary with no reference to the real world. You can, like McTaggart, find echoes of real events and trends, but the Dead Marshes of Mordor might not be an allusion to industrial destruction of the environment as much as an eerie echo of the trenches which Tolkien saw on the Western front. The fact that there are so many of these echoes (and the sheer breadth of them) militates against any simple, one-dimensional interpretations which claim to tell you the 'real meaning' of the book.

If you want to believe Frodo is a Christ figure (the name may derive from an Old Norse king called Frothi who ruled in a Christ-like fashion), you can – but some readers also find Christ-like elements in Gandalf and Aragorn (the latter's name means king tree in Elvish). You'd be on roughly the right lines; Tolkien may well have agreed with Elisabeth Carey, noting, as he did, that, "The Lord Of The Rings is of course a fundamentally religious and Roman Catholic work; unconsciously so at first but consciously in the revision."

That could end the debate, but with the current fashion for uncovering what authors may have subconsciously put into their novels, expect this one to run and run.

Tolkien's wizards look like druids and sometimes dispense some pretty sinister magic

and them. They also decreed that it would be divided into three volumes. Only **3,000** copies of the first, The Fellowship Of The Ring, would be printed and published, in August 1954, followed by 3,250 of *The Two Towers* in November, and 7,000 of *The Return Of The King* in October 1955. '**A Long-expected Party**' had finally arrived.

✦ The Lord Of The Rings ✦

The Lord Of The Rings is a single novel of a great quest, not a trilogy of serial novels. Allen & Unwin insisted on dividing it into **three volumes**, a strategy **Tolkien** regretted, but one which kept the size and costs of the book manageable. It was also a marketing ploy to get three separate sets of reviews and tempt along readers who would be daunted by its length if presented with the complete novel at once; some people still prefer three slimmer books to a single edition for convenience. Separate titles The Fellowship Of The Ring, The Two Towers and The Return Of The King were agreed upon, although Tolkien's preference for the third was **The War Of The Ring** because it doesn't give anything away. Each volume was divided into two books, with Tolkien's exhaustive, elaborately detailed historical, cultural and genealogical appendices and indexes at the end of the third volume. (These have been omitted in some cheaper editions that have appeared over the years.)

The entire story is set during the **Third Age of Middle-earth**. It is our Earth, imagined at a time long ago and far away. In the peaceful Shire, the race known to men and other big folk as halflings, the **hobbits**, enjoy a comfortable, bucolic lifestyle that evokes an insular and entirely untroubled, pre-industrial England. The wizard Gandalf learns that Sauron the Great, the Dark Lord, has arisen and that **Bilbo Baggins's** magic ring is the greatest of the rings of power wrought in an earlier age. The only way to destroy the Ring and thwart Sauron's bid for world domination is to cast it into the Crack of Doom within **Orodruin**, the fire-mountain. Eighty years after the events in *The Hobbit*, Bilbo's heir Frodo and three companions set out across Middle-earth to return the Ring, pursued by the Black Riders of the Enemy before they reach the help offered by the elven-wise in **Rivendell**. There a company from the free peoples of Middle-earth is formed to safeguard the Ring-bearer: the men are Aragorn, secret heir to an ancient kingship, and Boromir from the land of **Gondor**; the elves are represented by Legolas; the dwarves by the fierce Gimli; with Gandalf and the hobbits Sam, Merry and Pippin to accompany the surprise Ring-bearer, Frodo.

Together they face many perils, but the Fellowship is broken in a tragic sequence of events. Frodo, accompanied by the faithful Sam, continues on to the Crack of Doom in **Mordor**, while his former companions brave their own adventures, each finding a role as they wage the **War of the Ring**, always seeking to confront the Dark Lord and distract him from the indomitable little hobbit's tortuous path and purpose.

"I WILL TAKE THE RING," HE SAID,
"THOUGH I DO NOT KNOW THE WAY"
Frodo speaks up at the Council of Elrond

✦ The Fellowship Of The Ring ✦

THE PLOT Bilbo Baggins celebrates his **eleventy-first birthday** with a party at which he prankishly slips on his magic ring, never to be seen in **Hobbiton** again. Departing on his final journey to the elvish haven of Rivendell, he leaves the Ring and his property to his young nephew Frodo. Gandalf the wizard cautions Frodo to keep the Ring secret and safe. Nearly **20 years later**, having traced the history of the Ring, Gandalf returns and explains to Frodo that it is the One Ring – the greatest ring of power, forged by the Dark Lord Sauron and used by him to enslave the wearers of lesser rings. **Sauron** is searching for it, needing the power invested in it to overcome all opposition. It must be destroyed to save the Shire and Middle-earth from the dominion of Sauron and eternal darkness. Frodo and Gandalf agree Frodo should take the Ring to **Rivendell**. Gandalf chooses Frodo's gardener Samwise Gamgee to accompany him, whilst Frodo's exuberant young cousins Peregrin 'Pippin' Took and Meriadoc 'Merry' Brandybuck insist on accompanying them both.

On their journey out of the Shire, the hobbits find themselves pursued by sinister horsemen clothed in black – the ringwraiths of Sauron, ringbearers corrupted and enslaved to Sauron's will. An inn where the hobbits take refuge is attacked by the riders at night, but they are saved by a mysterious stranger called Strider, a friend of Gandalf who offers to guide them to Rivendell. On the journey they are ambushed and Frodo is stabbed with an evil blade by a Black Rider. Their enemies are swept away by elvish magic at the Fords of Bruinen, but Frodo only just escapes death after last-minute healing from the elf lord Elrond.

In Rivendell, Elrond hosts a council to decide the fate of the Ring. Gandalf is also there, having escaped from the treacherous Saruman the White – an ancient wizard of his order who has been corrupted by Sauron and is now scheming to acquire the Ring for himself. After Frodo volunteers to take the Ring to Orodruin, a volcano in the heart of Mordor, there to cast it into the fire and destroy it, the council decides to give Frodo eight companions on his journey: Boromir from Minas Tirith, Strider (now known as Aragorn), the elf Legolas, the dwarf Gimli, Merry and Pippin, Gandalf and Sam. Bilbo gives Frodo his old sword Sting and a mithril armoured shirt to take with him.

Having failed to cross over the Misty Mountains due to terrible weather, the company decides to take the difficult and dangerous path through the ancient dwarvish mines of Moria. During the journey, Frodo notices that Gollum – the evil, skulking creature from whom Bilbo originally took the Ring – is following them. Disaster strikes near the exit, where the company is attacked by orcs and cave trolls and Gandalf is lost battling a fearful demon of the deep called a balrog. Led by Aragorn, the grieving company reaches the magical elven wood of Lothlórien, where the Lady Galadriel gives them hope, wondrous gifts and, for Frodo, a fearful vision of the Eye of Sauron. The company journeys south by boat to the falls of Rauros, where they are beset by orcs. Corrupted by its evil influence, Boromir attempts to wrest the Ring from Frodo, who puts on the Ring to become invisible and escape. He realises he must leave the company and set out for Mordor.

Tolkien's Influences
THE LITERATURE BEHIND THE LITERATURE

THE ELDER EDDA

The great work of medieval Icelandic literature (in Old Norse) is a collection of 38 poems written down between the 11th and 13th centuries. Fourteen of them are awe-inspiring myths of creation, life and the end of the universe; 24 are legends of the hero Sigurd the Volsung, dragon-slayer, a variation of the Teutonic fifth-century hero Siegfried.

THE VOLSUNGA SAGA

Or Song Of The Volsungs, an Icelandic prose chronicle (also in Old Norse) of Sigurd, written in the 12th or 13th century. Sigurd (whose family were the Volsungs) was born after his father, a king, was slain. In manhood he wrought the broken pieces of his father's sword, Gram, together and with it slew Fafnir the dragon. He also found the Helm of Dread, which made him invisible. But everything ends badly for everyone because of the curse on a dwarf's gold ring Sigurd found in Fafnir's hoard.

BEOWULF

English literature's earliest major work is the epic poem of the heroic, chivalric dragon-slayer, written in Anglo-Saxon by one or more poet-writers in the sixth century. In The Hobbit, Bilbo steals a cup from under the sleeping Smaug, an idea Tolkien may have got from Beowulf's sport with Grendel.

CRIST

A cycle of religious poems by the eighth-century Northumbrian poet Cynewulf, who primarily wrote on the lives of saints. Anglo-Saxon (or Old English) was the literary language of England until the Norman Conquest. Lines from this inspired Tolkien's origination of The Silmarillion.

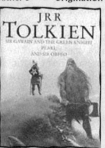
Pages of chivalry

THE KALEVALA

Finland's epic is a collection of medieval song, poetry and chants gathered from peasants and written down in the 18th century. The incanted sound of the language has excited many writers – Henry Wadsworth Longfellow's Song Of Hiawatha imitates the rhythm of The Kalevala, as do some of Tolkien's songs and poems.

SIR GAWAIN AND THE GREEN KNIGHT

A specialty of Tolkien's, this medieval romance verse was written in the 14th century (in Middle English) and presents Gawain – the only knight of King Arthur's Round Table to accept the challenge from the mysterious Green Knight – as the embodiment of the loyal, chivalric ideal.

ANDREW LANG

Tolkien's childhood introduction to fairy tales came courtesy of Andrew Lang's perennially popular Blue, Red, Green etc Fairy Books. And it was in the Red book that he first encountered Sigurd and the dragon Fafnir. He gave the books to his own children, and in 1938 delivered the Andrew Lang Lecture (available as the essay 'On Fairy Stories') in which he crystallised his thoughts on "sub-creation" and fantasy.

the wood Beyond the world

william morris

Morris major

WILLIAM MORRIS

The Pre-Raphaelite artist, designer, illustrator and nature lover – something of a 19th-century, one-man Renaissance – was also a poet and translator who wrote medieval-styled heroic romances. His fabulous The Wood Beyond The World is generally acknowledged as the first real heroic fantasy novel. As an Oxford undergraduate, Tolkien used part of a £5 prize he was awarded in English to buy Morris's translation of The Volsunga Saga and his novel The House Of The Wolfings.

LORD DUNSANY

Familiar to Tolkien and CS Lewis, Dunsany was an Anglo-Irish baron and British officer whose ancestral home was a 12th-century castle in County Meath. Steeped in Celtic legend and song, and inspired by Morris, he wrote influential poetry and short stories combining fairy-tale elements with sophisticated adult themes. His lovely, classic, fantasy novel The King Of Elfland's Daughter encapsulates his own imaginative mythology.

Tolkien's Heirs

THE INFLUENCE OF JRR TOLKIEN JUST GOES ON AND ON…

RICHARD ADAMS

Mythology, creatures going on a quest for the greater good (even if they are rabbits, not hobbits), the source for a powerful feature-length cartoon… the parallels between Richard Adams's most famous novel, Watership Down, and The Lord Of The Rings abound. Happily, Tolkien's work managed to make it to the screen without the involvement of Mike Batt (composer of Bright Eyes) or Art Garfunkel.

STEPHEN KING

The undisputed master of the thriller and spinner of horrific yarns freely admits that his novel The Stand owes a huge debt to Tolkien: "I thought I'd try to make Middle-earth America after the plague." According to King, Stu Redman is an American Frodo who sits around a gas station before embarking on his quest. For more on the links between Stephen King and Tolkien go to

www.geocities.com/Meredith_
Burwood/influence.html

TERRY PRATCHETT

The acclaimed author of the Discworld books puts it succinctly when he says: "We are all standing on Mount Tolkien, influenced by him in some way."

URSULA LE GUIN

The sci-fi maven is most famous for her Earthsea books and her best work is, like Tolkien's, marked by the suspicion that her fantastical world is a product of the past as much as of the future. Le Guin hopes the current sci-fi boom "might even lead to Tolkien being given his rightful place in the academic literary canon."

DAVID EDDINGS

This former English professor and grocery clerk makes no secret of his debt to Tolkien. Titles like The Belgariad and The Malloreon (a bit too close to ersatz-JRR for some) leave little doubt as to his inspiration. Like

Lord of the Downs

Tolkien, Edding infuses his best work with a marvellous, detailed vision of a very different world.

RAYMOND E FEIST

The Californian writer is more than just another Tolkien readalike; his Riftwar series has some fine moments. But you should start with Magician: Apprentice; by the time the Riftwar Legacy starts, the quality control has seriously started to fall apart.

JK ROWLING

For a sensible discussion of the similarities between the two most famous fantasy series of the last 100 years, see http://greenbooks.theonering. net/guest/files/050102.html The most obvious starting point for any discussion about the influence Tolkien may have had on Rowling is to look at the comparative roles of the two scarred orphan heroes, Harry Potter and Frodo.

PHILIP PULLMAN

Sorry JK Rowling, but the most critically rated series of fantasy novels published in the not-too-distant past is actually Pullman's Dark Materials trilogy, which tells the story of plucky heroine Lyra, her daemon Pantalaimon and her best friend Will. The final part of the trilogy, The Amber Spyglass, even won the Whitbread Book Of The Year award. Asked directly about his work's relationship to The Lord Of The Rings, Pullman told the BBC: "I don't think I was doing the same sort of thing as Tolkien. He started by inventing the language the elves speak, he invented a world in which that language could naturally come about and found himself writing stories about that world. I just wanted to tell a story about a girl and a boy growing up, and found myself writing a fantasy about different worlds because that seemed to be the best, most vivid way I could tell that story. On the other hand, I live in Oxford as Tolkien did, I have written a big book in three volumes as he did, and there are fantastical elements in both, so I can see similarities."

STEPHEN DONALDSON

One of the the most gifted writers to be inspired by Tolkien, although some found his trilogy The Chronicles Of Thomas Covenant The Unbeliever just too Tolkien-like for comfort.

"...HOWEVER THE FORTUNE OF WAR SHALL GO,
MAY IT NOT SO END THAT MUCH THAT WAS FAIR AND WONDERFUL
SHALL PASS FOREVER OUT OF MIDDLE-EARTH?"

Théoden foresees the inescapable

✦ The Two Towers ✦

THE PLOT Back to his senses, Boromir dies fighting to save Merry and Pippin who are kidnapped by Saruman's orcs. Legolas and Gimli place the body of Boromir in a boat and entrust it to the river Anduin. Knowing that Frodo is beyond their help – and that Sam has gone with him – Aragorn, Legolas and Gimli set off after the other hobbits. They follow Saruman's orcs for several days, but are unable to catch up. They eventually run into a group of riders from Rohan, the leader of whom, Éomer, tells them the orcs have been killed. He gives them horses and permits them to explore the burning pile of bodies on the edge of the forest Fangorn on condition they come to Rohan's capital, Edoras, afterwards. The three find hobbit tracks suggesting Merry and Pippin escaped the massacre... but no trace of the hobbits themselves. Instead, they meet Gandalf, who has been reincarnated after his battle with a balrog. The four make their way to Edoras. There they find king Théoden, who has become apathetic, suspicious and old before his time thanks to the crooked tongue of his counsellor **Gríma Wormtongue** – a secret spy of Saruman. Gandalf reveals Gríma's true colours and throws him out, thereby freeing Théoden from his influence and persuading the king to take action against Saruman. Rohan musters its men and rides to Helm's Deep, an ancient mountain stronghold, to await attack by Saruman's forces. Saruman's army is defeated, and the riders dash to Saruman's tower at Isengard – only to bump into Merry and Pippin.

The hobbits have wound up at Isengard after escaping the orcs on the edge of Fangorn and meeting Treebeard, the great ent – an enormous tree-like creature. The story they tell of the Ring and Saruman's treachery rouses Treebeard, and he persuades his ents to march on Isengard. There they smash the gates and confine Saruman in the tower by flooding the ring of Isengard. There is a happy reunion with Gandalf, Aragorn and co before Gandalf speaks to Saruman and casts him from the wizards' order. During this, Gríma, who is holed up in the tower, throws a heavy stone from the

In Middle-earth, wizards can come back from the dead – as long as they change colour

window. Pippin is unable to resist looking into this 'palantír', an ancient Númenórean communication device, and is almost interrogated by Sauron before Gandalf drags him away.

While all this is going on, Sam and Frodo continue their journey, stalked by the wretched Gollum. Frodo catches him and holds him as a guide. Gollum appears to be 'tamed', promising not to hurt them and agrees to lead them to Mordor – to which he claims to know a secret entrance. By chance, the trio have an enlightening encounter with a company of men from Gondor, led by Faramir, brother of Boromir, who is intent on ambushing armies marching to swell the forces of the Dark Tower. Faramir's news of war breaking out in Gondor and Rohan adds to Frodo's urgency. He is warned of the dangers of Cirith Ungol, Gollum's path into Mordor, but having seen the impregnable black gates of Sauron's land Frodo has little option but to go along with Gollum. The hobbits are lured by Gollum into the tunnel lair of Shelob, a vast and disgusting spider who stings Frodo and paralyses him. In fury, Sam inflicts terrible wounds upon Shelob but is unable to save his master. Believing Frodo dead, Sam takes the Ring and grapples with Gollum, whom he scares off. He resolves to go on alone, only to discover – too late – that Frodo was merely stunned by **Shelob's** poison, not killed. He is still alive and has been taken by orcs into Mordor.

◦ ❖ ◦

> "I AM WOUNDED WITH KNIFE, STING AND TOOTH,
> AND A LONG BURDEN. WHERE SHALL I FIND REST?"
> **Frodo prepares for the final journey**

❖ The Return Of The King ❖

THE PLOT At Minas Tirith, besieged citadel of Gondor, the storm of battle approaches, and the heroes make their way there by different routes, experiencing different adventures.

Aragorn, who it transpires is the rightful heir of Gondor, takes the Paths of the Dead – an ancient right reserved for Elendil's heir, who can summon a shadow army of men who broke an oath to fight with Gondor against Sauron in a previous age. Legolas and Gimli accompany him on this dreadful journey, where they gather a host of ghosts and fall upon the hordes of Mordor outside the gates of Gondor.

Merry pledges to serve Théoden, who is interested in hobbits and is kind to him. There is no horse small enough for him to ride, however a young rider called Dernhelm offers to take him. Unknown to Merry, Dernhelm is actually Éowyn, Théoden's niece. She has fallen in love with Aragorn, but he is pledged to Arwen and urges her to remain at Edoras. In bitterness and despair, she determines to ride to battle and death.

Pippin, taken to Minas Tirith by Gandalf, becomes a soldier of Gondor answerable to the Steward, Denethor, and his son Faramir. Denethor reveals to Gandalf that he, too, has looked into a palantír and seen the crushing hosts of Mordor. When Faramir is hit by a dart from a winged ringwraith as he returns to the city, Denethor despairs and determines to commit suicide. He commands his men to burn him on a pyre with the unconscious Faramir. Just in time, Pippin and Gandalf are able to save Faramir, but his father Denethor burns.

In lieu of Denethor, **Gandalf commands the last defence**, and battle is joined on the Pelennor Fields in the greatest clash between Sauron's armies and the armies of the West. On the battlefield, the king of the ringwraiths slays King Théoden before being struck down by Éowyn, aided by Merry. Both are wounded and taken to join Faramir in the Houses of Healing, where Aragorn later saves them both. While recovering, Éowyn falls in love with Faramir.

Despite grievous losses on the Pelennor, the Alliance wins the day. The decision is made to press on, taking the attack to Sauron's gate in a bid to draw attention away from Frodo and Sam. They hope to give the ring-bearer a chance of success or – as seems more likely – die in the attempt.

Despite Frodo's capture, all is not lost: Sam's determination and the Ring help him to rescue Frodo, whose efforts to resist the evil temptation of the Ring get more agonising as they inch towards Mount Doom. On the brink of the Crack of Doom, he is able to resist no more – and puts on the Ring in the heart of Sauron's empire, claiming it for his own. As he does so, however, Gollum – who has followed them since Cirith Ungol – springs up, wrestles with the invisible Frodo and bites off his ring finger to claim the Ring. In his jubilation, he dances on the edge of the abyss, misses his balance, falling into the flames.

The Ring's destruction undoes most of Sauron's power, and he is finished. His armies collapse and are defeated by the allies. Aragorn claims the throne of his ancestors as King Elessar, reuniting the kingdom. Retracing their steps homeward after many partings, the hobbits' final duty is to restore the tranquillity of the Shire. It has fallen into ugly disorder under Saruman, who has escaped the ents' vigil at Isengard. Saruman is killed and things put right, but two years later Frodo the weary ringbearer sails away with Gandalf. With them go the aged Bilbo, Elrond, Galadriel and others, departing Middle-earth forever.

So ends the Third Age and so begins the rule of men.

✦ The Appendices And Indexes ✦

While not essential to the story, Tolkien's dense addenda provide all sorts of background information, reference material, trivia and 'what happened nexts' – hours of happy, if complicated, wallowing for readers

A Hobbit's Gotta Do What A Hobbit's Gotta Do...

It is a stony heart indeed that is not moved by Frodo's small voice announcing to the grave Council of Elrond: "I will take the Ring, though I do not know the way." Who could fail to be amazed when Merry saves Éowyn at Pelennor Fields by driving his sword up into a towering Black Rider? And there's something wrong with anyone who doesn't cry when Sam finds the tortured Frodo in the Tower of Cirith Ungol: "Mr Frodo, my dear! It's Sam, I've come!"

In The Lord Of The Rings Frodo's courage is unsurpassed by anyone's, barring that of his faithful Sam. Even the duo of Merry and Pippin grow from silly kids into selfless heroes. It is incongruous given their cosy, common lives in the Shire (and Tolkien's puzzling affection for their banality), but there is nothing comical about them when they or their friends are in a tight spot.

This rejection of conventional romantic adventure, deviating from the norm of mythical warriors, is Tolkien's tribute to men he saw in the desolation of the Somme; to humble and sick, weary, ordinary men who in fear, fury or sheer bloody-mindedness performed extraordinary acts.

Tolkien thought this a very English attribute; others would not define it by nationality. But this elevation of the small person is one of the novel's most lovable virtues.

"But even as hope died in Sam, or seemed to die, it was turned to a new strength. Sam's plain hobbit face grew stern, almost grim, as the will hardened in him, and he felt through all his limbs a thrill, as if he was turning into some creature of stone and steel that neither despair nor weariness nor endless barren miles could subdue"

From The Return Of The King, Book Two, Chapter III – Mount Doom

"My Sam Gamgee is indeed a reflection of the English soldier, of the privates and batmen I knew in the 1914 war, and recognised as so far superior to myself"

JRR Tolkien on Samwise Gamgee

Frodo is tempted to kill Gollum but is overcome by pity, a virtue justly rewarded later

Tolkien's fictional women are supremely mysterious, and the heroes tight-lipped and virtuous

who just can't get enough of Middle-earth. These draw very heavily on the legends, histories and lore of The Silmarillion and it can all be a little overwhelming, but these are the best bits to dip into.

Appendix A, Annals Of The Kings And Rulers, Section I, The Númenórean Kings, sub-section V – for the romantic, bittersweet fairy tale of Aragorn and Arwen, from his upbringing under a secret identity with Elrond and their love-at-first-sight meeting to their years together in Gondor, his death and her lonely end (this is dramatised as her vision of the future in Peter Jackson's film of *The Two Towers*).

Appendix A, Section III, Durin's Folk – tells the story of Thrór, Thráin and Thorin Oakenshield; and ends by recounting the fate of both Gimli and that of his beloved friend Legolas.

Appendix B – for a chronology called 'Later Events Concerning The Members Of The Fellowship Of The Ring'. Appendix C provides the family trees of the Baggins, Brandybuck, Took and Gamgee clans, from which we learn titbits such as a daughter of Sam's married Pippin's son Faramir.

Appendices E and F – for those who want to pore over runes and learn

Tolkien: The Man And The Myths
WHERE MYTHOLOGY MEETS MORALITY

Myths are people's attempts to understand the why of things, from creation and nature to the nature of man and the existence of evil. Legends and folk tales are an ancient and traditional form of entertainment and the wisdom of life, but myths are bound up within a religious framework, expressing beliefs and truths. A people's mythology illuminates their view of the world and their place in it. And to linguists, myths are a kind of language and a key to a culture.

Tolkien thought "History often resembles myth because they are both ultimately made of the same stuff." In other words, that they are both a record of things believed to be true, which is not the same as a record of facts.

It was central to the grand concept underlying his own mythology – of the elven jewels of the Silmarilli; of the blessed realm Valinor; of the evil power Morgoth and his servant Sauron; of his imagined version of our world as Middle-earth, its peoples and its wars – that it should be strange and distant, but true. Tolkien intended his books' invented mythology to complement his religious beliefs and understanding of morality; his stories are supposed to embody "the underlying reality or truth".

Although he obviously studied mythology (and knew certain mythologies, such as the Norse myths, better than almost anyone else alive) he could get very testy when critics or fans tried to draw comparisons between his books and specific myths. A comparison often drawn in his lifetime was with the Nibelungenlied, the classic German work of mythology from the Middle Ages, which Richard Wagner adapted for his Rings Cycle of operas.

When a commentary to a Swedish version of his masterpiece described it as "in a certain way 'der Nibelungen ring'", he shot back: "Both rings were round and there the resemblance ceases." He was almost as upset when his friend CS Lewis once told him that "myths are lies, though breathed through silver." "No," Tolkien insisted, "they're not."

To read more on Tolkien's views on myth, track down his fine essay 'On Fairy Stories', available, for example, in Tree and Leaf (HarperCollins).

A Guide To Bits You Might Want To Skip...

These songs and poems were intended to be read aloud or sung (some are available on CD, actually read by Tolkien), but you're not going to do that on the bus, are you? If you want to get on with the story here are some 'turn that page' alerts...

THE FELLOWSHIP OF THE RING
Book One, Chapter III
Three Is Company
As soon as you see the words "They began to hum softly..." you could let your fingers stroll past A Walking Song until you reach: "'Hush!' said Frodo..."

Book One, Chapter V
A Conspiracy Unmasked
Pippin sings a bath song. Is he a three-year-old? Jump from "A bath!" to Chapter VI and you miss only mushroom gluttony and Merry and Pippin insisting they're coming along on the journey.

Book One, Chapter VII
In The House Of Tom Bombadil
Tolkien's aged Auntie Jane of Bag End loved Tom Bombadil. But his exclamatory turns of phrase

are reminiscent of a thigh-slapping Winnie the Pooh, and when he rescues the hobbits from a scary scrape in Chapter VIII – Fog On The Barrow-downs, he insists on singing. Skim to Chapter IX to meet Strider and get down to business (you may want to skip the two-page song "There is an inn..." here as well).

Book One, Chapter XII
Flight To The Ford
Sam's performance of Rhyme Of The Troll is, as advertised, "just a bit of nonsense." Two pages of it.

Book Two, Chapter I
Many Meetings
Bilbo's three-page verse is a variation of Tolkien's first thoughts towards The Silmarillion. If you don't care for the lore of yore, read fast.

THE TWO TOWERS,
Book One, Chapter I
The Departure Of Boromir
We're all sad that brave Boromir is dead, but instead of singing laments, Aragorn and Legolas really need to hustle.

more about Tolkien's invented languages.

Of the Indexes, **IV, Things**, is particularly useful for looking up definitions and references when you're on page 900-and-something and can't quite remember what the herb athelas is used for, which palantír is which, whose emblems are a ship, a star, a tree, and so on.

✦ The InterpretationGame✦

It's about good versus evil, **creation versus destruction**, and the miraculous grace of love. It's about the human condition. Read most simply as a cracking adventure and epic fairy tale, the novel's hundreds of millions of readers – in the 30-plus languages into which it has been translated – usually get that without needing to be told.

In 1939 Tolkien delivered the Andrew Lang Lecture at the University of St Andrews; it was later published as his essay 'On Fairy Stories'. Since he was deeply into writing *The Lord Of The Rings* at the time, much of what he had to say about fantasy and myth-making clearly applies to the novel. The essay can even be seen as an introduction to the novel and its principal themes. One of the points he puts forward is that "Even fairy stories as a whole have three faces: the **Mystical** towards the **Supernatural**; the **Magical** towards **Nature**; and the **Mirror of scorn and pity** towards **Man**." Man is born to suffer and die, and is therefore vulnerable to sorrow, failure and evil. Man must confront the reality of evil and ugliness to escape them, to be redeemed from them, to finally know joy.

The Lord Of The Rings is not, as persistently claimed, an allegory of **World War II**, a cautionary parable about the dawn of the atomic age, or a reactionary call for a feudal society (see page 298). Tolkien always maintained that "I much prefer history, true or feigned" and he strenuously denied that *The Lord Of The Rings* had "any allegorical significance or contemporary political reference whatsoever." What it did have, he stated, was a basis in his own life experience. "The prime motive was the desire of a tale-teller to try his hand at a really long story that would hold the attention of readers, amuse them, delight them, and at times maybe excite them or deeply move them. As a guide I had only my own feelings for what is appealing or moving…"

James Joyce vs John Ronald
ULYSSES: THE 20TH CENTURY'S PRE-EMINENT NOVEL NO MORE?

In a blitz of pre-millennial list-making, such literary figures as Gore Vidal, American historian Daniel J Boorstin and novelist AS Byatt drew up a list of the 100 greatest English-language novels of the 20th century. James Joyce's Ulysses came out top. (The Lord Of The Rings didn't even make the list, but it was named the 20th century's finest in an Amazon.com poll in 1997, with some 25,000 votes). Although the most famous passage in Ulysses – published in 1922, and immediately banned as pornographic – is a meditation by one of its characters on the toilet, the book has certain parallels with The Lord Of The Rings.

The title is the most obvious connection. Joyce, like Tolkien, knew his mythology, and named the book after the Greek hero in the Odyssey. (Joyce's Ulysses is a middle-aged advertising salesman called Leopold Bloom.) You should – if you haven't already – read Ulysses as a bawdy, life-affirming masterpiece, but you'll have to come to grips with the scholarly allusions; Joyce's style is as allusive as Tolkien's.

Joyce shared Tolkien's fascination with linguistics, creating a language (and a stream-of-consciousness technique) to tell his story of a single day in Dublin. Instead of Elvish, Joyce's novel is full of strange twists on the language, one of the more explicable sentences being: "I was blue mouldy for the want of that pint."

The two authors were very different. Tolkien looks the very picture of an Oxford don, while the image of Joyce sporting an eye-patch and rakish moustache pretty much sums up his attitude to life. Yet both have produced masterpieces which, detractors insist, they have trouble reading all the way through – while Ulysses may be, as The Times noted, "intensely alive, full of Rabelaisian humour, with a highly developed sense of time and a fantastic imaginative faculty," it, as the same reviewer continues, "has many repellent or merely boring passages."

The Lord Of The Rings is easily the better read of the two novels. With Joyce's masterpiece having been enthroned as 'the greatest novel of the 20th century' for so long, the dictates of media fashion and academic debate mean it could soon be deposed.

Tolkien's imagination was fired by monsters; Joyce's – so critics said – by the monstrous

It appealed to Tolkien that the act of what he called **sub-creation** could take readers into an imagined reality that conveyed truths he thought forgotten or obscured in the overwhelming reality of modern life. His religious faith is also at the heart of his work: "Fantasy remains a human right: we make… because we are made, and not only made, but made in the image and likeness of a Maker."

◦ ✦ ◦

✦ Themes And Subplots ✦

Literati have always tended to sneer at *The Lord Of The Rings*. Because it has its basis in Tolkien's own life and his idiosyncratic conservative, liberal, medievalist, humanist, tree-loving, paganism-embracing Catholicism, it is outside the modern intellectual, literary and social mainstreams, or it is antiquated in its fascination with mystery and magic. The great science-fiction fantasy writer **Ursula Le Guin** says critics have "a deep puritanical distrust of fantasy."

But the bottom line is that hundreds of millions of readers like Tolkien. *The Lord Of The Rings* is borrowed more often from libraries than works by **William Shakespeare, Charles Dickens** and **Jane Austen**. In the 40-odd years before Peter Jackson's film adaptation prompted a new Tolkien craze and attracted the latest generation of readers, *The Lord Of The Rings* had already sold an estimated 50 million copies.

There are strong themes in the books, which people continue to respond to. One is the sense of community, and loyalty to it, that steels hobbits, men, dwarves, elves and ents to defend the Shire, the magic, the forest. Another – despite Tolkien's specific and cherished aim of giving the English their own great, Anglo-Saxon-like mythology – is the universally loved and hoped-for idea that **even a very small individual can do something big**, that a humble but determined someone can make a difference, that impossible odds can be beaten. **Faith is tested**, but hope never dies. The environmentally aware and ecologically alarmed find inspiration in the richly detailed presence and power of nature in the novel – from the uncontrollable, elemental forces that affect characters and impact on the plot, to the healing herbs, the fine magical soil that is Galadriel's gift to Sam and the tiny flower called **elanor**.

Contrary to some critics' objections that the concept of evil in Tolkien is simplistic, *The Lord Of The Rings* characterises evil not just as a concept – symbolised in the grand design of Sauron to unmake the world and re-fashion it – but as everyday moral problems everyone recognises, whether the **malicious slanders** of Wormtongue, the savage tree-felling or even the petty, neighbourhood envy and greed of the spoon-filching Otho and Lobelia Sackville-Baggins.

Some people complain the novel is misogynist as there are **few women** (and absolutely no sex). And these few females are sketchy figures. Galadriel is remote and intimidatingly enchanting. Arwen drifts through sacred woods being darkly lovely and serene. Éowyn is a plucky warrior princess, but she wants to die because Aragorn is already taken. (She conveniently perks up when wooed and 'tamed' by Faramir, who encourages her to take up gardening.) The ents have misplaced their ent-wives. Dwarves habitually boast of their paternity but never mention having wives, sisters or daughters in their mines. Orcs, mercifully, are spawned without any need for females. Middle-earth is **a man's world**.

But this is hardly surprising. Tolkien was close to few women apart from his mother, wife and daughter. He did have friendships with bright female students and colleagues but, like many of his generation, he was schooled by and among men, bonded with soldiers at war, and was most relaxed and intellectually stimulated among pipe-smoking, beer-hoisting academic cronies. Moreover, his surrogate family and some lifelong friends were priests. The charge of neglecting women in his work can be levelled at many leading writers of the 20th century. It's probably best, in this context, to accept 'man' as acting for humankind.

✦ What Happened Next? ✦

Within six weeks of its publication in 1954 The Fellowship Of The Ring had to be reprinted. (Anyone in possession of a copy from that first small printing is sitting on the most valuable first edition in world literature of the last 50 years.) Allen & Unwin had expected to lose £1,000, but sales were steady. Tolkien's first cheque for his share of the profit in 1956 was for more than £3,500, **substantially higher than his professor's salary**. The belated financial success propelled him thereafter into unending tax problems, but he could at least indulge his taste in fine, Bilbo-style waistcoats. Foreign language editions began to appear, closely examined by Tolkien, who could find fault with and make corrections to Swedish, Dutch and many other translations. Fan mail snowballed into an avalanche as he tried to respond personally to as many people as he could. Tolkien made his publishers agree to fend off approaches for the film rights – he disliked drama – unless from someone who would treat his books with respect or make him an offer he couldn't refuse. The film rights were eventually granted to United Artists in the late 1960s.

In 1965 the American publishers **Ace Books** produced a pirated edition of *The Lord Of The Rings* as a single paperback, triggering a lengthy copyright dispute. Appropriately, since Tolkien was a great proponent of reading aloud, word of mouth turned this into a student rage. Tolkien's earliest American fans, particularly the many who had received letters from him, formed a fan club, enlisted the Science-Fiction Writers Of America to the cause and went into action, forcing booksellers to carry the authorised three-volume paperback edition from **Ballantine Books**. Ace eventually capitulated and offered Tolkien back royalties on the 100,000 copies they had sold. The affair created quite a stir in the press and the Ballantine edition sold in excess of one million copies.

Tolkien became a bestselling author, the book displacing *The Catcher In The Rye*, *The Great Gatsby* and *The Lord Of The Flies* as the top must-read on American campuses. Flower Power, psychedelia, the hippy back-to-nature counter-culture and the proliferating arts and crafts Renaissance Faires enthusiasts all adopted *The Lord Of The Rings* as their emblematic literary work, sealing Tolkien's cult status. His characters, runes and imagery were incorporated into pop music, poster art and graphic design. Fantasy literature underwent a rebirth, enjoying a brief, rare respectability. Would-be Tolkien imitators have come and gone, none rivalling him in popularity, or in his singular combination of scholarship and wonder.

In his book **Defending Middle-earth, Tolkien: Myth & Modernity**, the writer Patrick Curry says of *The Lord Of The Rings'* continuing appeal: "Tolkien's Middle-earth gleams with the light of an ancient hope: peace between peoples, and with nature, and before the unknown."

THE MOTION PICTURE TRILOGY

THE EPIC TALE OF THE LORD OF THE RINGS
ON THE BIG SCREEN

Gandalf and Frodo mosey into Hobbiton: the Shire is quiet – too quiet

"THE CYCLES SHOULD BE LINKED TO A MAJESTIC WHOLE,
AND YET LEAVE SCOPE FOR OTHER MINDS AND HANDS, WIELDING
PAINT AND MUSIC AND DRAMA. ABSURD"

JRR Tolkien

"THIS IS A GIANT UNDERTAKING, BUT I CONSIDER THIS A PERSONAL FILM.
IT'S MY FILM OF A LIFETIME"

Peter Jackson

Tolkien's hope of stimulating people's imaginations with his great creative labours of love *The Silmarillion* and The Lord Of The Rings was certainly realised. There have been countless enthusiastic outpourings of art and music, albeit many that emphatically would not have been to his taste, including wizards sculpted in lard, **Leonard Nimoy** (*Star Trek*'s Mr Spock) surrounded by gyrating go-go dancers, performing a pop ditty called Bilbo Baggins, and some incongruous heavy-metal rock homages. But for decades it did seem absurd to attempt a dramatic adaptation of *The Lord Of The Rings* for the screen because of the sheer enormity of it, not merely in length but in the creation of such a detailed other world. Tolkien himself – no fan of drama or movie in any case – said he could not see how a film could be made.

The film rights to the novel were acquired by **United Artists** at the end of the 1960s, but the studio was going broke and was unable to make anything of it. In the 1970s the rights were acquired by **Saul Zaentz**, a respected producer with a taste for taking on tricky literary adaptations (he won Best Picture Oscars for *One Flew Over The Cuckoo's Nest*, *Amadeus* and *The English Patient*). British film-maker **John Boorman**, for one, was interested in making it, but he was defeated by the apparent inevitability of having to compress the novel unsatisfactorily into one movie. (Boorman's sole science-fiction film, *Zardoz*, was poorly received but his single fantasy epic, 1981's Arthurian reworking *Excalibur*, was unusual and spellbinding, suggesting he might indeed have been able to make a compelling movie of *The Lord Of The Rings* given the resources.)

Since there was little else Zaentz could do with the 'property', he produced **Ralph Bakshi**'s ambitious, under-rated and ill-fated animated adaptation *The Lord Of The Rings* (1978). Running for two hours, it is notable for the voice of John Hurt as Strider/Aragorn, and took the story

What The Critics Said

THE GOOD, THE BAD AND SOME VERY UGLY FILM REVIEWS

"History should quickly regard Peter Jackson's The Fellowship Of The Ring as the first instalment of the best fantasy epic in motion-picture history."
Empire magazine on The Fellowship Of The Ring

"Warning! Film contains intense combat and fantasy horror scenes, long-haired men smoking unfeasibly long pipes, women with pointy ears, and lots and lots of interminable nerdish nonsense."
The Guardian on The Two Towers

"The movie is touching the minds of young people and winning a new generation of readers for Tolkien, and has been able to capitalise on a mood, a sentiment that is in the air, that humanity is embarking on perilous times."
World Socialist magazine on The Fellowship Of The Ring

"I love Fellowship Of The Ring and The Two Towers the way you can't think of anything but that object of your affection. It's just sick how much I love these films. It is dangerous, it scares me, because I get the genuine sense of worry that I'll never find

films I'll love this intensely again."
Ain't It Cool News

"The Two Towers is why Hollywood exists; its scope is tremendous, its heartening mixture and careful balance of technology, story and nature at times nothing short of breath-taking"
Entertainment Today on The Two Towers

"The battles and sieges are conducted with the ferocity of the Crusades, Agincourt and Stalingrad, and they are led up to and orchestrated in a manner that recalls the great movie epics of Fritz Lang and Sergei Eisenstein."
The Observer on The Two Towers

"Most of us are happy enough these days to go to the movies and not get screwed, so rarely does a movie even keep its promises, much less surpass them. That's why this is something of a miracle. It makes the great potentialities of movies seem realistic and achievable."
Salon.com on The Fellowship Of The Ring

"Brooding, intense and handy with a blade, Mortensen is the film's greatest strength – Han Solo to Wood's Luke Skywalker."
BBC Films on The Fellowship Of The Ring

"Jackson emphasises all the things that Lucas seems to have forgotten – a complex heroic arc with valiant heroes taking on vast forces in absolute black-and-white terms; a dense textural depth and background in the three-dimensional creation of a wholly imaginary world and its people; a wondrous sense of awe; and just the right balance of humour and romance."
Sci-fi, Horror And Fantasy Film Review on The Two Towers

"Jackson continues to make Middle-earth seem astoundingly real."
Boxoffice Magazine on The Two Towers

"It's a shame Rohan looks like a tiny hamlet. And there's something Monty Pythonesque in the way Princess Éowyn's (Miranda Otto) royalness is conveyed by her being the only person in Rohan with clean hair."
The New York Post on The Two Towers

"Though filmed with awesome detailing, the battle is long drawn out – and no matter how grand the spectacle, one gets tired of so much action."
The Hindu on The Two Towers

"Even the film's absurdities – such as the way Liv Tyler's radiant elf Arwen speaks Elvish as though it were some kind of pidgin Finnish – are endearing."
New York Magazine on The Fellowship Of The Ring

"A Middle-earth version of Conan The Barbarian."
Roger Ebert, The Chicago-Sun Times on The Two Towers

"What it lacks – at least until the climax – is the first film's wow-factor. We are now accustomed to the environs and inhabitants of Middle-earth."
BBC Films on The Two Towers

"First the good news: The Two Towers isn't necessarily better than The Fellowship Of The Ring, but everything great about the first film has been dutifully amplified here to umpteenth degrees. Now the bad: everything less than stellar about the first film has also been magnified."
Slant Magazine on The Two Towers

up to the battle at Isengard (about half-way through). Sadly Bakshi was unable to raise the finance for his follow-up to complete the tale.

Bakshi's interesting, if not entirely successful, mix of traditional animation and drawings traced over live-action footage demonstrated some of the challenges facing any would-be *The Lord Of The Rings* film-maker. The cost of battle scenes involving thousands of warriors was prohibitive; the technology to create the wondrous settings or the illusion of a cast of thousands was not yet developed enough; and depicting the likes of hobbits, elves and much-loved heroes to the satisfaction of passionate readers with their own mental images of these characters was **asking for trouble**. Getting around the physical characteristics of a multiplicity of races including orcs, Gollum and 3ft 6in hobbits who would have to interact with each other seemed to preclude a live-action version that wouldn't be shunned by Tolkien fans.

But in New Zealand an 18-year-old amateur movie-maker named **Peter Jackson** had seen Bakshi's picture and been sufficiently enthused to read the book. "'No one's made a live-action version,'" he recalled thinking. "'I can't wait until the movie comes out.' Twenty years later no one had done it,

> JACKSON HAD BEEN SUFFICIENTLY ENTHUSED BY THE CARTOON VERSION TO READ THE BOOK

so I got impatient." Actually he didn't wait quite 20 years. It was in 1995, during post-production on his paranormal horror-comedy *The Frighteners* (starring Michael J Fox) at his own special-effects company in Wellington (Weta Ltd, named after a New Zealand insect), that Jackson saw the possibilities offered by CGI technology.

It took Jackson a year to unravel the tangled rights situation of *The Lord Of The Rings*. It turned out that they were still held by Zaentz, who gave him his blessing to run with his idea. Armed with an early screenplay for the first of a **two-film proposal**, he approached Miramax Films' Harvey and Bob Weinstein, producers of hip repute, pitching the idea of two feature movies. Cautious, they were willing to gamble on only a single film. So Jackson met with New Line Cinema Corporation's **Robert Shaye**, a Tolkien devotee who also happened to love Jackson's work. He made Jackson an incredible offer, which amounted to 'you need to make three pictures to do it properly, so here's $270 million'.

There was now the small matter of a screenplay, restructuring the hoped-for two films into the dream-come-true trilogy. Adapting

The cover for Ralph Bakshi's 1978 animated version of The Lord Of The Rings

Cartoon Capers

•

Peter Jackson wasn't the first director to take The Lord Of The Rings trilogy to the big screen.

In 1978 Ralph Bakshi, director of the ground-breaking X-rated cartoon Fritz The Cat (and the inspiration for Comic Book Store Guy in The Simpsons), sought refuge from the storm of critical abuse that greeted Coonskins (his Song Of The South parody) in sci-fi, filming an adult cartoon of the first two instalments of The Lord Of The Rings before he ran out of money.

Bakshi's cartoon version was not hugely popular, either with Tolkienites or with fans of Fritz The Cat. To make it, Bakshi effectively traced (rotoscoped) the animated movements from live-action figures. The result was a strange creation which lacked the vim and vigour of his earlier animated movies but which was not without power.

There are many obvious flaws. Some of the animation is a bit crude. The character Saruman appears to have two names (he's often referred to as Aruman after research showed that audiences kept mixing up Saruman and Sauron). The editing is a bit dodgy and the scars where the budget was suddenly cut are all too obvious. Enough blunders then to justify one reviewer's threat: "If I ever meet Ralph Bakshi, I shall kick him square in the privates." The case against is memorably, and lovingly, detailed in the review on http://flyingmoose.org/tolksarc/bakshi/bakshi.htm

Yet the battle scenes (which borrow footage from the classic Alexander Nevsky) have genuine menace, and the evil, as personified by Sauron and his henchmen, is genuinely dark. Even the combination of live-action tracings and straight animation, as BBC Films note, "echoes Tolkien's own drawings."

If you're a purist, you may find this movie infuriating. If you're not, you probably won't find it as enthralling as the Jackson version, but it's worth a look. The characters are brilliantly voiced by (among others) John Hurt, William Squires, Annette Crosbie and Anthony Daniels (the voice of C3PO). If you think the Jackson version might be a bit too heavy for your child, this could be an acceptable substitute.

The Lord Of The Rings presented the daunting multiple task of respecting Tolkien's work, pleasing fans of the book who had their own visions of Middle-earth's characters and events, and making an entertaining, commercially viable trilogy of films. If they were to recover their colossal costs, the movies would have to appeal to a wide mainstream audience, including people who had never read or enjoyed the books. If the first film released failed to find favour the project would be a catastrophe. And no matter how great or revered they are, books are seldom filmable without major alterations to structure, character, point of view and tone. Being what is called 'faithful to the spirit' of the original work is always a vague, subjective enterprise, but Jackson undertook adapting *The Lord Of The Rings* with his wife **Fran Walsh** and playwright **Philippa Boyens**. "The more time you spend in Tolkien's world the more complex it grows," observed Boyens. "It was all there for us, but the scope was tremendous."

In pondering what was most important to keep, they decided to highlight the major themes of the complete *The Lord Of The Rings* and to emphasise these from early in the first film: **good versus evil**, nature versus the unnatural, and the power of friendship against an overwhelming outside threat. Jackson stated his intent: "What we are trying to do, as we adapt *The Lord Of The Rings* into a film medium, is honour these themes. And whilst you can never be totally faithful to a book, especially a book over 1,000 pages, we have tried to incorporate the things that Tolkien cared about when he wrote the book, and make them the fabric of the films."

> "YOU CAN NEVER BE TOTALLY FAITHFUL TO A BOOK, BUT WE'VE TRIED TO INCORPORATE THE THINGS TOLKIEN CARED ABOUT"

Other decisions were made in the interests of a balanced, well-paced drama. These included quickening the initial hobbitry, liberating the soulful love story of Aragorn and Arwen from the appendices and bringing it into the main narrative, and giving the women more to do amid the male-dominated sword and sorcery.

A **prologue** at the beginning of the first film also evolved (it would be revised repeatedly and finalised only late in the post-production period). Inspired by the traditional James Bond device of a major action sequence to draw people quickly into the story, it was intended to convey the terrible force and evil of Sauron, establish the importance of the One Ring and track its journey through history. Other portions of the script

No pointy shoes for Gandalf, but he couldn't escape the pointy ears surrounding him

continued to be revised throughout filming, as the actors fleshed out their characters. During editing, cuts would make other adjustments as repetitions, complications of a multi-layered plot and elements that slowed the rhythm of the picture became apparent.

No sooner was the production announced than Tolkien's international fandom became excited, concerned and agitated, feeling personally involved with a depth of passion not demonstrated for the screen adaptation of a novel since *Gone With The Wind*. The Internet buzzed with speculation, opinion and debate about potential casting. (Rumours that Sean Connery would be or should be Gandalf, for instance, swiftly circled the globe.) The international film community, meanwhile, was agog at the news that all three movies would be filmed simultaneously over a single intensive 18-month period.

While this made sense on both practical and artistic grounds, it was an unprecedented undertaking, and one that demanded an extraordinary commitment from principal cast and crew (more than 2,500 people) as well as the logistical forward planning of an army going to war. (*Back*

From The Set
NEWS FROM THE MAKING OF THE MOVIES

Ian McKellen had read The Hobbit but admitted "I wasn't even aware of The Lord Of The Rings." He made up for it by having a special pocket made in his Gandalf costume so he could carry it around with him. He also decided his character had to wear boots after getting an email from a fan who said, "Can you make sure Gandalf wears boots? I don't want to see him in any pointy shoes."

Elijah Wood (Frodo Baggins) was only slightly more au fait with the books. "I'd read The Hobbit, a beloved book from my childhood, but I didn't finish the trilogy while we were making the movies." His enthusiasm for the role was great enough for him to voluntarily dress in breeches and a flowing shirt and run out into the hills for his audition tape.

John Rhys-Davies, who plays Gimli, took six to seven hours each day to put his make-up on at the start of the film "but we got it down to three-and-a-half hours at the end; just having it touched up could take 25 minutes."

Billy Boyd, who plays Pippin, says, "My memory of The Two Towers really is me and Dom [Monaghan, who plays Merry] being stuck 15ft up Treebeard for a couple of months. You had to be harnessed for safety and it got to the point where you couldn't get down for tea breaks." Monaghan had a specially tough shoot: he had to wear a fat foam suit and drink three litres of water a day so he wouldn't dehydrate.

Sean Astin meanwhile needed to gain 30lbs in weight to play Sam Gamgee

Some members of the cast and crew had tattoos to celebrate the completion of the films. Boyd says "We were in New Zealand, the home of tattoos, so it seemed like the thing to do." The tattoo was of the Elvish symbol for 9 – McKellen's tattoo is on his shoulder, Wood's on his stomach.

Viggo Mortensen got so into character on set that Jackson once referred to him as Aragorn for more than 30 minutes without him realising. The actor also requested the script be rewritten so he could use more Elvish words.

Andy Serkis (Gollum) was ruled ineligible for a Best Supporting Actor Oscar nomination, because his onscreen character involved computer-generation.

For Pete's Sake

PETER JACKSON – FILM-MAKER AND KIWI HOBBIT

Writer-director Peter Jackson was evidently born to make movies, but he has affinities with burrowing, home-loving, family-oriented hobbits. The bearded, bespectacled, burly 5ft 7in Jackson was of a size, shape and countenance to blend in with his hobbit and dwarf actors on set – even if his habitual garb of shorts not a giveaway. Married to Fran Walsh since 1987, Jackson has two children, Billy and Katie, two dogs and a home a few minutes from his studio.

Jackson was born on Halloween, 31 October, in 1961 in Pukerua, North Island, New Zealand. By the age of eight he was using his parents' Super-8 movie camera to make his own mini-opuses. He left school at 17 and, unable to find employment in New Zealand's small film industry, he apprenticed as a photoengraver and worked on a Wellington newspaper and in a photo lab. He bought a 16mm camera and, financed entirely from his own wages, he wrote, produced, directed, starred in and did the make-up and editing for what began as a sci-fi comedy short with a cast of friends.

Over the course of three years

the film grew to short feature length and the New Zealand Film Commission was persuaded to fund its completion. It emerged as Bad Taste, the tale of aliens on Earth to serve mankind – as fast food. Bad Taste hit the film festival circuit in 1987 and became a worldwide cult hit for its quirky, gory hilarity. Quirky and gory have since become synonymous with Jackson's body of work, which includes Meet The Feebles, an insanely gross, adults-only 'backstage' satire starring a cast of depraved puppets, and Braindead, a cheerful tale of zombie flesh-eaters wreaking havoc in a sleepy New Zealand street. The latter won 16 international sci-fi and horror-fantasy awards, including the prestigious Saturn.

Jackson found a wider circle of admirers with Heavenly Creatures (1994), an inspired dramatisation of a real murder that stunned New Zealand in the 1950s, when teenagers Pauline Parker and Juliet Hulme brutally killed Pauline's mother. Drawing sensational performances from young Melanie Lynskey and Kate Winslet (in her star-making vehicle), Jackson's departures from the dark (and

Director Peter Jackson – set to take on King Kong now he's finished with hobbits

sometimes darkly funny) realism into exhilarating, beautifully created depictions of the girls' rich fantasy world served notice that here was the man who could tackle The Lord Of The Rings. His 1996 paranormal horror-comedy The Frighteners, in which Michael J Fox's psychic investigator hunts a phantasmic serial killer, failed commercially, but was original and imaginative, exploring ingenious computer effects with style and wit.

A self-made industry in himself, with a production company (Wingnut Films), an effects company (Weta Ltd) and a studio (Three Foot Six) in Wellington, Jackson's eight years of living in Middle-earth haven't exhausted his native creative impulses. "I absolutely want to do Bad Taste 2. I want to go back and do a splatter movie. I'm still that person." After The Lord Of The Rings, his next film is a new version of King Kong, a homage to the 1933 original he cites as a favourite and to the 1950s special-effects wizard Ray Harryhausen, who was his early inspiration.

To The Future II and *III*, and subsequently *The Matrix II* and *III*, had been shot back-to-back, but in both cases some time after the first films had become runaway hits, thus guaranteeing profitability for the further instalments.) "I felt that in order to do the tale's epic nature justice, we had to shoot it as one big story, because that's what it is," said Jackson. "I look forward to the day when audiences can sit down and watch all three films in a row, because it is one big story and adventure."

At the other end of the production process, composer Howard Shore would similarly view his opportunity to score the trilogy as one great work, his equivalent of creating an epic opera. Since Tolkien's many songs and poems in the book would not be able to be kept, Shore incorporated some of the literature into the music where appropriate.

Also Worth Considering...
BBC's RADIO 4 DRAMATISATION OF THE LORD OF THE RINGS

In 1981 BBC Radio 4 broadcast an epic, atmospheric 13-part, 13-hour dramatisation of The Lord Of The Rings, adapted by writer and broadcaster Brian Sibley, directed by Jane Morgan and featuring music by Stephen Oliver.

It boasted a great voice cast including Peter Jackson's future movie Bilbo, Ian Holm, as Frodo, Michael Hordern as Gandalf, Robert Stephens as Aragorn, Bill Nighy as Sam, Peter Woodthorpe as Gollum and Royal Shakespeare Company actor Gerard Murphy as the narrator.

Even at four hours longer than Jackson's film trilogy, material had to be left out. But Sibley did a brilliant job of telling the story excitingly and coherently, cleverly beginning with the capture of Gollum by Sauron's servants and his squealing denunciation of Baggins as the thief of the Ring, setting off the search for the Ring-bearer while in the Shire Frodo is oblivious to the approaching danger.

The recording – available on audio cassette and CD – is the BBC's top-selling spoken-word title worldwide, with more than 100,000 copies sold. In New Zealand copies were given to members of the film cast who had not read the book. And when the serialisation was last broadcast on Radio 4 (on Saturday afternoons from January to March, 2002), it brought record audiences of nearly a million to the station.

In the Mines of Moria, for example, dwarvish singing and chanting is heard (although, in fact, it is performed by a Pacific male voice choir, augmented by grunting rugby players). A 60-strong mixed voice choir, a boys' choir and soloists were also incorporated to add emotional nuances in Middle-earth's range of cultures and settings.

Jackson's resolve to film in his native **New Zealand** with a core of people who included his **regular collaborators** (some of them in tune with his sensibilities since they were teenagers) was also questioned. However, the location has proved to be one of the films' great assets, offering not just spectacular scenery but a pool of eager technicians and actors from New Zealand and Australia, and unprecedented nationwide co-operation and pride invested in the project's success. Other collaborators, excited by the scale of the production, were lured without real difficulty from Europe and North America.

ELIJAH WOOD, PROMPTED BY ONLINE GOSSIP, SENT JACKSON A HOMEMADE AUDITION VIDEOTAPE

The director had few fixed views on the casting process, saying, "I'm never envisaging Sean Connery as Gandalf or Anthony Hopkins as Bilbo, I just see the characters the same way anyone does when reading a book." But Jackson had decided that all the hobbits would be cast in **Britain**, reflecting their inherent Englishness and underlining, beyond their obvious physical distinctiveness, the different nature of the Shire-folk from the other cultures of Middle-earth. Auditions found small, boyish **Dominic Monaghan** and **Billy Boyd** (actually a 30-year-old Scot) for Merry and Pippin, with the bonus of **Orlando Bloom** (then still at drama school) for the elf Legolas, but no Frodo. Prompted by the casting gossip from Ain't It Cool News website-guru Harry Knowles, the young but experienced US actor **Elijah Wood** (conveniently on the small side at 5ft 7in) sent Jackson a homemade audition videotape and immediately landed the role of the Ring-bearer. This paved the way for another American, **Sean Astin**, as his sidekick Sam, although he was ordered to put on 30lbs to clinch the part.

Height and slimness influenced the casting of principal elves such as American **Liv Tyler** for Arwen and Australian **Hugo Weaving** as Elrond, although landing the Antipodes' hottest actress to play Galadriel meant **Cate Blanchett** would find herself in difficulty while trying to glide through forest glades in 12-inch platform boots that any 1970s glam-rock fashion victim would have envied.

British veterans of international recognition, **Sir Ian McKellen**, **Ian Holm** and **John Rhys-Davies** were early recruits as Gandalf the Grey, Bilbo and the dwarf Gimli, meeting with general approbation on Internet message boards. McKellen, Brian Sibley notes in his book on the making of the movie, soon began to own his character. As Jackson says, if somebody wanted to know if Gandalf would do this or that, or what shape his staff was, they could "just go to Ian McKellen and ask him". Holm, who had played Frodo in the major BBC Radio adaptation of *The Lord Of The Rings* nearly 20 years earlier, was a particular Tolkien enthusiast, likening Bilbo to **Hamlet**: "He's an eternal character."

Dashing action man and a Bond villain in *Goldeneye*, **Sean Bean** was enlisted as Boromir, whose brother Faramir would be played by rising Australian actor **David Wenham**. Later the news that cult-movie icon **Christopher Lee** would join the production as Saruman the White was greeted with universal acclaim. It was doubly appropriate, as he proved to be the only person involved in the films who had actually met JRR Tolkien and he was a passionate expert on Tolkien's work.

The thorniest pivotal role was that of Aragorn. British actor **Stuart Townsend** was cast, but at only 28 even he shared in the misgivings about his suitability. These were dismissed by Jackson, until two weeks into filming when it all ended in tears. The older, ruggedly handsome Danish-American actor **Viggo Mortensen** was hurriedly contacted in New York. He declined, then changed his mind on the advice of his son Henry, who knew the book very well. Rushed to New Zealand and on to the set, he quickly became a legend on the production for his complete immersion in it, and was hailed by a relieved Jackson as his 'miracle man'.

Producer **Barrie Osborne** says the casting process, despite a few setbacks, was simpler than many imagined: "We went for the most appropriate actors to play the roles. We weren't under any pressure to cast 'star names' simply in order to open the movie because, after all, we had a novel with a hundred-million readers that would open the movie."

The mood on set, despite all the obvious difficulties with filming such an epic, was perhaps best summed up by **John Rhys-Davies** who, after only a couple of days of filming, declared "We are making a masterpiece! Gentlemen, we are making a film that will be bigger than Star Wars, a film that in twenty years' time people are going to list in their top ten movies!"

✦ Bringing Middle-earth To Life ✦

The realistic creation of a fantasy requires fastidious attention to detail. The film-makers' first step was to engage conceptual artists **Alan Lee** (who did the 76 watercolour illustrations for the anniversary editions of *The Hobbit* and *The Lord Of The Rings*) and **John Howe** (whose Tolkien work includes the jacket illustrations for HarperCollins' editions of the trilogy, calendars and posters). The two men made hundreds of sketches of Middle-earth's races, creatures, landscapes and structures. These evolved into storyboards, scale models and sets – both full-sized and miniature – under production designer **Grant Major**. "They gave us the look and feel of Middle-earth," he explained, "and they brought the most intimate knowledge of Tolkien lore to their work."

The sets were built at Jackson's Three Foot Six studios in Wellington, and in many cases pre-fabricated for shipping to locations. They ranged from country village structures for earthy Hobbiton (where flower and vegetable gardens were planted a year in advance of filming so they could grow naturally) to the art-nouveau-influenced elven kingdom of Rivendell, and from the underground mining realm of Moria with its dwarvish inscriptions on the walls, to the giant spider Shelob's foul lair and the labyrinthine city of Minas Tirith in Gondor.

Richard Taylor, director of Weta and the special-effects maestro on all of Jackson's films, was made the supervisor of all the

A WHOLE YEAR WAS SPENT PERFECTING FOAM-LATEX HOBBIT EARS AND CREATING THOUSANDS OF GELATINE ELF EARS

creatures, miniatures, armour and special make-up effects. He set up six departments in the Weta workshops and employed nearly 150 predominantly youthful colleagues to develop a cohesive realism.

Creatures and **Make-up and Prosthetics** were two of these departments, in which a whole year was spent perfecting foam-latex hobbit ears and feet (1,600 pairs were worn out by the four main characters). Other duties ranged from creating thousands of **gelatine elf ears** and 10,000 facial appliances to making 200 orc heads from latex-foam silicone and yak hair, and a tar-like 'orc blood' for battle wounds. Further responsibilities included producing animatronics such as Saruman's fiendish genetic experiment goblin warriors, making an uncannily realistic silicone duplicate of Sean Bean (as the fallen Boromir, to be placed in a boat and sent over the Falls of

After 16 months in this make-up, the cast no longer needed to search for their anger

Rings And Things
DIRECTORS' CAMEOS, ACTOR'S JOKES AND GANDALF'S TRAINERS

Such is the scale of the movies, it's easy to miss some of the movie-makers' running gags, motifs and, perish the thought, even the odd goof. Here's a very quick guide to stuff you should keep an eye out for.

THE DIRECTOR'S CAMEOS
In The Fellowship Of The Ring, Peter Jackson is the belching peasant outside the Prancing Pony Inn in Bree. In The Two Towers, he can be glimpsed wearing chain mail at Helm's Deep – opinions differ on whether he's throwing a spear or a rock. His kids also appear in the credits as "cute Rohan refugee children". In The Fellowship Of The Ring, the portraits above the fireplace in Bag End are of the director and his producer/wife Frances Walsh.

OTHER CAMEOS
That's art director Dan Hennah getting suited-up in armour at Helm's Deep in The Two Towers. Concept designer Alan Lee also appears at the same spot: he's the Rohan collecting weapons.

RELATIVELY SPEAKING
Viggo Mortensen's son Henry is said to have appeared in some battle scenes during the shoot.

CREDIT WHERE IT'S DUE
Appearing on the credits for The Two Towers is "He maungärongo ki te whenua/He whakaaro pai ki ngä tängata katoa." It's a Maori greeting, wishing the land and people all the best.

SHARPE PRACTICE
Sean Bean, famous for playing eponymous British soldier Sharpe in the long-running ITV series set in the Napoleonic Wars, touches the sword of Elendil and says "Still sharp." The rascal.

SPORTING LIFE
When Shadowfax first appears in The Two Towers, Gandalf appears to be wearing sports shoes – the stripes, laces and a circular logo are visible.

LOOK WHO'S TALKING
Ian McKellen based his Gandalf accent on Tolkien's. The poet WH Auden once wrote to Tolkien to say that hearing the author read his work was like hearing "the voice of Gandalf" – a feeling the actor clearly agreed with.

The Casting Couch
HOW CREATIVE DIFFERENCES, WHIMS AND PREGNANCIES SHAPED THE FILMS

It's a good job that actor Stuart Townsend is engaged to actress Charlize Theron. That might just have come as at least some consolation for his having to give up the part of Aragorn four days into filming, handing over to Viggo Mortensen following "creative differences".

Orlando Bloom was originally supposed to play Faramir, but he was called back and cast as Legolas.

David Bowie, who obviously enjoyed his role in the Rings-lite Jim Henson movie Labyrinth, is rumoured to have wanted to play the part of Elrond. The role finally went to Hugo Weaving, whose roles in The Lord Of The Rings and The Matrix trilogy make him a bit of a cult movie hero at present.

Christopher Lee was the first actor to be cast (as Saruman), but then he is the only member of cast and crew to have met the author. Lee re-reads the books once a year.

Irish actress Alison Doody was first offered the part of Éowyn, the White Lady of Rohan, but had to decline as she had just given birth to her second daughter. Miranda Otto eventually won the part.

Pregnancy also prevented Björk from accepting the film-makers' repeated offers to write and sing Gollum's Song.

Rauros), and air-brushing characters' make-up onto the actors.

In **Armour & Weapons**, meanwhile, experts on medieval warfare liaised with blacksmiths, sculptors and leather-workers to produce thousands of stunt weapons, mock chain mail made of rubber pressure hosepipe, and 48,000 separate pieces of armour, from the elves' fine and elegant accoutrements to the black orc armour, inspired by insect exoskeletons.

Over in **Miniatures**, teams were divided to work across such diverse tasks as sticking 75,000 scale-model plastic medieval soldiers on boards to make blocks of armies, and scattering herbal tea on the floor of miniature forests. Also on their 'to do' list was constructing 'big-atures' (as they came to call them) – such things as a 30ft model of Sauron's Dark Tower, Barad-dûr, the seven-tiered citadel of Minas Tirith, and a detailed large-scale Corsair ship for *The Return Of The King*.

Other experts in **Special Effects** and **Model Effects** handled such intricacies as creating the trolls, orc archers and a wolf battering-ram attack on the gates of Minas Tirith for Visual Effects Miniatures Director of Photography **Alex Funke** and his team.

Simultaneously, the separate arm of Weta Digital was undertaking the major challenges of computer-generated creatures. Gollum, Treebeard, the Balrog, 'scary' Bilbo and Galadriel (when they feel the effects of the Ring) and the eye of Sauron were among the delights and terrors created and digitally manipulated by artists, modellers, editors, compositors and software engineers. Gollum, originating in the filmed performance of character-actor **Andy Serkis**, was also transformed into the baleful, melancholy menace of the finished movie by state-of-the-art computer animation and motion-capture technology.

Finally, **Visual Effects** (supervised by **Jim Rygiel**) were given challenges ranging from making the magical inscription on the Ring glow with ominous light to staging the massive battle sequences in *The Two Towers* and *The Return Of The King*. **Stephen Regelous** wrote a revolutionary new software programme called Massive, creating randomised 'agents' that have individual personality traits and respond to their environment – the closest thing yet to artificial intelligence in digital characters – to move and fight like tens of thousands of warriors. **John Alitt** invented a device called Grunt to 'render' Massive's skeleton motion-data agents into complete costumed computer-generated images.

On top of this, locations were scouted that would look like our Earth might have looked 7,000 years ago, for Middle-earth. A multiplicity of ingenious scale tricks were painstakingly co-ordinated by the visual effects, production design and camera teams to blend diminutive hobbits, squat, medium dwarves and Big Folk seamlessly into the same frames. And a veritable army – costume designer **Ngila Dickson**; make-up and hair designers **Peter King** and **Peter Owen**; stunt co-ordinator **George Marshall Ruge**; legendary sword-master **Bob Anderson**; wranglers for the specially trained corps of horses; more than 26,000 extras (including Maoris in blond wigs among the Riders of Rohan and a division of New Zealand's army); Elvish dialogue coaches; and 2,400 production crew – all had to be prepared for 274 days of principal photography between October 1999 and January 2001.

"I DIDN'T WANT TO MAKE YOUR STANDARD FANTASY FILM.
I WANTED SOMETHING THAT FELT MUCH, MUCH MORE REAL.
TOLKIEN WRITES IN A WAY THAT MAKES EVERYTHING COME ALIVE
AND WE WANTED TO SET THAT REALISTIC FEELING OF AN ANCIENT WORLD
COME TO LIFE RIGHT AWAY WITH THE FIRST FILM, THEN CONTINUE TO
BUILD IT AS THE STORY UNRAVELS"

"WE CONSTANTLY REFERRED TO THE BOOK, NOT JUST IN WRITING THE
SCREENPLAY BUT ALSO THROUGHOUT THE PRODUCTION. EVERY TIME WE
SHOT A SCENE I RE-READ THAT PART OF THE BOOK RIGHT BEFORE,
AS DID THE CAST. IT WAS ALWAYS WORTH IT, ALWAYS INSPIRING"

Peter Jackson

✦ The Lord Of The Rings ✦ The Fellowship Of The Ring (2001)

THE PLOT The voice of Galadriel (**Cate Blanchett**) narrates the history of the Ring, the Last Alliance of Elves and Men against Sauron at the end of the Second Age, and the events in *The Hobbit* that brought the Ring to the Shire. Sixty years later Bilbo's (**Ian Holm**) birthday brings Gandalf the Grey (**Ian McKellen**) to the Shire. As young Frodo (**Elijah Wood**) becomes the bearer of the Ring, in Mordor a dark army prepares for the enslavement of Middle-earth, and the ringwraiths set out seeking the Ring of absolute power. Frodo and a company of hobbits, men, the wizard, a dwarf and an elf become the Fellowship of the Ring, sent towards the Dark Lord's territory to destroy the Ring. But in the Mines of Moria after a desperate fight Gandalf falls into an abyss with the demon **Balrog**. The corrupting influence of the Ring breaks up the Fellowship. Boromir, after being tempted by the power of the Ring, dies bravely defending hobbits Merry and Pippin from the raiding uruk-hai, but they are taken prisoner. Accepting the Ring-bearer's fate is in his own hands, Aragorn, Legolas and Gimli pledge faith with each other and race after the captives, as Frodo and Sam set their faces to Mordor.

Frodo Baggins succeeds his uncle Bilbo as the Ring-bearer

Christopher Lee
CINEMA'S FAVOURITE DARK LORD

When Christopher Lee was honoured with a Lifetime Achievement Award in 2002, the 80-year-old éminence grise of British film said that his only remaining ambition was to live long enough to see the finished The Return Of The King. He was particularly proud of the film trilogy and his part in it, as well he might have been, given that the wizardly fight between his Saruman and Gandalf the Grey was one of its highlights.

Born 27 May 1922, in London, the 6ft 5in Lee was classically trained as a singer, worked as a clerk and served in the RAF during World War II before entering films as a bit player from the Rank Organisation's famous 'charm school'. Since then he has been in a remarkable 240 films, from Sir Laurence Olivier's Oscar-winning Hamlet to George Lucas's Star Wars trilogy (Lee's battle with Yoda as Count Dooku in Star Wars Episode II: The Attack Of The Clones helped make him the surprise action-darling of two blockbusters that year).

But it was as a horror icon that Lee found international fame, playing a compelling Dracula for Hammer Film Productions ten times, the sinister Fu Manchu five times, and the Mummy and Frankenstein's creation as tragic terrors. But he tired of his genre typecasting and cult identification with what he likes to refer to as "theatre of the fantastique". Among his other many films and screen personae Lee is particularly fond of the British spine-chiller The Wicker Man, in which he played the local lord; Rasputin; his Bond-villain turn as three-nippled assassin Scaramanga in The Man With The Golden Gun (his frequent golf partner Ian Fleming had wanted Lee to play Dr No); and Jinnah, in which he is outstanding as the founder of Pakistan.

Lee bought the first volume of The Lord Of The Rings when it was first published in 1954. He was thrilled a few years later when a mutual acquaintance introduced him to Professor Tolkien in the Oxford pub The Eagle And Child. Every year for nearly 50 years he has re-read the trilogy, and was respected as the Tolkien authority on the set of The Lord Of The Rings. "People would try to catch me out, but they never did."

✦ The Lord Of The Rings ✦
The Two Towers (2002)

THE PLOT Splintered into separate groups, the members of the Fellowship continue their own heroic journeys. Gandalf's descent into the fire with the Balrog has ended not in death but a transformation. Frodo and Sam discover they are being stalked by Gollum and capture him as their guide into Mordor. At Isengard the corrupted wizard Saruman builds his unnatural army, bent on ruling Middle-earth with the Dark Lord Sauron. Merry and Pippin escape their captors and flee into the mysterious Fangorn Forest, where they find an ally in Treebeard the ent – the oldest species in Middle-earth. The progress of Frodo and Sam through the Dead Marshes as the Ring strengthens its hold over Frodo, and their encounter with Faramir of Gondor, is interwoven with Gandalf's reappearance as Gandalf the White and the efforts of Aragorn, Gimli and Legolas in the troubled land of Rohan, where siblings Éomer and Éowyn, their bewitched uncle King Théoden and his people come under attack by Saruman's forces. At Helm's Deep, elves fight alongside men once more, while the ents make their march on Isengard. In the midst of big battles with the armies from the Two Towers – Orthanc and Barad-dûr – all hopes lie with the two small hobbits.

✦ The Lord Of The Rings ✦
The Return Of The King (2003)

THE PLOT Having been defeated at Isengard, where Saruman's forces and the duplicitous spy from Rohan, Gríma Wormtongue, were surrounded, Sauron's gaze is turned to Gondor. As his forces mass there in siege, Aragorn must decide how to unite the people of Rohan with those of Middle-earth's last stronghold at Minas Tirith, reclaim his throne from Gondor's embittered steward Denethor and lead the free peoples of Middle-earth in a new alliance – a final, defiant stand that is doomed unless the Ring-bearer is able to complete his task. Frodo and Sam, desperate for a quicker route to Mount Doom, have been tricked by

Gollum into the dark lair of the monstrous spider Shelob, whose paralysing attack on Frodo leaves Sam with an agonising choice and the burden of the Ring. Gollum still has a key role to play in the story of the Ring. And victory carries the price of grievous partings as one age of Middle-earth comes to an end.

THE FINAL INSTALMENT We know what the plot is – well, all of us who have read the books do – but what else can we expect from the third part of the trilogy? The pleasing news is that Shelob, scarier than all the eight-legged principals in *Arachnophobia*, will make her appearance – she is in the second book but will take a bow, as it were, in the third instalment. Yet, according to **Elijah Wood** (Frodo), there's more to the thrills than a contest with a giant spider. "It's a full-on war movie," he told *MTV.com*.

"Pete [Jackson] said he reckons it's going to be the most massive war movie ever shown on film. It's a massive boast but I'd say it's pretty close to that."

> "THE GREAT THING ABOUT TOLKIEN IS THAT WHERE THERE'S GREAT TRIUMPH, THERE'S ALSO GREAT LOSS"

So move over *Saving Private Ryan*, The Return Of The King is coming through. The battle scenes alone are reported to contain 200,000 digital participants; Jackson's special-effects company Weta Digital had to spend another $5 million on digital hardware for the final instalment, which contains about 1,200 special-effects shots.

Yet this being Tolkien, the war stories are underpinned by a tragic, emotional tale with something to say about the nature of good, evil and the corruption of power. **Dominic Monaghan** (Merry) says: "*The Return Of The King* is the bringing together of a lot of stories, and what the Fellowship has to sacrifice to save Middle-earth is huge. So you see these people facing the consequences of their actions."

In another interview Wood says, "the third film is the darkest and the saddest of the three. Everyone loses a little bit. The great thing about Tolkien is that where there's great triumph, there's also great loss. The third movie is a conclusion and a very ironed-out thing."

How much the actors themselves know about the fine detail of the third instalment is unclear. **Christopher Lee** is also, for example, said to have filmed five different death scenes for the character of Saruman, and doesn't really know which one Jackson will end up using in the final cut. There was also some additional shooting required.

Your Shopping List
ARGONATH BOOKENDS, GOLLUM STATUES AND RICK WAKEMAN

If visits to the nearest multiplex haven't satisfied your appetite for The Lord Of The Rings, here are some fine accompaniments to enjoy in your home.

DVD/VHS MOVIES
Fellowship Of The Ring
(Extended version)
Thirty-minutes longer, most of it more orc blood and gore, but still no Tom Bombadil. It does offer the making of the movie however.
Four-disc collector's box set
How did anyone live without the Argonath bookends which accompany this extra, extra special DVD collection?

The Two Towers
(Extended version)
If the cinema release wasn't long enough for you, here are more than 30 extra minutes, plus hours of behind-the-scenes footage.
Five-disc collector's box set
All of the above plus a booklet on how Gollum went from page to screen, and a Gollum statue.

Lord Of The Rings
(1978 animated version)
Featuring the voices of John Hurt as Aragorn and C3PO (sorry,

Anthony Daniels) as Legolas. The animation by Ralph Bakshi is fantastic but it's a paltry two hours long and leaves Frodo and Sam stuck in Mordor.

National Geographic –
Beyond The Movie –
The Lord Of The Rings
This hour-long documentary looks at every possible influence in the creation of Middle-earth, from Tolkien's home in Sarehole to Finnish mythology.

A Film Portrait of JRR Tolkien
Narrated by Judi Dench, this documentary was produced to celebrate both Tolkien and The Lord Of The Rings, featuring interviews with the author and his family – insights worth having.

Master Of The Rings
This mixed bag of a documentary veers from serious discussions of the influence of Beowulf to Yes keyboardist Rick Wakeman's 'insight' into The Lord Of The Rings phenomenon. Billed as "the definitive guide", but at only 80 minutes it's probably not, though the art by the Hildebrandt brothers compensates for any shortfalls.

Number Crunching
IN MOVIELAND YOU CAN NEVER HAVE ENOUGH FIGURES

270,000,000 the total budget, in dollars, to produce the motion picture trilogy.

12,500,000 the number of plastic rings used in chain mail in The Fellowship Of The Ring.

1,600,000 the number of times The Fellowship Of The Ring trailer was downloaded within the first 24 hours of its release on the Internet.

25,000 the number of cricket fans used to create the war cries of the orcs during the Helm's Deep battle sequence in The Two Towers.

1,600 the number of latex ears and feet produced for the hobbits.

1,460 the number of eggs served to cast and crew for breakfast on each day of shooting.

274 the number of days of shooting it took to film the three parts of the trilogy, back to back.

66 weight, in lbs, of Gimli's armour.

30 the number of pounds in weight Sean Astin had to gain for the role of Samwise Gamgee.

20 the number of hours the Helm's Deep battle footage in The Two Towers lasted before it was cut.

16 the number of months the shoot was spread over.

10 the number director Peter Jackson chose to have tattooed on his body in Elvish.

8 the number of members of the Fellowship who had the Elvish number 9 tattooed on their body. Only John Rhys-Davies declined, sending his stunt double instead.

7 the number of months it took to build the Helm's Deep battle set.

5 the number of different death scenes for Saruman that were shot, to prevent anyone guessing events.

2 the number of hours it took Sean Bean (Boromir) to climb to the top of the snowy mountain set for The Fellowship Of The Ring. Everyone else went by helicopter but Bean is afraid of flying.

1 the number of times Christopher Lee reads The Lord Of The Rings every year.

Henry V would have been proud of this turn out at Agincourt

Annie Lennox revealed in July 2003, on an Australian TV show, that "I was asked if I would sing the title track for the next *Lord Of The Rings* film which looks like it's going to happen. I was working in the studio with them a couple of days ago." Lennox's scoop soon blazed across the Internet, but hadn't been officially confirmed as this book went to press.

Jackson, working on production this summer, sounded very much as if he were missing the trilogy already: "Each movie has a very different tone, feel and structure so I've never really felt like I've been trapped in a Groundhog Day for seven years working on one project."

"We're shooting, we're cutting, the visual effects have a way to go, we haven't started recording the music yet – the premiére still seems a long way away from where I am at the moment. I have just experienced my last day of shooting **Elijah Wood** as Frodo and my last day of shooting **Viggo Mortensen** as Aragorn. Those, to me, are more profound than what my personal last day is going to be."

Of *The Return Of The King* he said, "It is the movie that I want to be most proud of, so I am working very hard to make sure that happens.

Christopher Lee as Saruman, with one of his most destructive creations

When people look back at the three films, I want The Return Of The King to be the one that really lingers with them in terms of the emotional experience. I want it to be the reason why we made the other two films."

✦ The Finished Trilogy ✦

When The Lord Of The Rings: The Fellowship Of The Ring opened in theatres in December 2001 it was to near-unanimous acclaim. The film took $860 million at the box office worldwide, and among a raft of honours it was nominated for 13 Academy Awards, winning four (for cinematographer Andrew Lesnie, for composer Howard Shore's score, and Best Visual Effects and Best Make-up for Richard Taylor and his teams). The soundtrack became a platinum seller and the DVD broke records when it was released in August 2002. It was a triumphant validation for work that was a collective labour of love.

And, at least as important as its enthusiastic reception, The Fellowship Of The Ring made audiences anxious to see what happened next. Much of the credit goes to cast and crew but some, too, goes to Tolkien himself. The poet WH Auden noted in his laudatory review of the first book in the trilogy, "on the primitive level of wanting to know what happens next, *The Fellowship Of The Ring* is at least as good as [John Buchan's thriller] *The Thirty-Nine Steps.*"

The Fellowship Of The Ring was embraced in its context as the first film of a bigger epic. Magnificent though they were, elements like the scenic splendours of New Zealand and the fabulous production design would not have been enough in themselves to make the film work so successfully, but the magic is there in a 'Frodo-centric' interpretation of a tale that excels in conveying the spell of the Ring.

There were criticisms that the three-hour film was sprawling, but it was already apparent that here was the first part of a landmark fantasy epic likely to stand out as unique in film history. Jackson also brought out some of the tale's gentle, yet often overlooked, sense of humour – in Gimli's dwarf-tossing gag and in the exchanges between Merry and Pippin.

The Lord Of The Rings: The Two Towers, released in December 2002, feels every bit the 'second act'. Peter Jackson held to his intention that eventually all three films are meant to be seen consecutively, and makes no concessions to any viewer who might take in the second film without having seen The Fellowship Of The Ring – even eschewing a typical 'the story so far' prologue or encapsulating earlier events with any exposition.

The seductive and destructive nature of power is the pervasive theme as the splintered Fellowship confront it on all fronts. Some of the three-hour second film's strengths are only fully appreciated when seen as the middle part of the whole story – darkening the mood and widening an understanding of the land and cultures as the enemy begins to wreak a serious amount of havoc on Middle-earth and as the corrupting influence of the Ring grows in power.

The Lord Of The Rings And Star Wars
TWO PARALLEL FICTIONAL UNIVERSES

Jean Tang, writing for the American news and opinion website Salon.com, noted that "The Lord Of The Rings and Star Wars share a long list of structural and thematic similarities. They're both mythical creature fantasies hellbent on rescuing good from the clutches of evil. Both feature circumstantial heroes who make Oz-like journeys and come of age in the process."

Tang went on: "Both movies feature mentors who duel bad guys atop narrow passageways, as well as secondary villains – Darth Vader and Saruman the White, both deserters to the dark side, both fond of telekinetic violence – who provide the more visible nemesis. Along the way, both heroes encounter women in white gowns, cynical older-brother types, sidekicks playing for laughs and faceless cannon fodder (storm troopers and orcs).

"Both make use of mystical languages, mystical spiritual beliefs and pivotal scenes in bars and in watery mucky-mucks (compare the swamp at the gates of Moria with the garbage chute in the Death Star)."

The similarities keep multiplying, some suggest that Gollum is the thinking man's Jar Jar Binks (for a fuller list see opposite), but perhaps the most ironic parallel is that both George Lucas – the genius behind the Star Wars movies – and Tolkien believed that religion has a profound role to play in society.

Lucas once noted, "I would hate to find ourselves in a completely secular world where entertainment was passing for some kind of religious experience."

Yet he and Tolkien have created fictional worlds which have inspired quasi-religious devotion among millions of fans.

There is also the welcome, dread appearance of the poisonously malicious spy Gríma Wormtongue (**Brad Dourif**) in Théoden's bedevilled court; the first encounter in the whole cycle with a human woman (Australian actress **Miranda Otto** as the heartsick but courageous Éowyn); the first meeting with determined Faramir, the younger brother of the lost Fellowship comrade Boromir; and the breathtakingly complex creations of Gollum (the unique combination of actor **Andy Serkis's** disturbing movement and voice with ground-breaking computer

The Lord Of The Rings vs Star Wars
THOSE REMARKABLE PARALLELS IN FULL

Gollum	Yoda (greenish, raggedy midget with a speech impediment).
Magic swords	Lightsabres
Gandalf	Obi-Wan Kenobi
Éowyn	Princess Leia
Saruman	Darth Vader
Sauron	Emperor Palpatine
Bilbo digs his magic sword out of an old wooden box, and gives it to Frodo.	Obi-Wan digs Anakin's lightsabre out of an old wooden box, and gives it to Luke Skywalker.
Gollum bites off Frodo's finger, which plunges into the abyss with the Ring.	Darth cuts off Luke's hand, which plunges into the abyss with Luke's lightsabre.
Galadriel foretells the future, and Sam must decide whether to help his friends or not. Galadriel warns that she's seen only one possible future.	Yoda foretells the future, and Luke must decide whether to help his friends or not. Yoda warns that he's seen only one possible future.
Saruman tries to convince Gandalf to join the evil wizards, thereby bringing order to Middle-earth.	Darth tries to convince Luke to join the dark side, thereby bringing order to the galaxy.
Mundane name and special name (Strider and Aragorn).	Mundane name and special name (Ben and Obi-Wan).
Mysterious figure throws back hood of robe to reveal that he's Gandalf.	Mysterious figure throws back hood of robe to reveal that he's Obi-Wan.

wizardry) and the fantastic Treebeard (voiced with electronic enhancement by the booming Welsh bass John 'Gimli' Rhys-Davies).

But the film is most amazing for its spectacular action sequences, with an awesome **Battle of Helm's Deep** that is unlikely to be rivalled, being impossible to surpass for the realism with which the computer-generated armies clash gruesomely. For lovers of fantasy the film has everything: romance (Arwen and Aragorn's story beautifully elaborated), tragedy, action thrills, spectacle and some good humour in a story of war, grief and despair compounded by the trials of Frodo and Sam.

Even critics like **Roger Ebert**, who bemoaned what they saw as the shift of emphasis away from the hobbits, felt obliged to concede, "*The Two Towers* is one of the most spectacular swashbucklers ever made." Viggo Mortensen (Aragorn) worked on the swordplay as soon as he arrived on set – with Bob Anderson, who once taught Errol Flynn how to wave a sword to fine cinematic effect. Mortensen was a dedicated student: he was once stopped by a policeman while carrying his sword home for some extra practice.

Roger Ebert also noted that, "Jackson, like some of the great silent directors, is not afraid to use his entire screen, to present images of wide scope and great complexity. He paints in the corners." The sweep of Jackson's lens is such that the movies cry out to be seen on as big a screen as possible yet also, remarkably, retain their power when watched on the most modest TV set. Ebert's observation was echoed by one of the actors, Ian McKellen saying of the three movies, "It's a **Fritz Lang** epic!" Indeed, the creator of the 1930s futuristic science-fiction masterpiece Metropolis would probably have been impressed by this epic fictional world. Others, seeking similar comparisons from movie history, likened the films to the work of John Ford and David Lean. A few critics saw the bucolic hobbit homeland as inspired by **John Constable**'s paintings while others referred to the apocalyptic visions of good and evil created by **Hieronymus Bosch**, the 15th-century Dutch painter of bizarre portrayals of hell.

While *The Fellowship Of The Ring* is a notably family-friendly movie, The Two Towers markedly ups the intense combat and fantasy-horror content. After seeing The Return Of The King (due for release in December 2003 as this book went to press), it should be evident that the films, like the books, are not a work conceived or executed for children. *The Return Of The King* is an inherently sombre spectacle, taking the now familiar and best beloved characters to their **final face-off with the ultimate catastrophe** and the savage hordes of darkness

– and the hardship, cruelty and slaughter are relentless.

There is little room for light-hearted respites, although there is always love, a vast amount of uplifting heroism and unquenched hope – obviously justified in an inevitably cathartic celebration, since the king must return and good must triumph over evil.

Viewed in a single nine-hour stint – more when scenes deleted for theatrical release are incorporated on DVD – the majesty, intensity and collective force of emotion harnessed to effects in Jackson's audacious venture is staggering, exhausting and unlikely ever to be equalled. Even the normally cynical *The Onion*, the American satirical website and newspaper, noted: "It's thrilling as swords clash and arrows fly, but it also never abandons the underlying sadness of Tolkien's world, in which each victory only forestalls the transition to a meaner age." *The Onion* was offering its verdict on *The Two Towers* but the point applies to the trilogy as a whole, this being (as the review noted in closing): "a tale from a fantastic imagined past rich with resonance for the human present."

If Tolkien's book often reads as if he is describing fantastic scenes with the authority of an eyewitness, the same is just as true of the movies; there's an inevitability about the way Jackson uses the camera which seems to deliberately echo the author's technique.

In the end, the scale of the achievement is rather aptly summed up by one Tolkien fanatic's detailed and enthusiastic review of The Two Towers (see *www.tolkienonline.com/docs/8442.html* for the full article), in which the aficionado notes: "My biggest complaint is simply that the movie is far too short."

✦ Cautionary Notes On The Source ✦

Although it may come as a shock to Tolkien's multitude of admirers, there are still many people who have never read The Lord Of The Rings. A whole new readership has become aware of the book in the wake of Peter Jackson's blockbuster trilogy. So to prepare readers coming to a rather large book of The Lord Of The Rings only after seeing the movies, these notes may be useful to avoid literary culture shock.

No matter how beloved they might be of readers, some characters,

A Western Lord Of The Rings

HOBBITS, HEROES, VILLAINS AND COWBOYS

JRR Tolkien might have been slightly irritated by the idea that his tale has some echoes of the archetypal Hollywood Western. He was, after all, no great fan of America and knew little of Hollywood. In 1965 he attended a lecture by the English poet Robert Graves and he noted, "after it he introduced me to a pleasant young woman: well but quietly dressed, easy and agreeable and we got on quite well." The agreeable young woman turned out to be Ava Gardner. Tolkien had never heard of her and she had never heard of him.

Yet in essence the simple, but arduous, quest facing Frodo and his eight allies – a magnificent nine rather than seven – is similar to that of many Western heroes: to defend their world against evil, whatever the cost.

Tolkien rarely watched television and probably watched few movies, but you can imagine him liking a self-consciously adult, yet great, Western like George Stevens's Shane. Alan Ladd plays the eponymous hero who, like Aragorn, has endured a kind of exile but commits to the right side in a battle of good and evil

though he knows he'll pay a tragic price – in Ladd's case, a life of continued exile, spent wondering when he will fatally confront a gunslinger faster than he is.

His opponent in the film is a black rider (and a mercenary to boot) played by Jack Palance. It's possible to imagine, too, Tolkien sympathising with the small farmers of this Western shire, against the monopolistic cattle barons. The fellowship of small farmers is fractured by the power of evil, many trying to flee the conflict. And Stevens's epic sense of landscape echoes the grandeur of the land through which Frodo and his allies must progress.

Ultimately, these echoes may be explained simply by the fact that Tolkien and the great Western directors like Stevens and John Ford were drawing on the power of myth. But specific vignettes highlight the comparison: Aragorn (who Viggo Mortensen says reminded him of the sheriff in High Noon) saying, "Let's go hunt some orc" at the close of the first film; Aragorn, Gandalf and Legolas riding the range; Gandalf's mosey into Hobbiton in the Shire's answer to a wagon...

including Tom Bombadil, master of the Old Forest, were shed if they didn't contribute to the main story of the Ring. In Bombadil's case he can be said to slow the hobbits' progress to Bree inexcusably for an adventure film.

While some material has been cut for the films, to add weight to characters such as Arwen – marginalised at best by Tolkien in a book with no interest in sex appeal or gender equality – material had to be created.

Thus, for example, in the film *The Fellowship Of The Ring*, Arwen is given an eye-catching warrior princess sequence, plucking the wounded Frodo from the Fellowship and racing on horseback with him to the safety of Rivendell, pursued thrillingly by the nine evil ringwraiths. She also chants the sublime elven spell that turns the river water into white steeds, routing the riders at the boundary of Rivendell. True, the water stallions are in the book – beautifully conjured by Tolkien – but Arwen hasn't appeared by then, and her role in the book (still hauntingly persistent in the films) is to give Aragorn the heart and will to fulfil his overwhelming destiny.

Viggo Mortensen was encouraged to compose and sing The Song Of Beren And Lúthien, a neat way of making exposition painless, telling the story of mortal man Beren and elf-maiden Lúthien which is mirrored by the lovers Aragorn and Arwen. No one could quarrel with a scene like this, whether or not the Aragorn of the book is a fellow given to a soulful melodious moment by the campfire.

The Ring also develops a presence and character of its own in the films, dramatically interacting in a sense with the characters (and eventually acquiring its own voice, called Black Speech, voiced by Royal Shakespeare Company veteran Alan Howard). As a well-considered, chillingly executed device, one feels Tolkien would have appreciated this notion.

The restructuring may come as a surprise, but the need to do it is apparent from a reading. *The Fellowship Of The Ring* concludes with Frodo and Sam running away from the Fellowship, seeking their path into Mordor and leaving the others oblivious. To create a fitting finale for the first film (the fate of Boromir and the decision thrust upon Aragorn, Legolas and Gimli), the beginning of The Two Towers has to be included.

The Two Towers is itself divided into two books (Books Three and Four of the novel) and so is the action. Book Three is concerned with the events overtaking the three hunters, Gandalf's reappearance, Merry and Pippin's adventure with Treebeard and the ents, the situation in Rohan and the battles at Helm's Deep and Isengard.

Book Four returns to Frodo and Sam for ten chapters of their perilous trek, climaxing in the encounter with Shelob and the separation of the two hobbits. But filmgoers would not be prepared to wait an hour and a half (at least) into *The Two Towers* without a glimpse of Frodo and Sam, or want to watch each separate adventure in Book Three play out to their ends before catching up with other key characters. So Jackson did the cinematic thing, ambitiously interweaving the stories.

The Return Of The King does exactly the same thing. Book Five is taken up with men, elves, dwarf, wizard, politics and battles, leaving the fates of Frodo and Sam precariously in the balance until Book Six. So Jackson saved Shelob for the final film instalment, when the doings in Mordor and beyond are interconnected to their conclusion.

✦ What Happens Next? ✦

The Lord Of The Rings' journey to the big screen has finally come to an end. As journeys go, it hasn't been quite as arduous as that undertaken by Frodo and his fellow hobbits, but it hasn't been easy either, peppered with false starts, false hopes and false dawns. The wait was, though, ultimately worth it. The director himself seems, in interviews, to be gripped by a sense of nostalgia for the heroic enterprise which has occupied him for so much of the last seven years, however he also admits to "a certain amount of relief that creeps into thinking that we're almost done and will be able to spend our lives focusing on something that's not based on hobbits, wizards and elves."

Jackson's next project is King Kong. Meanwhile, for fans of hobbits, there has, of course, been an animated version of Tolkien's The Hobbit, made for TV in 1977 and directed by Jules Bass and Arthur Rankin Junior. Re-released on video in 2001, this version was praised by some Tolkien fans but dismissed by a few critics as too bland and inoffensive for its own good. In the 1970s the relative failure of the cartoon (and the vicissitudes of the Ralph Bakshi animation of *The Lord Of The Rings*) only served to justify the prevailing cliché that all Tolkien's books really were utterly unfilmable. Yet the cast of voices included director John Huston (as Gandalf the Grey), Otto Preminger (the Elvenking) and Don Messick – better known for voicing Muttley in Wacky Races and Scooby Doo.

What's My Motivation?
THE CAST ON PLAYING THEIR PART

Sir Ian McKellen "You can't think about Gandalf being 7,000 years old because that's beyond anyone's experience: you have to play an old man who's got arthritis, who's cold, wet and tired; a man who has a daunting job to do, who enjoys a drink and a smoke."

Viggo Mortensen "I was afraid. Practically speaking, I was still reading the book within days of joining this project, but as I read I saw that, brave as Aragorn seems to be, he is much conflicted and dealing with a lot of self-doubt. I recognise something of the roles played by Toshirô Mifune in Kurosawa's pictures, as well as those taciturn characters played by Clint Eastwood or Gary Cooper in High Noon."

Billy Boyd "Pippin comes from a family that is known for being a bit adventurous and likely to fly off the handle. What's more, he does have a habit of doing the wrong thing at the wrong time. Although to be fair, as the story develops, we see Pippin going through all kinds of experiences and becoming more mature."

Sean Bean "He's (Boromir) a much wiser man. He understands the complexities of Middle-earth and its cultures much more clearly than when he first sets off. He seems to have found his spirituality, his soul. Even though he's been ripped apart, he's not going to let the Ring defeat him."

Elijah Wood "I was out of my element, as Frodo was out of his carrying out this responsibility on this journey. Everyone felt like that and felt that their journeys mirrored that of the characters."

Viggo Mortensen "There is a tendency to say 'This is good and this is evil and I shall do something about it.' It isn't that simple. Tolkien has Gandalf say something to the effect that there was no evil in the beginning; Sauron was not always so. Aragorn says to Legolas, 'Good and evil have not changed since yesteryear and nor are they one thing among dwarves and elves.' Even though Tolkien was a devout Christian, the books don't assert that there is a heavenly reward for doing the right thing. Doing the right thing is its own reward."

After watching both Bakshi's animation and the cartoon of *The Hobbit* you can see why, when rumours of Jackson's trilogy were first mooted, Richard Cranshaw of the Tolkien Society said: "Tolkien himself never thought a film could be made of the book. We feel that no movie could ever capture the full depth and flavour of the book." Cranshaw's caution, understandable at the time, has been superseded by the acclaim for Jackson's work, yet his point is still relevant. The other Tolkien books pose something of a problem for the wannabe scriptwriter and adaptor, nor, given the uneventful nature of Tolkien's life once he became an Oxford don, are we likely to see a big screen biopic of the man himself.

It's entirely possible that, given Hollywood's current predilection for prequels and sequels, a studio will want to make a movie out of *The Silmarillion*. Given the acclaim which has greeted Jackson's trilogy, directing such a film would surely be one of the toughest jobs in Hollywood. Jackson's achievement in creating such a definitive version of Middle-earth means that it's impossible to imagine any other studio or director wanting to remake the trilogy in the next decade or two. Still, this is the movie business and things almost as strange have happened.

Quote Credits

All quotes in this chapter from: New Line Cinema, Paul Fisher at CrankyCritic.com, Empire Magazine (January 2002), Berlin Talent Campus Lecture by Peter Cowie (February 2003), Science Fiction Weekly, www.great-scot.net and FilmForce.ign.com

THE CHARACTERS

TOLKIEN'S CREATIONS:
FROM ARAGORN TO WARGS

Aragorn: as taciturn as Clint Eastwood and as decent as Gary Cooper onscreen

"That's where I got the idea for The Hobbit"
**JRR Tolkien to Arthur C Clarke over lunch, pointing
to his diminutive editor**

Middle-earth is so wonderfully, lovingly – even geologically – realised that it's easy to forget that there are also strong characters in The Lord Of The Rings. On one level, this isn't too surprising – there's some merit in the argument by **Raymond E Feist**, author of the Riftwar Legacy fantasy novels, that: "Frodo and the hobbits were 'people': simple, peaceful, graceful and humble. They were archetypes bordering on stereotypes: Frodo the plucky hero; Sam the good and faithful; Gandalf the eminence who could not possibly be more grise; and Merry and Pippin, as hale a pair of well-met fellows as you'd find in **Percival C Wren**'s Beau Geste, uncertain why they were a part of the drama but willing to put aside personal safety for friendship." But, as is usually the case with **Tolkien**, the reality isn't quite that simple.

The characters must be more than stereotypes because we care about them. Many have symbolic significance – there is a slew of Christ figures and at least one **Satan** – yet they also have personal significance, sometimes heavily disguised (and sometimes not), for the author. Take Sam Gamgee, a character variously seen as the hero of the book and, as even Tolkien admits, so irrepressibly stout and true that he almost becomes an irritant. His role comes into focus when you recall **Tolkien**'s admission that "My Sam Gamgee is a **reflection of the English soldier**."

Tolkien laboured mightily over their naming – even the names he doesn't discuss are significant (see **Tom Shippey**'s exploration of the origins of 'Frodo' on page 85). And yet, as movie critic **Roger Ebert** notes, "The Lord Of The Rings is not about a narrative arc or the growth of the characters, but about a long series of episodes in which the essential nature of the characters is demonstrated again and again and again."

✦ Aragorn ✦

Son of **Dúnedain** chieftain Arathorn (who was slain by orcs) and the direct descendent of Isildur and the exiled Northern kings, Aragorn – lean, grim, wise and something like a Norse King Arthur – was raised in secrecy in **Rivendell** by Elrond, who called him Estel (which is Sindarin for hope). When he was 20, Elrond told him who he was. About this time Elrond's daughter Arwen returned from Lórien and Aragorn fell in love with her at once. Preparing to fulfill his destiny and reunite the Dúnedain kingdoms, Aragorn went into the wilderness, leading the **Rangers of the North** for many years against the minions of Sauron, protecting the Shire and, in disguise, serving the rulers of **Gondor** and **Rohan**. He sought and captured Gollum for his friend Gandalf, and later went to **Bree** at Gandalf's summons to protect the hobbits, taking them to Rivendell and the Council of Elrond. There the sword that was broken, Isildur's sword, was forged anew for Aragorn and renamed Andúril, **Flame of the West**. Aragorn's role in the Fellowship and the War of the Ring is quite faithful to the book in the films. Aragorn has many names. His Ranger nom de guerre was Strider. Galadriel called him Elessar, which is Quenyan for **elf-stone** (because he wore Arwen's emerald brooch); the people of Gondor hailed him this, fulfilling Galadriel's prophecy, and Aragorn took this name when he assumed kingship.

✦ Arwen ✦

Daughter of Elrond and Celebrían, granddaughter of Galadriel and Celeborn, **Tolkien's** archetypal elven princess Arwen (whose name is Sindarin for royal maiden) lived 3,000 years in elven realms before meeting Aragorn. They pledged themselves to each other on the hill of **Cerin Amroth** in Lórien, but Elrond would not agree to their marriage until Aragorn became king of Gondor and Arnor. Her dark beauty reminded her people of Lúthien (who also loved a mortal man) and they called her Arwen **Undómiel**, or Evenstar, because they knew such beauty among their kind would soon pass away from Middle-earth. Arwen's role in the films is slightly more active, riding to the rescue of Frodo from the Black Riders. In the books and films her love gives Aragorn the heart

Arwen otherwise known as Evenstar, and the future Queen of Gondor

Faramir - Captain of the Rangers of Ithilien and brother to Boromir

to bear his hardships, assume leadership in the **War of the Ring** and reunite his ancestral kingdoms. By marrying Aragorn, Arwen surrendered her right to pass over the Sea and thus became mortal. They had a long and happy reign, Arwen bearing Aragorn a son and several daughters. Although his life span was more than twice that of ordinary men, Aragorn died at a time of his choosing and Arwen returned to silent Lórien, making her grave on Cerin Amroth.

✦ Bilbo Baggins ✦

The hobbit Bilbo discovered a taste for adventure when the wizard Gandalf mischievously – or prophetically – recruited him for a dragon-slaying quest. (It was possibly a taste inherited from his mother Belladonna Took; the Tooks, who sometimes exhibited an un-hobbitlike wanderlust, were rumoured to have a touch of fairy in their bloodline.) After his return to the Shire, secretly in possession of a ring that made him invisible and kept him unnaturally youthful, he took to such eccentricities as writing poetry and visiting **elves**. Eventually he used the Ring to vanish at his eleventy-first birthday celebrations, before leaving it to his young cousin Frodo and setting forth. The time period is compressed in the films, so we do not gather the scholarship, elven lore and history acquired and recorded by Bilbo during his decades as an elven friend. He does give Frodo the mithril-mail and the sword Sting he received on his journey with the dwarves, gifts which save Frodo's life. Rapidly ageing and badly affected by his possession of the Ring, Bilbo's status as a one-time Ring-bearer earns him the privilege of leaving Middle-earth with Gandalf, Frodo and a company of the **elven High Kindred** led by Elrond and Galadriel.

✦ Boromir And Faramir ✦

Captains of **Gondor** and sons of Denethor II, Steward of Gondor, proud warrior Boromir was the elder son and his father's favourite, sharing his reluctance to give the crown of Gondor to Isildur's heir should he return, while the gentler, more learned, wiser Faramir, overshadowed by his brother, tried and failed to please his father with his bravery against enemy raiders and in the **Siege of Gondor**. Both brothers shared

Finding Tolkien

"I am, in fact, a hobbit in all but size"

While you should sometimes be wary of taking such statements straight from a novelist's mouth, in this instance JRR Tolkien may have a point

As Humphrey Carpenter notes in his biography of Tolkien, author and Bilbo Baggins are both middle-aged, with a slightly contradictory fondness for sensible clothes and bright colours (Tolkien particularly liked to wear colourful waistcoats) and plain homespun food. The hobbit house was even called Bag End, the name locals gave to the farm run by Tolkien's aunt in Worcestershire.

Like his creator, Bilbo finally achieves his long-held ambition to write his own book – although in his case it's an autobiography.

You could even argue that, as Bilbo is distracted from his book by the Ring, so JRR was distracted from the serious business of writing more masterworks by fan mail and his own cult status.

Frodo Baggins, the principal character, shares fewer traits with his creator. He does, though, share Tolkien's appetite for food, drink and good cheer. Perhaps the most dramatic resemblance is that, like Tolkien (who had lost both his parents by the time he was 12),

Frodo is an orphan. Again, it's possible to read too much into this: the wholly or semi-orphaned hero(ine) is a classic motif in fairy-tales like Cinderella and Pinocchio, myths like King Arthur and novels like The Wizard Of Oz (where Dorothy is effectively orphaned on the yellow brick road), Great Expectations and Oliver Twist.

The practice, in modern literary criticism, of finding an author in a character can be taken too far. Yes, The Lord Of The Rings is full of characters who share some traits with the author – just as it is full of characters who owe something to the people the author knew. For example, hobbits are, Tolkien told us, shrunken-down versions of the rural people he knew and admired in Warwickshire and of the World War 1 soldiers, whose superhuman courage in adversity he saw first hand in battle.

But it's part of the art of a great novelist like Tolkien to ensure that some kind of alchemy takes place. Characters taken too literally from life seldom convince or enthral.

Bilbo Baggins - the original hobbit ring-bearer and adventurer

Elrond - an Eldarin lord of great power and wisdom and father to Arwen

a mystifying dream ("Seek for the sword that was broken..."), which prompted Boromir's journey to Elrond in search of its meaning. At the Council of Elrond, Boromir learned Aragorn's identity and joined the Company of the Ring, whose spell overcame him in a murderous attempt to wrest it from Frodo. Remorseful, he defended Merry and Pippin from orcs and died urging Aragorn to save his people. Faramir encountered Frodo and Sam on their journey to Mordor, learned something of their story and was reluctantly persuaded to let them continue on their way. He comes into his own in The Return Of The King, falls in battle, is healed by Aragorn, and rewarded for his loyalty and valour with titles, lands and the love of Éowyn.

✦ Elrond ✦

Son of Eärendil and half-elven Elwing, Elrond fought in the Great Battle at the end of the First Age and was permitted by the ancient angelic powers, the Valar, to choose elven-kind as his race. In the Second Age, as a wise and powerful elven lord, he founded the haven Imladris (Rivendell), fought in the War of the Last Alliance of Men and Elves that overthrew Sauron, and was given the greatest of the three elven rings of power, Vilya, which was the gold and sapphire ring of air. In the Third Age he wed Celebrían, the only child of Galadriel and Celeborn, who bore him Arwen, along with twin sons Elladan and Elrohir (somewhat sidelined in the movies, but friends who fought alongside Aragorn in the book). Celebrían was captured, tortured and poisonously wounded by orcs, rescued by her sons and sailed out of Middle-earth; but Elrond remained to help the Dúnedain survive and resist for generations Sauron's insidious recovery of power, bent on rallying the peoples of Middle-earth in the cause of Sauron's final destruction. The War of the Ring ended the Third Age and ushered in the Age of Men, so Elrond, sorely grieved by his parting with Arwen, passed over the Sea.

✦ Éomer And Éowyn ✦

The handsome blonde children of King Théoden's sister Théodwyn in the Nordic and Anglo-Saxon-flavoured Land of the Mark (called Rohan by their allies in Gondor), Éomer became his uncle's heir after the death of

A Rough Guide To Elvish
THE LANGUAGES OF THE LORD OF THE RINGS

"Naneth lîn mant hû nin" is, as the cognoscenti amongst you will doubtless already know, Sindarin for "Your mother ate my dog." Granted, it isn't the kind of phrase you are likely to use very often outside Middle-earth, but then part of the charm of learning any new language is that instead of acquiring a really useful vocabulary you end up parroting phrases like "My brother is a lieutenant in the Italian navy" from a phrasebook.

Sindarin is just one of the Elvish languages which JRR Tolkien invented for The Lord Of The Rings trilogy. In these post Star Trek days, it's tempting to see Tolkien's languages as a kind of higher Klingon but, although you can buy a Klingon dictionary, Klingon lacks the linguistic logic Tolkien brought to his invented language.

Tolkien was so fascinated by his new languages that it is a wonder he ever found time to finish the books. That said, as he wrote to his American publishers in 1955, his work was "fundamentally linguistic in inspiration". In other words, if he hadn't been the kind of boy who had learned Latin, French and

German from his mother, acquiring a reasonable mastery of Greek, Middle English, Old English, Old Norse, Gothic, modern and medieval Welsh, Finnish, Spanish and Italian while at school and, as an academic, developed a working knowledge of Russian, Swedish, Danish, Norwegian, Dutch and Lombardic, his books wouldn't be with us today.

He created five alphabets (Rumil, Tengwar, the Cirth – of which there are many variants, Goblin and the Runes of Gondolin) and up to 12 languages; for a full listing and a bit on the use of each see www.geocities.com/Athens/Parthenon/9902/langlst.html.

His cousins, Mary and Majory Incledon, had invented their own language, called Animalic, which, as the name suggests, traded mainly on animal names. With Tolkien, Mary created something called Nevbosh (it meant "new nonsense" and was a blend of heavily distorted French, Latin and English). As a schoolboy, Tolkien's curiosity reached such a point that he was soon tracking down dry-as-dust books about languages which had nothing to do with the curriculum.

The serious invention of language began soon after his mother's shockingly sudden death, and you don't have to be Freud to see some psychological explanation. In inventing languages, he was honouring the parent whose Latin lessons were still among his most cherished memories and, of course, creating a fairy-tale world which made the grim reality of being a virtual orphan more tolerable. At the same time, although he went further in inventing languages than most children of his age, he didn't see his gift as especially unusual. He had always believed that children were actually far more creative than teachers or parents gave them credit for – indeed child psychologists now believe that playing with nonsense words at a very early age helps stimulate a child's intelligence.

In 1915, while completing his degree and waiting to be summoned to war, what he called his "nonsense fairy language" became more complex, influenced by his recent re-reading of Finnish. The creation (and constant revision) of languages would henceforth be a life's work.

The two most developed languages are Quenya, clearly inspired by Finnish, and Sindarin, which owes something to Tolkien's childhood joy in discovering Welsh. If you are as fascinated by these languages as he was, both have literally thousands of words, and therefore a vocabulary large enough for you to write short essays. Tolkien has left behind a lot of verses in both and grammatical rules – though sadly not all the rules have been published.

JRR Tolkien didn't sit in his study and think "'gazumblatt!' – that would be a great exclamation in Sindarin." As his third son Christopher pointed out, he invented words according to a set of logical rules (for more information on this go to www.uib.no/People/hnohf/vice.htm, and the article called 'Tolkien's Not So Secret Vice'). Some people actually use these languages – indeed, Lisa Star, in her online journal 'Tyalië Tyelelliéva' declares that she wants to lead a revival in the Elvish language. There's certainly enough verse written by Tolkien's admirers for an enterprising publisher to compile an anthology of Elvish verse, and Star runs her very own Elvish language poetry prize. If Tolkien was alive today, he might be flattered. Or he might want to correct her grammar.

his cousin Théodred, although he and his unhappy sister Éowyn bore disfavour and insult when Théoden was bewitched by the poisonous counsellor and spy Gríma Wormtongue. The arrival of Gandalf and Aragorn restored sanity and purpose in the court, and ever-loyal Éomer, who forged a lasting friendship with Aragorn fighting side by side at the **Hornburg** and after, proved a valiant leader of the strong, fair Riders of the Mark, the Rohirrim (Sindarin for horse lords), throughout the War of the Ring. Éowyn's despair from **unrequited love** for the sympathetic Aragorn and her courage as a shield-maiden inspired her to ride in battle with the Rohirrim as the youth Dernhelm; in this disguise she confronted the Lord of the Nazgûl and slew him, but was overcome by the **Black Breath**. Healed in body and mind by Aragorn, her heart turned joyfully to the admiring Faramir, who is created Prince of Ithilien. And as King of the Mark, Éomer remained a lifelong friend and ally to King Elessar (Aragorn).

✦ Frodo Baggins ✦

The orphaned, dreamy hobbit Frodo was adopted by Bilbo, inheriting **Bag End** and the Ring when Bilbo departed. Seventeen years later (but only months in the film, to keep things moving), Gandalf dispatched Frodo from **the Shire**. On the desperate journey he and his companions were relentlessly pursued by Black Riders, but Strider came to their aid and the injured Frodo reached **Rivendell** in time to be saved. Shy, quiet and true, Frodo bravely undertook the destruction of the Ring, to which he demonstrated remarkable resistance. After the Company of the Ring's trials Frodo struck out on his own, although he was grateful when the loyal Sam insisted on accompanying him. His pity for Gollum, an untrustworthy guide on the harrowing passage into **Mordor**, led him to a near-fatal encounter and capture, but he reached the fires of **Mount Doom**, only to be overcome by the Ring's spell at the last. Miraculously spared in the ensuing cataclysm, he was honoured through the long, bittersweet journey home, only to find **the Shire** in need of purging of the evil wrought in his absence. Finally the wounds Frodo had sustained as Ring-bearer became too grievous too bear. Leaving his record of events and his property to Sam, he joined the **Last Riding of the Keepers of the Ring** to go across the Sea.

Frodo Baggins: Bilbo's nephew and his successor as the ring-bearer

Galadriel or 'lady of the light' as played by Austrailiam actress Cate Blanchett

✦ Galadriel ✦

Stately, strong-willed and golden-haired Galadriel (Sindarin for lady of light) was the eldest of her kind in Middle-earth. For her part in a rebellion against the Valar she was banished from crossing the Sea. Wedded to Celeborn the Wise, she had one child, Celebrían, who married Elrond. In the Second Age she founded the forest realm of Lórien, where she was Queen of the Galadrim (tree-people), and shielded it from Sauron with the help of her elven ring of power Nenya, the mithril Ring of Water or Ring of Adamant. She was able to see into the mind of Sauron without him knowing hers, and she gave Frodo a glimpse into her magic mirror to steel him for his task. For her long resistance to Sauron, her kindness to the Company of the Ring, and her refusal of the One Ring, Galadriel was at last permitted to leave Middle-earth and Lórien was virtually abandoned. Celeborn, who led the Galadrim army during the War of the Ring (a 'supporting role' in the book appendix and films), joined his grandsons, Elrond's sons, in Imladris after a time but, tired of his life in Middle-earth without Galadriel, finally followed her over the Sea.

✦ Gandalf ✦

The Wizard Gandalf the Grey was one of the Istari (he was the second most-powerful Istari after Saruman), sent in the guise of old men by the Valar to Middle-earth in the Third Age to act as advisors to the free peoples in the fight against Sauron. When Gandalf arrived in Middle-earth the seafaring elf Círdan, Lord of the Grey Havens, gave him the third elven ring of power, Narya, the red-stoned Ring of Fire (which may account for his fireworks artistry). More than anyone else he travelled and worked tirelessly to foster resistance to Sauron on many fronts. Elven friend (he was called by them Mithrandir, Sindarin for grey pilgrim) and fond teacher of Aragorn, Gandalf had great compassion and loved the overlooked parts of Middle-earth, such as hobbits and trees. He acquired his elven sword Glamdring (Sindarin for foe-hammer) on Bilbo's adventure with the dwarves, and wielded it in the War of the Ring. After being taken from the Company in his death-battle with the demon balrog he was sent back transformed into the invulnerable Gandalf the White. He tamed Shadowfax, greatest of horses on Earth, and upon him revealed his implacable grandeur halting the Lord of the Nazgûl at the **Gate of Gondor**. His work done, Gandalf took ship over the Sea with the Keepers of the Ring.

✦ Gimli ✦

The dwarf Gimli was the son of Glóin (one of Bilbo's companions on his great adventure) and accompanied his father to the **Council of Elrond**, where he joined the Company of the Ring. He guided the Company through the **Mines of Moria**, where he was excited by its marvels and devastated by its tragic disclosures. Doughty Gimli fought ferociously alongside Aragorn to the end of the War of the Ring. Afterwards he kept a promise to Legolas and accepted Treebeard's invitation to explore **Fangorn**, despite his unease in forests. Later he brought dwarves to the caverns of **Helm's Deep**, where he became Lord of the Glittering Caves and built great works in **Rohan** and Gondor, including gates of mithril and steel at Minas Tirith to replace those smashed by the Lord of the Nazgûl. His **dwarvish detestation of elves** was overcome by his friendship with Legolas and his adoration of Galadriel. As a dwarf, his eventual departure over the Sea with Legolas was unprecedented.

✦ Gollum ✦

Unhappy Gollum's real name was Sméagol and he was a river-dwelling **hobbit** of the Stoor breed, who were fishers and swimmers. His cousin Déagol found the Ring while they were fishing in a river, and was murdered by Sméagol who was overcome with uncontrollable desire for the Ring. Under the influence of the Ring, Sméagol became odious to his family (who took to calling him Gollum, after the sound he made in his throat since he had found the Ring) and he was soon driven from his home. He wandered into caverns under the **Misty Mountains**. Hundreds of years passed as he degenerated into the foul thing of the dark he was when he lost the Ring to Bilbo. Obsessed to madness with the thief Baggins and the recovery of his 'preciousss', Gollum dared to re-enter the world above, but was captured and questioned in turn by Sauron, Aragorn and Gandalf, bringing the whereabouts of the Ring to light. After escaping the custody of the **woodland elves** he was inexorably

Gimli played by John Rhys-Davies, who multi-tasked as the voice of Treebeard the Ent

Legolas, played by Orlando Bloom became the unlikely friend of Gimli the dwarf

drawn to Frodo, trailing the Fellowship from **Moria** onwards and caught by Sam and Frodo in the hills bordering Rohan and Mordor. Frodo's pity for the wretched Gollum, a gaunt, lantern-eyed, unnerving thing, re-awakened flickers of Sméagol's better personality, but his enthralment with the Ring inspired deceit and nearly finished the hobbits. He emerged a tragic figure with a vital, if unintended, role in the destruction of the One Ring.

✦ Legolas ✦

The elf Legolas (whose name is Sindarin for green leaf) was the son of Thranduil of the Woodland Realm in **Mirkwood** (the elven king who imprisoned Bilbo's dwarf companions in *The Hobbit*). On the elves' behalf he journeyed with disturbing news of Gollum to Rivendell, where he joined the Company to represent the elves. Fleet-footed, keen-sighted and a formidable archer and knife-fighter, Legolas was the only member of the Company who did not quail when Aragorn summoned an army of the dead, having no terror of the ghosts of men. His first sight of the port of **Gondor** awakened his yearning for the Sea, but after the **War of the Ring** he brought elves from the Greenwood to Ithilien to make the countryside of Aragorn/Elessar's realm fair again. When Elessar died, Legolas built his own ship and sailed over the Sea, taking Gimli with him, marking the final exit of the Fellowship of the Ring from Middle-earth.

✦ Merry And Pippin ✦

The young hobbits Meriadoc 'Merry' Brandybuck and Peregrin 'Pippin' Took were happy-go-lucky, occasionally dopey cousins who loyally went along on Frodo's journey with their usual boundless enthusiasm but no understanding of the terrors that awaited them. Nevertheless they showed the strength of the Shire-folk, maturing from jolly sports into heroes of great heart and determination. Insistent on joining the Company of the Ring they endured the travails with their Fellows until they were captured by orcs (Boromir died trying to save them). They escaped their captors by keeping their wits and fled into **Fangorn Forest**, where they were befriended by Treebeard the ent (whose hospitable draught greatly increased their height) and sparked the ents' march on Isengard. Merry joined the service of Théoden and came to love him. Refusing an order to remain behind, he rode with the Rohirrim and distinguished himself at the **Battle of the Pelennor Fields**. Pippin entered the service of Denethor in Minas Tirith, saved Faramir's life and slew a troll. Both hobbits enjoyed high honours, renown and the friendship of kings for their deeds and they prospered back in the Shire. In old age they made a final journey together to Rohan and Gondor, where they died, eventually to be laid in state beside King Elessar.

✦ Sam Gamgee ✦

Son of the Bagginses' colourful old gardener Hamfest Gamgee, stout-hearted Samwise, or Sam, was the archetypal country man, a lover of home, family and growing things; but his selfless devotion to his master Frodo made him the doughtiest of companions in extremity. Fiercely protective of Frodo, mistrustful of everyone – particularly Gollum – until they proved their worth, he was ever frank and sensible while retaining a **childlike wonder** for elven beauty and thrilling at the sight of an **oliphaunt** (elephant). In the darkest hours of the quest Sam, believing Frodo dead, made the agonising decision to leave him and take the Ring to its destruction himself. On discovering his mistake, the indomitable hobbit rescued Frodo enabling them to complete their task. Back in the Shire he was instrumental in restoring order and used his gifts from Galadriel to make the land bloom. He married his sweetheart Rosie Cotton and the couple cared for Frodo at Bag End until Frodo sailed from Middle-earth, leaving his property to Sam, who named his first son Frodo. Sam and Rosie had 13 children, several named after War comrades. After his wife's death it is believed that Sam passed over the Sea, for he, too, had been a Ring-bearer.

✦ Saruman ✦

The greatest wizard of Gandalf's order, Saruman the White, also called Saruman the Wise, was head of the **White Council**, a group of wizards and elven-wise (including Elrond and Galadriel) who shared information of Sauron's rise and plotted together against him. Saruman convinced the

Merry and Pippin - Frodo and Sam's erstwhile hobbit friends

Saruman the White, head of the White council whose emblem was the white hand

Council that the One Ring lay in the Sea and would never again be found in Middle-earth. Gandalf had misgivings about that but never suspected the dreadful truth: that Saruman's pride and love of power had overcome his wisdom and he had fallen into darkness, seeking the Ring for himself and breeding warrior orcs called uruk-hai. Using the palantír (or seeing-stone) of Orthanc, Saruman was ensnared by Sauron. Possessing great power himself, his low, melodious voice could enthrall, quieting, confusing and corrupting men's hearts. Released by the ents after his defeat at Isengard, Saruman and his stooge Gríma Wormtongue embarked on the ruin of the Shire, where he was known as Sharkey, before the returning hobbits kicked them out and Gríma killed him. Much of Saruman's activity is actually recounted at second-hand in the book; his role is more visible in the movies, capitalising on his presence.

✦ Sauron ✦

The Enemy, the Dark Lord Sauron (whose name means abominable in Quenya) is the Lord of the Rings. Once one of the beings who served the Valar, he was seduced to the cause of evil by Morgoth. His master was overthrown at the end of the First Age, but in the Second Age Sauron began to stir, made the land of Mordor his stronghold, built the dark tower of Barad-dûr and, appearing fair and wise, instructed the elven-smiths to forge the rings of power. He himself forged the One Ring in Orodruin. His forces overran much of Middle-earth, laying waste, and created the Nazgûl, men enslaved by the nine rings. The host of the Last Alliance of Elves and Men overthrew Sauron, ending the Second Age. But in the Third Age evil things multiplied once more and the Nazgûl reappeared as Sauron again grew in power, rebuilding Barad-dûr, gathering all the rings and seeking the One Ring. His body having been ruined in the Second Age, he most often manifested himself as a fiery eye; his emblem was a red eye. At the destruction of the One Ring and the ruin of Barad-dûr, Sauron's dark shadow filled the sky and was blown away, although it took some time to rout all his servants and allies.

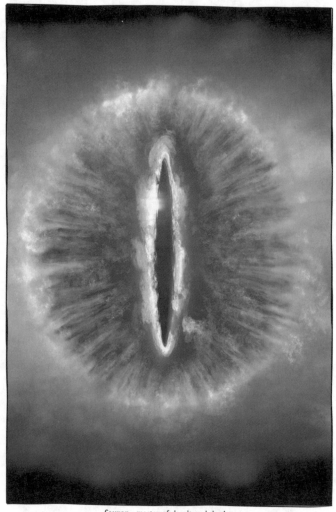

Sauron - master of deceit and destiny

✦ The Supporting Cast... ✦

✦ Balrogs ✦

Balrogs were demons (spirits of fire with whips of flame) who were mostly destroyed in the Elder Days, but a few did manage to survive deep underground. The balrog in **Khazad-dûm** was unintentionally released by mining dwarves and preyed on **Durin's Folk** until they abandoned the mines to the balrog and to Sauron's orcs. Gandalf destroyed the balrog in his epic death battle.

✦ Beren And Lúthien ✦

Mortal man and elf maid whose love, griefs and heroism are told in **The Silmarillion** and celebrated in song and legend in **The Lord Of The Rings**. Aragorn sings of them in the film of *The Fellowship Of The Ring*. Both Elrond and Aragorn were their descendants.

✦ Black Riders ✦

The Nine who scoured the Shire and beyond seeking the Ring were revealed to be the Nazgûl, which means **ringwraiths** in the **Black Speech**. Once men, they were given rings of power by Sauron, who enslaved them as his messengers, scouts, tormentors and military leaders. Their chief was the Lord of the Nazgûl, also known as the **Witch King of Angmar** (as he is billed in the movie *The Return Of The King*). People exposed to them could be infected by the **Black Breath**. It was Éowyn, with the help of Merry, who slew the Lord of the Nazgûl; the others were undone when the One Ring was destroyed. The Black Riders look scary for one very simple reason: they *are* scary. After all, Black Breath rhymes terribly appropriately with Black Death. And they don't really care what happens to the land after they've ridden through it either.

The Black Riders - slaves of the nine rings and messengers of Sauron

✦ Denethor ✦

Unwilling to be supplanted by Isildur's heir, Denethor – the proud, bitter and grim Steward of Gondor – began using the **palantír** (seeing-stone) of **Minas Tirith** to see into Sauron's mind, only to fall into despair. The death of his favoured son Boromir made him even colder to his younger son Faramir, and he was hostile to Gandalf, but he thought it amusing to take Pippin into his service. Madness overtook Denethor in the **Siege of Gondor**, as Faramir lay comatose from the Black Breath; he decided to kill himself and Faramir, but the latter was saved by Pippin's action.

✦ Dwarves ✦

One of the free peoples of Middle-earth, the **dwarves** (whose own name for themselves was the **Khazad**) were created by one of the Valar. He made seven: the fathers of the seven folk. The greatest of these was Durin, whose folk made their hall at Khazad-dûm until they were driven out by **the balrog**. Durin's people fought beside **men** and **elves** in the **Last Alliance** and suffered much from Sauron, who wanted the last of the seven rings of power, possessed by the dwarf lords (whom he was unable to bend to his will). Short (about four-and-a-half feet), robust and proud, dwarves were miners, smiths and craftsmen; quick to anger, they warred often, but were a just people.

✦ Elves ✦

The Elder Children of Ilúvatar (God), firstborn and fairest of the four free peoples of Middle-earth, the elves (whose own name for themselves was the Quendi, the speakers) belonged to two groups: the higher, nobler Eldar and the lower, more numerous Silvan, who wandered the woods or lived in realms founded by Eldar lords (such as Elrond's haven Imladris). All were tall (about six feet), slender, beautiful and good, free from ageing or illness, although they could be slain. If they died they left Middle-earth but went to Valinor. Eventually most chose to sail over the Sea to Eldamar (Quenyan for elven home). They loved beauty, nature, knowledge and language, and taught the ents to speak and the Dúnedain to write.

✦ Glorfindel ✦

A great elven lord, second to Elrond in Rivendell, it was Glorfindel in the books who found Aragorn and the hobbits, speeding Frodo from the Black Riders and across the ford on his white elf-horse Asfaloth. (Arwen got the job in the movies.) Glorfindel was also at the Council of Elrond.

✦ Gríma ✦

Dubbed Wormtongue by the Rohirrim for his vicious murmurings, the duplicitous advisor and confidant to Théoden cast a spell over the king, lusted after Éowyn and reported information to Saruman, to whom he fled when Théoden regained his senses – just in time to be held with his master when the ents marched on Isengard. Released, Gríma did Saruman's dirty work in the Shire, but turned on him for his mistreatment and was in turn killed by roused hobbits.

Gríma Wormtongue - chief councillor to King Théoden and agent to Saruman

✦ Gwaihir ✦

Lord of the Eagles, Gwaihir (Sindarin for wind lord) once had a poisoned wound healed by Gandalf and repaid the kindness by saving him, Bilbo and Thorin's company in the **Misty Mountains.** Seeking Gandalf at Orthanc to bring him news, Gwaihir discovered his plight and bore him to **Rohan.** He later found Gandalf in a trance, naked on a mountain after his rebirth, and carried him to Galadriel for healing. At the **Field of Cormallen** Gwaihir led the eagles against the Nazgûl, bringing fear to the hosts of **Mordor** and unexpected-for hope to the army of the West. It was also Gwaihir who found Frodo and Sam, plucking them from the blazing Mount Doom.

✦ Hobbits ✦

One of the free peoples, although barely noticed by men – despite being related to them – until the **War of the Ring,** when their resilience and pluck won them great respect. Also called halflings, they established **the Shire** in **Eriador** during the Third Age to pursue their own peaceful, provincial farming out of the way of the world. A few hobbits felt the desire to travel or have some adventure, but they were generally thought peculiar. Small (between two and four feet) and nimble but sturdy, hobbits learned their crafts and writing from men, but invented pipe smoking themselves.

✦ Imrahil ✦

Prince of Dol Amroth, castle and port of **Gondor,** handsome Imrahil was descended from the Dúnedain and the **elves.** A **great warrior** who sat in counsel with Gandalf, Aragorn, Éomer and the sons of Elrond, he distinguished himself as one of the Captains of the West in the **Battle of the Pelennor Fields** and at the Black Gate, and he commanded **Minas Tirith** in the confusion following Denethor's suicide.

✦ Morgoth ✦

The malicious cosmic rebel Melkor, later called Morgoth (which means **Dark Enemy of the World,** or **Black Foe of the World**), was something of a Lucifer figure in *The Silmarillion*. It was he who created orcs, dragons, trolls, pestilence and many foul things to plague Middle-earth, and he who lured Sauron from the angelic powers of Light.

✦ Men ✦

The Younger Children of Ilúvatar were inferior to the elves but were given the Gift of Men, free will, as well as the Doom of Men, death. They soon multiplied in many cultures, most wild and ignorant, but the Edain or elven friends were taught much by the elves and the Dúnedain of the West became the kings of men. In the War of the Ring Sauron's forces included the short easterlings and the tall, dark haradrim with their oliphaunts, while Saruman enlisted the primitive Dunlendings wildmen from the North. The Fourth Age saw the inexorable dominion of men, as the other races dwindled or passed out of Middle-earth.

✦ Orcs ✦

The evil goblins of Middle-earth were first bred by Morgoth using elves he imprisoned and tormented; they multiplied to become the most numerous of the enemy's minions and fighters, used by Sauron and Saruman. They were short, squat and intolerant of sunlight, cannabilistic and hard to kill. Orcs were tribal, and as likely to attack each other as the free peoples and animals, but under Sauron's control they presented a formidable army. Critics have come up with various theories about who the orcs actually are: none of them really add much to the pleasure of reading the book.

✦ Radagast The Brown ✦

One of the order of the Istari, Radagast, master of shapes and the lore of herbs and beasts, friend of birds, brought Gandalf the news that the Black Riders were abroad looking for the Shire, and that Saruman summoned him. Fortunately Gandalf asked him to send birds to Orthanc with further news, providing his means of escape when he was Saruman's prisoner.

One of thousands of orcs an evil race of Middle-earth

✦ Shelob ✦

The monstrous **ancient spider** Shelob, bloated on the blood of **elves** and men, had a lair with many tunnels under **Cirith Ungol** (Sindarin for pass of the spider) – the way through the mountainous border of **Mordor** used by the Nazgûl and through which Frodo and Sam (directed by Gollum) hoped to slip undiscovered. Since Sauron's rise she had had little to feed on but orcs and she lusted after sweeter meat, which Gollum had promised to bring to her. Shelob caught Frodo, but was unprepared for the wrath of Sam, who blinded her with the Phial of Galadriel and grievously wounded her with **Sting**, so that she crawled away in agony. Her fate remains unknown.

Théoden - put under Saruman's spell but went on to battle again at Hornburg

✦ Théoden ✦

King of the Mark, the kingdom also called **Rohan**, Théoden declined into a dark paranoia and physical degeneration under the influence of his counsellor Gríma, but was healed by Gandalf. His courage and leadership restored, he sent the Rohirrim against Saruman's forces at **Helm's Deep** and, after a desperate race to **Gondor's** aid, he led them heroically at the climactic **Battle of the Pelennor Fields**, hailing Éomer as the new king with his dying breath when he was slain by the Lord of the Nazgûl.

✦ Tom Bombadil ✦

The hobbits encountered Bombadil – **Master of the Old Forest** – en route to **Bree**. An old being of power and lore, mysterious origins and a joyful nature, he came to their rescue, but in his pleasure in the woods and song and his woman Goldberry he had no care for anything beyond the forest. The Ring had no power over him. He was called Oldest by the **elves**, to whom he was an ancient enigma. Left out of radio and film versions, Bombadil played no role in the War of the Ring, and the hobbits looked for him later in vain. Gandalf left them to find him, but what they might have said to each other is unknown.

✦ Treebeard And The Ents ✦

Eldest of the ents, the **tree shepherds** who were the oldest beings in **Middle-earth**, Treebeard was **guardian of Fangorn Forest**, named after him. (The elves called him Fangorn, Sindarin for beard-tree). Described as above 14ft in height and resembling an old tree with a low thrumming voice (and, of course, a beard), Treebeard and the other ents may have been spirits who inhabited trees; certainly they came to resemble the kind of trees they tended. Treebeard befriended Merry and Pippin when they escaped the orcs and then mustered the ents, angered by Saruman's depredations, to march on Isengard. The ents were ultimately doomed to become more like their trees in extreme age and to dwindle because they lost the ent-wives (who taught men agriculture before they vanished).

Orcs are generally short, squat and bow-legged and are weakened by sunlight

✦ Uruk-hai ✦

A type of orc bred by Sauron in **Mordor** and by Saruman at **Isengard**. The uruk-hai were used by them as soldiers, since they were man-sized, tolerant of sunlight and superior as spies, soldiers and commanders of orcs.

✦ Wargs ✦

Monstrous wolves, servants of Sauron and sometimes used as mounts by orc riders during frenzied attacks, as seen against Rohan refugees in the movie The Two Towers. In the novel a host of wargs attacked the Company near Moria but then mysteriously vanished, suggesting that they were conjured rather than real.

MIDDLE-EARTH

A ROUGH GUIDE TO THE SIGHTS IN TOLKIEN'S FICTIONAL WORLD

Maps play an often-underrated part in the enduring attraction of The Lord Of The Rings

"IT WAS NOT A PICTURE OF FRODO THAT TOLKIEN'S READERS
TAPED TO THE WALLS OF THEIR DORM ROOMS, IT WAS A MAP.
A MAP OF A PLACE THAT NEVER WAS"

George RR Martin, novelist and editor of The Twilight Zone TV series

Imaginary worlds have a controversial history. An obvious vehicle for satire, they have been used for centuries by writers to make political, social and religious comment. From works of pure allegory such as **Bunyan**'s *Pilgrim's Progress* to outright socio-political satire such as **Voltaire**'s 'contes', the fantasy world has a pre-eminent place in the didactic tradition. When **George Orwell** wrote *Animal Farm* and *1984* he was merely picking up where Voltaire, Thomas More (*Utopia*) and Jonathan Swift (*Gulliver's Travels*) had left off.

So long is the shadow cast by this literary legacy that all works of fantasy tend to be scrutinised for symbolism and deeper meanings. Why, after all, would a writer go to all that imaginative effort just for fun? What, in short, is the point?

Tolkien, like **Lewis Carroll**, has suffered from this attitude. Just as critics have found a thousand bizarre readings of *Alice In Wonderland*, so they have examined The Lord Of The Rings and The Silmarillion line by line. Sauron's Mordor is, of course, Hitler's Germany. The hobbits are the British. Isengard is Vichy France. The end of Númenor represents the warping of the higher values of the enlightenment. All such hidden meanings are gospel to those who discern them. They must be what **Tolkien** was trying to tell us, however much he himself denied it.

In truth, it's clear from even the briefest examination of *The Lord Of The Rings* that this enormous work of imagination stands alone in the fantasy tradition. The astounding geographical range, the breadth of time it spans and the painstaking elaboration of the tiniest details are unique. No other work comes close – nor does it need to. Satirists needn't devise new languages, new races, thousands of years of social and millions of years of geological history. These can exist for only one reason: to satisfy the intellectual thirst of a **mind-boggling genius**.

Epic seems too small a description for The Lord Of The Rings. Tolkien's imaginary world changes with the millennia: there are floods and earthquakes, continents split, landmasses appear and disappear, seas rise and fall. Huge migrations of peoples are common, and their languages evolve with them. Up to 20 distinct tongues have been identified in the corpus of Middle-earth history. Men, elves, dwarves, wargs, goblins, trolls, hobbits, ents, wizards… the species list is seemingly endless.

The inclusion of non-humans is also unique. Before Tolkien and his contemporary CS Lewis, only Gulliver had encountered aliens. Tolkien introduces us to elves, dwarves and hobbits, yet retains our belief and even reinforces it by setting them in a world that we can recognise. Unlike Alice's looking-glass world or Lewis's Narnia fantasy, where anything and everything is paranormal, Middle-earth looks and feels like our own world. It just happens to be full of elves as well as men. Tolkien pulls off the same trick as Ridley Scott in the first and best of the *Alien* trilogy: the movie is terrifying because it's so real. It's set in a spaceship where men and women smoke cigarettes, wear trainers and slacks and live in rooms that look like factory floors – no funny uniforms, no futuristic sets.

UNLIKE NARNIA, WHERE EVERYTHING IS PARANORMAL, MIDDLE-EARTH LOOKS AND FEELS LIKE OUR OWN WORLD

Tolkien well understood the importance of suspending his reader's disbelief, and he worked hard at it. Again unlike Narnia, there is little magic in Middle-earth. The Istari may be called wizards by the hobbits (through whose eyes Middle-earth is described), but Tolkien himself described them as "utterly distinct from sorcerer or magician", and Gandalf and company perform very few acts of magic. Galadriel is baffled that Frodo sees her mirror as magical. There is a powerful suggestion that what hobbits see as magic is in fact merely a manifestation of higher scientific knowledge. They are too primitive to understand.

So powerful is the push to make Middle-earth like our own world that Tolkien leaves open the possibility that it actually is. His maps of Middle-earth and Valinor look remarkably like Europe and America divided by the Atlantic Ocean, and his languages reflect north European linguistics. He even incorporates the Atlantis legend to hint that the events of *The Silmarillion* and *The Lord Of The Rings* take place in the pre-history of our own world. The groundwork is clearly laid for the departure of other species and the dominion of men.

Narnia makes no attempt at such realism. Driven by Lewis's Christian evangelism, events in Narnia are pure fantasy fiction. **Christian symbolism** pervades the books, which place evil squarely in the heart of men. The battles are about temptation, sinning and redemption. Moreover, Narnia is psychologically a darker world than Middle-earth. Trees have ears, talk is dangerous. The enemy is within men, summoned and nurtured by the seductive call of temptation.

Though Tolkien plays with this idea – notably in the corruption of Númenor by Sauron, and indeed the corrupting influence of Morgoth before him – the evil in Middle-earth is largely less Machiavellian. Tolkien personifies it for us, and sets up a less-complicated battle between black and white. Even Saruman is a faint-hearted double agent. Though there are faint echoes in Morgoth and Sauron of Satan in *Paradise Lost*, their motivation is never entirely clear. They are just the Bad Guys, and they're fighting the Good Guys. Take your pick, and fight accordingly.

The Lord Of The Rings is therefore truly a one-off. Though it borrows from the traditions of fantasy world, it sets an entirely new agenda. While Alice and Gulliver never knew where their journey was taking them, or what was round the next corner, Tolkien's characters can look at supremely detailed maps. Indeed, they can look at atlases of maps stretching back millennia, some describing lost worlds and continents. More's Utopia and Dante's Hell are mapped and detailed, but they are essentially dead – clear pieces of political or religious fiction. Tolkien's world is credible, vibrant, alive and real. So real it could even be true.

As novelist and TV writer/producer George RR Martin says, this geographical detail has always been part of the attraction. "The hallmarks of Tolkienesque fantasy are legion. But to my mind one stands high above the rest: JRR Tolkien was the first to create a fully realized secondary universe, an entire world with its own geography and histories and legends. The buttons in the 1960s might have said 'Frodo Lives!' but it was not a picture of Frodo that Tolkien's readers taped to the walls of their dorm rooms, it was a map. A map of a place that never was. Tolkien gave us wonderful characters, evocative prose, some stirring adventures and exciting battles… but it is the place we remember most of all. The setting becomes a character in its own right."

The elves' haven of Rivendell: thousands of suburban homes have been named after this haven

✦ Eriador ✦
(Excluding The Shire)

LANGUAGES Westron (common speech).

INHABITANTS Men, hobbits, elves, goblins, trolls.

SIGHTSEEING **Weathertop**, aka **Amon Sûl**, is the southernmost of the Weather Hills. It stands 1,000ft high, upon which the **Tower of Amon Sûl** was built. One of the **palantíri**, the seeing-stones, was set within it to enable the Númenóreans to communicate. The tower built upon the hill was burned by the Witch King of Angmar a millennium before the era of *The Lord Of The Rings*. The Witch King, now a ringwraith in thrall to Sauron, returns to Weathertop to confront Aragorn and wound Frodo with an enchanted Morgul knife.

The other big attraction in Eriador is Rivendell, home to Elrond and an important **elven** redoubt. Set in the foothills of the **Misty Mountains**, **Imladris** (its Elvish name) is a haven from the evils of the wider world, protected by Vilya, one of the three elven rings of power worn by Elrond. **Rivendell** is a place of contemplation, meditation and healing. As Tolkien wrote in the preface to *The Silmarillion*: "Elrond's house represents lore – the preservation in reverent memory of all tradition concerning the good, wise and beautiful. It is not a scene of action, but of **reflection**. Thus it is a place visited on the way to all deeds, or 'adventures'."

ACCOMMODATION No listing would be complete without mention of the Prancing Pony Inn at **Bree**, presided over by the rotund and convivial landlord Butterbur. It has rooms for both men and hobbits.

✦ Fangorn ✦

LANGUAGES **Entish**, a rambling and monotonous language that uses a hundred words where one would do. For example, A-lalla-lalla-rumba-kamanda-lind-or-burume means... hill.

INHABITANTS Trees – ancient and the oldest in Middle-earth, remnants of the great forests that once covered nearly the entire landmass. Also ents: huge, tree-like creatures who fulfil a pastoral role in the forest. They are slow breeders and dying out.

SIGHTSEEING A dark and creaky arboretum full of huorns, **half-ents** that can uproot and move around the forest to destroy anyone rash enough to set axe to tree. The forest is described as dark, gloomy and foreboding by just about everyone who visits. But don't let that put you off.

ACCOMMODATION Sleeping in the forest is dangerous, and cutting down trees or lighting fires is suicidal. **Ent** homes, such as Treebeard's at **Wellinghall**, tend not to be buildings but lush grottos formed from rock, tree branches and natural clearings. There's nowhere to sit because ents aren't very bendable, but there is always a water-feature. Drinking from it makes your hair curl and adds a few inches to your height (if you're a **hobbit**, at least).

✦ Gondor ✦

LANGUAGES Westron (common speech).

INHABITANTS Men, originally from the island kingdom of **Númenor** – destroyed by the treachery of Sauron. Elendil, the leader and founder of **Gondor**, fled **Númenor** and established a kingdom in **Arnor** and Gondor based largely on the ideals of his lost society. **Gondor** is a bitter and ancient enemy of Sauron. It was Isildur, son of Elendil, who cut the One Ring from Sauron's hand and, unable to bring himself to destroy it, left it to Frodo and posterity to deal with.

SIGHTSEEING **Minas Tirith**, the greatest and brightest city of Gondor. Set on a hill 700ft high, the city itself rises 300ft to the peak of its centrepiece, the Tower of Ecthelion. The tower is the holy of holies for men of Gondor – the main room, the Tower Hall, containing the palantír of Minas Anor. In front of it stands a courtyard with a fountain and the withered white tree of **Nimloth**, a cherished heirloom that once stood in Númenor. Surrounding the tower are seven concentric walls – 40,000ft long in total

Minas Tirith: Gondor's greatest city even has its own conference facilities

The Orthanc tower: translated from Rohirric, Orthanc means 'the cunning mind'

– that required two million tons of stone to build. The outer wall is made of the same mysterious, hard, black stone as the **tower of Orthanc** in **Isengard**.

ACCOMMODATION Much of Gondor is now sadly decaying, after many years of retreat from **Mordor** and its allies. The southern coastal port of **Dol Amroth** is only a shadow of its former glory, as is the old settlement of **Pelargir**. Once the capital of Gondor and called the Citadel of the Stars, **Osgiliath** is now just a ruin after being destroyed by internal strife and fire, and an army directed by Sauron when he returned to **Mirkwood**.

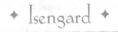

✦ Isengard ✦

LANGUAGES **Westron, Orkish.**

INHABITANTS Werewolf-like creatures called wargs, goblins, orcs and uruk-hai – half-man-half-orcs bred by Saruman to be fiercer, stronger, tougher and nastier. Can withstand daylight, unlike standard orcs. All are answerable to Saruman, a wizard of Gandalf's order.

SIGHTSEEING **Isengard** stands on a plain at the foot of the Misty Mountains, in the **Gap of Rohan** – also known as **Nan Curunír** (Sindarin for valley of the wizard). The star turn of **Isengard** is Orthanc, the 500ft tower of black stone built by the men of **Númenor**. These were a race of 'super' men, who boasted both extraordinary intelligence and great longevity (Aragorn is one of their direct descendants), who fled from their home island of **Númenor/Westernesse** (or **Atalantë** in High Elvish) after the corruption and destruction of their society by Sauron. **Orthanc** is tall, hard and impregnable, fashioned from an unknown rock too strong even for **ents** to break. It stands in the circular **Ring of Isengard**, once a beautiful place of pools, a waterfall and tree-lined avenues, but destroyed by Saruman to make way for his underground armouries, factories and orc barracks.

ACCOMMODATION None, unless you've been invited into Orthanc by Saruman or you care to share the orcs' quarters underground. Neither prospect is particularly appealing.

✦ Lothlórien ✦
aka Lórien Or Laurelindórinan

LANGUAGES Sindarin, one of the two principal elven languages.

INHABITANTS Elves, of the highest order. Traditionally suspicious of other elves, and indeed pretty much everyone else, **Lórien** elves are reclusive and tend to stay within the confines of their forest kingdom. Visitors are not only unwelcome, they risk being shot. Even friends are blindfolded as they are led into the heart of the kingdom. The elves of **Lórien** are led by the ancient elven-queen Galadriel and her consort Celeborn.

SIGHTSEEING One of the loveliest parts of Middle-earth. Known as the **Golden Wood**, Lórien is painted in some of Tolkien's most lyrical descriptive language. It is full of rare and beautiful mallorn trees which spiral up to such heights that the tops are invisible. The beauty of **Lórien** is frequently described as magical, which indeed it is: Galadriel wields **Nenya**, one of the three ancient elven rings of power, and Lórien is largely maintained and defended by it.

ACCOMMODATION Elves live in 'flets', special wooden platforms built into the mallorn trees. These spiral up, one above the other, to heights of many hundred feet. There are no buildings in Lórien.

✦ Mirkwood ✦

LANGUAGES Westron and Sindarin.

INHABITANTS Many and varied. Not all of them terribly desirable – Frodo's forebear Bilbo Baggins and his dwarf companions were trapped and almost eaten by hordes of enormous spiders here. **Mirkwood** is also the heartland of the wood elves who, although they're suspicious of newcomers, are at least civilised. Perhaps the most (in)famous erstwhile inhabitant of Mirkwood is Sauron himself, who took up residence at the fortress of **Dol Guldur** (Sindarin for hill of sorcery) in the south-west of

The Golden Wood of Lothlórien, ruled by Galadriel

the forest before retreating to **Mordor**. He was long known as the Necromancer of Mirkwood, and those parts of the forest are dark and evil.

SIGHTSEEING There are two great sites on the visitors' map of the **Mirkwood** area. The **great halls** of the elven king Thranduil are described in detail by an awestruck Bilbo. The other attraction is the **Lonely Mountain** just east of Mirkwood. A barren outcrop of rock rising 3,500ft above the men's city of **Lake Town**, Erebor is an ancient dwarvish stronghold that was, until recently, home to the last great dragon, Smaug. Tourists interested in seeing Gollum should take the short trip to the **Gladden Fields**, west of Mirkwood where the Anduin joins the river Gladden, to see Sméagol's putative homeland. The forest itself is to be avoided: Mirkwood is vast and mostly unmapped. Like Russia, it has no roads – only directions.

ACCOMMODATION Only Thranduil's halls and the dungeons of **Dol Guldur** (where **Sauron** tortured the dwarf-lord Thráin to gain the last dwarvish ring of power – and where you wouldn't want to spend the night).

✦ The Misty Mountains ✦

LANGUAGES Just about all of them, since this enormous mountain range runs north-south through 900 miles and passes through many lands.

INHABITANTS Goblins, dwarves, orcs and men. There are also two notorious previous inhabitants: Gollum and, in the far northern realm of Angmar, the Witch King – an evil lord of men who took one of Sauron's nine rings of power and was subsumed by it to become the chief of his ringwraiths. The terrifying balrogs (one of whom drags Gandalf from Durin's Bridge) also came from the depths of the Misty Mountains.

The Misty Mountains are also the traditional homeland of dwarves, who fled to the northern limits of the range after digging too deep in Moria and disturbing the balrog. But the north, too, proved unsuccessful as a homeland, and dwarves have since been the people in search of a home: the dwarvish diaspora stretches from Erebor in the north-east to Dunland in the south-west.

SIGHTSEEING Where do you start? Caradhras, the highest peak in the range, would be on every rock climber's wishlist. But by far the biggest attraction is Moria, aka Khazad-dûm, the ancient realm of dwarves. Situated bang in the middle of the range near Lórien, Moria is 40-miles wide from the Hollin Gate to the Dimrill Gate.

Dwarves lived in Moria (aka 'the black pit' or 'the black chasm') for centuries, mining the fabled metal mithril and digging out a vast, incomparably magnificent series of halls, chambers and corridors, reaching down perhaps 12,000ft. Gimli the dwarf speaks with awed reverence of Moria's lofty past, when the huge halls were lit with flaming torches and millions of jewels and silvery strands of mithril glimmered in the naked, chiselled rock.

One of the great sights of Moria was the Endless Stair, a spiralling staircase reaching from 4,000ft below sea level to Durin's Tower on one of the Misty Mountains' great peaks at perhaps 11,000ft. Alas, it was ruined in Gandalf's battle with the balrog, along with Durin's Tower.

ACCOMMODATION Staying in Moria is certainly not advised – orcs, cave trolls and balrogs may prove unpleasant bedfellows. The Foreign Office would probably give similar advice for the goblin city further north.

Gimli the dwarf can talk for hours about Moria's illustrious past – if you let him

Middle-earth is just full of unexpected sights, huge gates, hobbit houses and the like

✦ Mithlond, Or The Grey Havens ✦

LANGUAGES **Westron, Sindarin.**

INHABITANTS The ancient elf-lord Cirdan, veteran of previous wars against Sauron and an old colleague of Elrond, Galadriel and Celeborn.

SIGHTSEEING **The Havens,** a town and harbour on the **Gulf of Lhûn** leading to the Great Sea of the West, play a critical role in the history of Middle-earth. In a previous age they were the main conduit for trade and immigration from the ancient elven land of **Valinor** and the island of **Númenor** (or **Westernesse**). What little is written about them suggests Plymouth meets Milford Haven – grey, salty and windswept.

ACCOMMODATION None known, but the **Grey Havens** are a transit stage, not a destination. In the age of *The Lord Of The Rings* they have become a departure point for elves forsaking Middle-earth to return to Valinor – whither Frodo and Gandalf eventually travel as well. A feeling of finality and sadness hangs heavily on them.

✦ Mordor ✦

LANGUAGES The Black Speech (a grossly distorted and harsh language invented by Sauron), Orkish.

INHABITANTS Orcs. Lots of 'em. Also the revolting great spider Shelob and just about every other nasty thing you can imagine, including Sauron.

SIGHTSEEING **Mount Doom** is the big attraction. Seven miles around at the base and 4,500ft high, **Orodruin** (as it is also known) was based by Tolkien on the Italian volcano Stromboli. At its core is the hottest fire in Middle-earth – the place where Sauron forged the One Ring, and the only fire hot enough to destroy it. Mount Doom belches ash, pumice and lava almost constantly, and the winding road to **Sammath Naur** (Sindarin for chambers of fire, containing Sauron's smithy and the **Crack of Doom**, near the peak) must be constantly rebuilt by armies of expendable orcs as the lava routinely destroys it. Around **Orodruin** is the black, featureless basalt plain of **Gorgoroth**, the result of laval outpourings over millions of years. Huge fissures divide the weird, misshapen hillocks of congealed lava.

ACCOMMODATION **Barad-dûr**, the home of Sauron, sits in the northern plains. A vast castle rising high up to the peak of its "dark and bitter crown", it was built by Sauron with the power he had invested in his One Ring. Impressive, but not frightfully welcoming: "Those who pass the gates of **Barad-dûr** do not return." Arguably as unpleasant is **Cirith Ungol**, the high mountain pass in the west, garrisoned by orcs and guarded by the enormous man-eating spider Shelob. The main body of Sauron's orc army is largely housed in barracks in the stronghold of **Udûn**, guarded by the enormous gates of the **Morannon** – the 'official' entrance to **Mordor**.

The only other building of note is **Minas Morgul**, once **Minas Ithil** – a great city of **Gondor** that fell to Sauron's armies and has become a ghastly caricature of Minas Tirith, which lies 20 miles to the west. A place of death and horror, **Minas Morgul** is home to yet more battalions of orcs. No place to spend the night – unless you like the thought of a grotesque, 40ft fell beast perching on the battlements outside your window.

✦ Rohan ✦

LANGUAGES Westron, Rohirric.

INHABITANTS Men. Imagine a cross between the Vikings and the Normans, and you've pretty much got the picture. The Riders of Rohan are descendants largely of men native to Middle-earth, and allies of Gondor.

SIGHTSEEING The city of **Edoras**, surrounded by a mighty wall, stands on the rising slope of a foothill of the **White Mountains**. Its palace, **Meduseld**, is near the top. This Valhalla-like hall, built of wood with a roof of gold, is the home to the King of Rohan and is known as the Golden Hall. It's rustic and quaint compared with, say, **Minas Tirith**, but still a fabulous work of quasi-Viking artisanship.

Upstream from Edoras is **Dunharrow**, an ancient fortress and Rohan refuge in the hills that leads to the **Dark Door** in **Dwimorberg**, the haunted mountain. This is the entrance to the Paths of the Dead, the dreadful

The Rohan, ruled by King Théoden, are Middle-earth's answer to the Vikings and Normans

The LORD of the RINGS

route taken by Aragorn to summon the cursed spirits of ancient allies of **Gondor**, who had failed to answer the call to assist them in a previous age.

ACCOMMODATION The most impressive building in **Rohan** is **Helm's Deep**, the mountain fortress constructed originally by the Númenóreans. Built into the rock of a foothill, **Helm's Deep** consists of a wall across the entrance to the valley, coupled with a redoubt constructed on a 40ft rock called the **Hornburg**. The **Deeping Wall** is 20ft high, with a parapet. The Hornburg has two strong walls surrounding two inner courts and a tower known as the **Burg**. It is an almost impregnable natural position, which Rohan is able to defend – albeit with enormous difficulty – against an enemy host far larger than its own force.

Next door to Helm's Deep is **Aglarond** (the Glittering Caves), which Gimli the dwarf falls in love with during his time at the Deep. These are astonishingly beautiful – so much so that even Legolas, a wood elf normally unimpressed by such things, is profoundly affected by them. Gimli himself settles at Aglarond after the fall of Sauron.

✦ The Shire ✦

LANGUAGES Westron.

INHABITANTS Hobbits.

SIGHTSEEING Tolkien's descriptions of the Shire make it sound suspiciously like southern or middle England – indeed, on the quasi-European map of Middle-earth, **Hobbiton** corresponds roughly to Worcester. The star attraction has to be the Bagginses' family home at **Bag End** – variously described as a "homely" and "comfortable" example of the burrow-building art. The downs, mills and streams sound very John Constable, although the tobacco plantations in the southern Shire suggest a climate rather warmer than Worcestershire's. The Shire is certainly old, settled and civilised: hobbits have lived there for almost 2,000 years, since their migration from their original home in the **Gladden Fields**, on the river **Anduin**. An ancient attraction is the **Emyn Beraid** (tower hills) in the west. Here are the ruins of the two white towers built by Elendil when he came to Middle-earth from **Númenor** to found a new kingdom in exile.

A hobbit's home is his castle: Bag End, home to Bilbo and Frodo, in Hobbiton

ACCOMMODATION Hobbit holes, for the most part. In the east, a comfortable home is run by the ever-mysterious Tom Bombadil – the **Master of the Old Forest** and the only character in *The Lord Of The Rings* over whom the One Ring of Sauron has no power. Little is known about him, but Gandalf hints that he is one of the oldest and most powerful beings in Middle-earth. Less attractive are the burrows of the barrow-wights, residents of the barrow-downs just beyond the Shire's eastern border. Created by the **Witch King of Angmar**, the wights are evil spirits who moved into the downs when they were abandoned by men after the Great Plague, 1,000 years before the events of *The Lord Of The Rings*.

✦ Wish You Were Here? ✦

Were Thomas Cook to set up shop in Middle-earth, probably the most tempting package holiday would be a cruise down the Anduin. Running from north to south through almost 1,000 miles, the Great River goes through, or passes near to, many of the great visual and historic sites of *The Lord Of The Rings*. A powered craft would be needed to explore upstream tributaries, but most of the journey would be downriver.

A 14-day cruise would take you from the **Gladden Fields** just north of Lórien to **Minas Tirith**. Starting in Gollum's homeland, where Isildur was killed by orcs and dropped the One Ring into the **Anduin**, the river winds along the western fringe of **Mirkwood**, passing down the eastern borders of Lórien. Here the boat would turn right into the **Silverlode**, a pleasant river flowing through **Lórien**, and journey upstream. When the water becomes too shallow for the boat, passengers could hike for a daytrip to the **Mirrormere** (a lake which is always still, but which does not reflect the faces of those looking into it) or visit the broken bridge of **Khazad-dûm** (the greatest of the dwarf halls), where Gandalf battled the balrog.

Returning downstream, the boat rejoins the Anduin and travels down to the Brown Lands and the Wold, rolling limestone hills given over to grazing and farming by **Rohan**. A day or two's cruising brings you to **Sarn Gebir**, a stretch of rapids in the cliffs of the **Emyn Muil** hill country. Enormous walls of rock rear up on either side, and travellers can witness the **Argonath**: vast stone statues of Isildur and Anárion (sons of Elendil, the first King of **Gondor**) carved there to mark its northern boundary. Mooring at **Parth Galen**, at the top of the **Rauros** waterfall, you can climb

Middle-earth vs Narnia
A HANDY COMPARISON FOR VISITORS

Compared to Middle-earth, which is thoroughly mapped by Tolkien, Narnian geography is curiously abstract. Even the main characters have difficulty finding places they've visited before. Indeed, the whole entry/exit thing is a mystery. Unlike Middle-earth, Narnia is connected to our world: people can step in and out.

The visitor to Narnia, however, will have pictures or drawings of some of the principal sights. While Tolkien mapped Middle-earth, he created very few pictures of buildings, countryside or even people. Narnia also has navigable seas and a maritime dimension (the Dawn Treader) largely lacking in Tolkien, but it seems much more compact than Middle-earth, though its countryside is rather similar to Tolkien's Eriador.

There are other important differences. Narnia steps into the improbable: many animals talk, whereas even Shadowfax, the noblest of Tolkien's dumb beasts, cannot. But other than talking animals, species in Narnia reflect our own – Lewis, unlike Tolkien, felt no need to invent botanical exotica. Showy, childish magic is also omnipresent in Narnia: Jadis the White Witch casts 'abracadabra' spells. The 'magic' of Middle-earth is more mysterious, less twee, and somehow more credible.

Even so, Narnia often feels scarier. Under Jadis, it's a totalitarian state ruled by an iron-fisted dictator, whereas most of Middle-earth is free – as long as you don't stumble into Mordor and Isengard. Narnian forests have ears and everybody is on one 'side' or another. You need passes, permissions, papers. Stick to the designated tour, or else!

If the worst happens, though, your chances are better in Narnia. Fall into the wrong hands in Middle-earth and the enemy will torture and kill you. Narnian enemies are more ambivalent. A deal may be struck. Narnia's despots are weak-willed, 'fallen' – apostles of Satan, not Satan himself. Convert or co-operate and you may be spared. That, for Lewis, is the essence of temptation.

On balance, Middle-earth is a more attractive destination. It's bigger, more beautiful and more detailed. Narnia is less credible, although even its more innocuous parts have a menacing quality that Middle-earth lacks.

Amon Hen for a spectacular view of the falls, a sheer drop of 2,500ft that fills the air with spray. You can sit here like Frodo and see over the whole of Rohan to the river **Entwash** and far off, in the south-east, the menacing shadow of the **Ephel Dúath** – the mountains bordering **Mordor**. At the top of **Rauros** sits the island of **Tol Brandir**, battered by the powerful current of the river as it plunges over the edge.

Travellers would have to descend the falls on foot by the **North Stair** and rejoin another boat on **Nen Hithoel**, the lake at the top of Falls of Rauros. From here the Anduin winds through the marshes of **Nindalf**, whence a minibus daytrip to **the Dead Marshes** allows travellers to experience the spooky sight of dead warriors lying under the water. It's even possible to travel to the **Morannon**, the shattered iron gate of Mordor guarded by the outlying sentinel hills of **Narchost** and **Carchost**.

A day or two's travel then brings you to **Minas Tirith**. Here the cruise ends with a visit to the **White Tower of Ecthelion** to see the brilliant new white tree guarding the entrance to Aragorn's throne room.

THE LOCATIONS

THE PLACES THAT PROVED INSPIRATIONAL, FROM SAREHOLE TO THE KAPITI COAST

Hobbits weren't known to follow the Barratt Homes school of house building

Sir Richard Francis Burton

According to St Augustine, "the world is a book, and those who stay at home read only one page." When the Catholic theologian made this bold statement in the fourth century, he evidently didn't allow for the works of JRR Tolkien. The author's simple English country life provided the basis for a book which allowed others to travel to a whole new world without leaving their front room. Whether his work would have been as successful without its variety of different landscapes and cultures, however, is debatable. The books' settings are as intrinsic to the appeal of *The Lord Of The Rings* as the characters: envisaging a hobbit hole is as essential to understanding the hobbit character as seeing what they wear and hearing how they speak. And Tolkien's own travels as a child, from South Africa to Birmingham, helped to shape the world of hobbits.

There is no mistaking that Tolkien used his own experiences in his writings. As he himself noted: "I take my models like anyone else – from such life as I know." Yet there remains some debate as to which places inspired which elements. Was Moseley Bog the inspiration for Fangorn or the Old Forest, or both? Should the Ribble Valley be considered the premier Tolkien spot in England, or Sarehole?

What is certain is that the adventures of Frodo, Sam, Aragorn and their fellow journeymen could only have been written by someone who had himself experienced and enjoyed adventures. Although much of Tolkien's adventures and travels arose out of sadness and grief (the death of his parents, for example), he still managed to draw something good from the circumstances: as he moved to new places, he was forced to explore and soak up his new surroundings.

One of the beauties of Tolkien's work, for British fans at least, is the accessibility of its settings. With the exception of Bloemfontein, the areas which most inspired him are right on their doorstep. This section isn't solely about the books, however. It also includes the locations of the film adaptations, which are as important as the original sources to today's generation of *Lord Of The Rings* fans. We are fortunate that director **Peter Jackson** and his team went to great pains to seek out the best locations in New Zealand to capture the rolling green fields, rippling streams and mystical forests of the books. Fictional England has never looked lovelier. Your efforts to reach these Tolkien-like destinations shouldn't be as arduous as Frodo's journeys but even if you travel no further than the printed page, this should give you a flavour of every location, from the Kapiti Coast in New Zealand to the Ribble Valley in Lancashire.

✦ Bloemfontein, South Africa ✦

Anyone wishing to follow in the footsteps of **Tolkien** should begin in Bloemfontein, the capital of the Orange Free State in South Africa. Tolkien was born on 3 January 1892 on the second floor of the Bank Of Africa building on **Maitland Street**, where his father worked as manager. The building no longer exists: it was destroyed in a flood in the 1920s and a furniture shop has replaced it. Bloemfontein cathedral, where **Tolkien** was christened on 31 January 1892, is still standing, however, and the font used in his baptism remains in use.

Although Tolkien spent only three years in the capital before returning to his mother's home town of Birmingham in 1895, the contrast between the arid, yet exotic, surroundings of South Africa and the quaint hamlet of Sarehole (the family's new home), was great enough to ensure Tolkien never forgot those early days. He himself remarked that England was an inspiring contrast to South Africa's climate and landscape.

Many scholars point to the similarities between the landscape of Bloemfontein, ramshackle and barren as it was then, and Middle-earth (and cite the beginnings of the Boer War during Tolkien's time in South Africa as influential). But the more unusual events of his short time there may have also had an impact on his work. Tolkien was probably too young to remember when, as a baby, he was 'borrowed' by the family's native houseboy Isaak to be proudly shown off at his *kraal* (the traditional African hut). Despite the ensuing alarm, Isaak was not sacked, and later showed his gratitude by calling his own son Isaak Mister Tolkien Victor. But the neighbours' pet monkeys attacking the Tolkiens' garden, the snakes lurking in the woodshed and being bitten by a tarantula would certainly have left their mark on any young boy's memory and coloured the imagination of the embryonic writer. Monstrous spiders with venomous bites, for example, appear in Tolkien's stories several times.

The fact that Bloemfontein was chosen as the setting for the South African première of *The Fellowship Of The Ring* illustrates its importance as a Tolkien location, and the local Tolkien society, The Haradin Society, are keen to promote the city as a top attraction for fans. In addition to an impressive Tolkien exhibition in its National Museum, Bloemfontein already boasts the Hobbit House and the Tolkien Trail. Hobbit House, opened in 1994 in the Westdene area of the city, consists of 12 themed rooms, each named after a different character, where guests are encouraged to "eat, sleep and live Tolkien". The Tolkien Trail begins at Hobbit House, and includes Tolkien's birthplace, the Bloemfontein cathedral and the cemetery where his father Arthur is buried.

The première in Bloemfontein was celebrated with a hobbit feast which included 'traditional' hobbit fare – meat, ale, fruit, bread and berries. There are also plans for an annual literary festival to be held on Tolkien's birthday, and for a statue of Tolkien within a new park development.

HIGHLIGHTS **If you can catch a hobbit feast – the one staged before the film première was intended by Mangaung Tourism (the local tourism promotion organisation) to be the first of many – this is a must for any Tolkienite. And where better to enjoy your stay in South Africa than at Hobbit House?**

PRACTICALITIES Bloemfontein airport only services domestic flights and, as flights to South Africa can be expensive, it's worth putting as much thought into planning your trip as possible. Ebookers (www.ebookers.com) and Expedia (www.expedia.com) claim to find you the best flight deals going. The ACSA (Airports Company of South Africa) at www.airports.co.za has information on internal flights to and from Bloemfontein, while www.linx.co.za/bloemfontein has non-Hobbit related information about the city. Hobbit House may prove more costly than standard accommodation, but can you really go all that way and not complete your Tolkien experience in style? For more information call Jake Uys on +27 (0)51 447 0663; he's the proprietor of Hobbit House and chairperson of the Haradin Society.

✦ Sarehole ✦

Tolkien's parents originated from Birmingham. His father Arthur moved to South Africa in the hope that working amid the country's booming gold and diamond industries would bring him promotion at the bank where he worked. Although Tolkien's mother Mabel was initially happy to move where her husband could be successful, she soon felt isolated and was concerned about the noticeable deterioration of the health of her elder son, John Ronald Reuel. She and her two sons therefore returned to the familiarity and cooler climate of the Midlands in April 1895. Tolkien's father was set to join them as soon as possible, but he died of rheumatic fever in February 1896, without having seen his family again.

Although Mabel's and Arthur's respective families both lived in Birmingham, the rapidly expanding city was not only too expensive for her meagre 30 shillings a week allowance, but also too polluted. Mabel wanted her children to grow up surrounded by nature and clean, fresh air, so during the summer of 1896 they moved to a tiny, brick-built cottage in the village of Sarehole. Although only a couple of miles south of the city, Sarehole then lay in the English countryside, with the picturesque River Cole trickling through it and only the occasional horse and cart by way of traffic. Tolkien himself later acknowledged the impact the move had on him. "It was a kind of lost paradise," Tolkien told the Oxford Mail in 1966. "There was an old mill that really did grind corn with two millers, a great big pond with swans on it, a sandpit, a wonderful dell with flowers, a few old-fashioned village houses and, further away, a stream with another mill."

Tolkien was not yet in school, so as soon as his brother Hilary was old enough, the pair explored their surroundings daily. Tolkien was in no doubt about the effect that these four years in Sarehole – "the longest-seeming and most formative part of my life" – had on him. "I was brought up in considerable poverty but I was running about in that country. I took the idea of the hobbits from the village people and children. They rather despised me because my mother liked me to be pretty: I went about with long hair and a Little Lord Fauntleroy costume. The hobbits are just what I should like to have been but never was – an entirely unmilitary people who always came up to scratch in a clinch."

The hamlet and its surrounding areas also helped to inspire the Shire. "The shire… is in fact more or less a Warwickshire village of about the period of [Queen Victoria's] Diamond Jubilee," Tolkien once said. Signs for Hob Lane are also frequent across the Warwickshire countryside.

Sarehole Mill in Warwickshire, where Tolkien learnt to appreciate the countryside

Tolkien Recordings

Whether it's parents reading to children at bedtime, or the dulcet tones of the Jackanoryesque reader on kids' TV, few things are as evocative as listening to someone read a book aloud. That's even more true when the adult in question wrote the book. Imagine the thrill, therefore, when HarperCollins released a recording of Tolkien reading passages from The Fellowship Of The Ring as part of a seven-volume millennium edition of The Lord Of The Rings. Recorded in 1952, it also includes a sample of Tolkien reading the Great Elvish poem in Elvish from Book II, Chapter VIII. The recordings were released along with works by other 20th-century authors such as Virginia Wolff and Robert Browning.

The recording has now been put onto a CD entitled Spoken Word – Writers (ISBN 0712305165), along with recordings by Wolff, Kipling and HG Wells, and can be bought from the British Library bookshop for £9.95. For more information go to www.bl.uk.

Remarkably, most of Tolkien's Sarehole still exists. The reasons for its survival, however, are a strange combination of industrial history and the altruism of local landowners. The mill – the mill of the Shire – and its dominating chimney stack were built in 1765, and Tolkien was so fond of it he left money to go towards its preservation. But ironically the mill was of more industrial significance than rural – for six years it had been rented by Matthew Boulton (James Watt's partner in harnessing the power of steam) who did various experiments there. By Tolkien's day it had gone back to pastoral uses before finally shutting in 1919, after which it became a target for vandals. When the city council began to think about preserving it some 40 years later, it wasn't hobbits they were interested in but Boulton.

The mill actually belonged to the council already. It, and the meadow, had been left to it in 1928 by a solicitor called Arthur Foster (the 'White Ogre' miller was his tenant), on condition they were not built on. Other landowners who loved the area followed suit (one even rented a stretch of riverside land so it could not be used for business). Tolkien was not aware of it, but as early as 1911 the altruists' aim was to create a riverside walk along the Cole. This idea is now being brought to fruition, in conjunction with the Tolkien Society, as a Tolkien Park, complete with a visitor centre, to celebrate the author's connection with the area.

Tolkien's childhood home, 5 Gracewell, still exists (now as 464A Wake Green Road). It is one of six preserved cottages which now form the Foster Trust Houses for the Gentlewomen of Moseley. Behind it lies Moseley Bog, which is not a marsh but a deep, densely grown wooded dell and part of the old Forest Of Arden. It's a protected site but the council does allow free public access. Tolkien was greatly affected by the rapidly disappearing countryside, writing in the foreword to the 1966 edition of the trilogy, "The country in which I lived in childhood was being shabbily destroyed before I was ten." Moseley Bog, however, was one site that "civilisation had missed": it was the inspiration for Tom Bombadil's home in the Old Forest. It is also thought to have played a role in shaping the forbidding forest of Fangorn and the mystical Lothlórien.

Just beyond Sarehole (in the direction of Stratford-Upon-Avon), is the village of Long Compton. Here the Barrow Downs can be found just as they are described by Tolkien – shrouded in fog.

HIGHLIGHTS As one of Tolkien's favourite childhood haunts, the Sarehole Mill is a must for Tolkienites. Today the mill is a museum, and Birmingham City Council help to organise Tolkien Weekends with information on Tolkien and dramatisations by Shire Productions of scenes from both The Lord Of The Rings and The Hobbit. It's also worth stopping off at nearby Hall Green, as the library there is brimming with information about Tolkien and has also previously organised Tolkien Weekends.

PRACTICALITIES For details of Sarehole Mill museum, visit www.bmag.org.uk/ sarehole_mill or call +44 (0)121 777 6612. For information about Hall Green Library's Tolkien Weekends, call +44 (0)121 464 6633. If you want to find out more about the proposed Tolkien Park and its progress, check out the Tolkien Society's website at www.tolkiensociety.org. Finally, although Tolkien's Sarehole home still exists, albeit under a different name, please note that it is now a private residence.

✦ Edgbaston ✦

As much as the Tolkien family loved Sarehole, remaining there was no longer feasible once Tolkien was accepted into King Edward's School in Birmingham in 1900. The family was poor and public transport did not extend out as far as Sarehole. For the first month Tolkien walked the eight miles a day to and from school to try to remain in the country, but this could not continue. Lodgings were found in Moseley, from where the city centre was accessible by tram, but it meant Tolkien's previous views of rolling fields were now replaced by the factory chimneys of Sparkbrook and Small Heath. Tolkien described his time there as "dreadful".

Within a short time, however, they had to move again, as the house was being demolished. Now they went even further into the city, to a small terraced house by King's Heath station. Here Tolkien took solace in the nature found on the railway banks, and found his imagination fired by such evocative Welsh names as Penrhiwceiber, Senghenydd and Nantyglo on the coal wagons being shunted nearby. But his mother failed to settle and they moved on, this time to the suburb of Edgbaston.

For all its urban characteristics, Edgbaston proved to be one of the most influential of Tolkien's early homes. The Birmingham Oratory, which Mabel had chosen as her new spiritual home and the new school for her sons, can still be visited today (by appointment only). It was here that the family met Father Francis Xavier Morgan, who took the boys under his wing after their mother's death from diabetes in 1904. Tolkien and his brother stayed in the area, living at a number of addresses including numbers 25 and 4 Highfield Road which can still be seen today. It was at the latter that Tolkien met and fell in love with his future wife, Edith.

The local Perrott's Folly also made a great impact on the young scholar. It was this extraordinary 96ft tower (built in 1758 by architect John Perrott) that allegedly came to mind when Tolkien was writing *The Two Towers* and creating the imposing Minas Morgul and Minas Tirith. (The other tower was that of the local waterworks.) The door to Perrott's Folly is a tiny 3ft high, ensuring only hobbit-size people can get up to the roof with ease. Both Perrott's Folly and Edgbaston Waterworks are still standing today, and there are plans to restore these local landmarks to their full glory.

The King Edward's School of Tolkien's day, however, is no more. This imposing Victorian gothic building – the work of Sir Charles Barry, who designed the Houses of Parliament – then stood near the entrance to New Street station. It was demolished when the school moved to its present premises in the 1930s, but a blue plaque marks the site.

HIGHLIGHTS To the layman, Perrott's Folly may look like a simple tower and Edgbaston Waterworks like, well, a waterworks, but to the fan's eye, the sight of the 'real' Minas Morgul and Minas Tirith arouses wonderment. A browse

The Bodleian Library in Oxford, otherwise known as Barad-dûr to Tolkienites

round Edgbaston can also give a greater understanding of both Tolkien's love of his surroundings and how they have come to be represented on paper.

PRACTICALITIES The Birmingham Oratory is still the heart of a working parish. For more information, visit www.birmingham-oratory.org.uk or, to make a viewing appointment (outside service hours), call +44 (0)121 454 0496. For more on Perrott's Folly or to make a donation to the restoration programme, call +44 (0)121 455 0422. For general information about Birmingham and the surrounding areas, call the Visitor Information Centre on +44 (0)121 643 2514.

✦ Oxford ✦

Oxford will always occupy an important, if not central, place in Tolkien's history. He studied, worked and taught at the university, and was later laid to rest in the city's Wolvercote cemetery.

According to Tolkien's biographer Humphrey Carpenter, "Already as the car bowled into Oxford [in 1911] [Tolkien] had decided he would be happy there." Exeter College is not the most beautiful of Oxford's colleges, but it represented Tolkien's first real home since his mother's death, and held an important place in his heart. It was only natural, therefore, for him and his new wife Edith to want to return there, rather than to Birmingham, following the end of World War I.

The couple began their married life at 50 St John's Street, before moving to 1 Alfred Street, now Pusey Street. Both are still standing today. Tolkien's first job after leaving university in 1919 was as an assistant on the *Oxford English Dictionary*, then at the Old Ashmolean Building on Broad Street (now the Museum of the History of Science). Tolkien spent just two years of his life working on the dictionary: it may not seem particularly significant, but as he once put it: "I learnt more in those two years than any other equal period of my life."

After moving to Leeds University for a four-year stint as Reader (a grade between senior lecturer and professor) in English Language, Tolkien returned to Oxford as the Rawlinson and Bosworth Professor of Anglo-Saxon and Fellow of Pembroke College. This time, 22 Northmoor Road became the Tolkien home, followed by number 20, a house previously owned by the bookseller and publisher Basil Blackwell. There they remained until 1947.

During this time Tolkien completed *The Hobbit* and nearly finished *The Lord Of The Rings* (he would complete it the following year). Here he also met **CS Lewis**, who would become a lifelong friend, and formed **The Inklings** group, which met at the Eagle & Child pub (more commonly referred to as the Bird & Baby). The pub is certainly worth a visit, and a plaque inside commemorates the scholarly group. Some also believe it inspired the Prancing Pony Inn in *The Fellowship Of The Ring*.

CS Lewis's rooms at Magdalen College, where the group also met, are less accessible, and the current occupiers are not always keen on visitors (a different room had to be used in the Anthony Hopkins-Debra Winger movie of Lewis's marriage, *Shadowlands*). Oxford's Bodleian Library (in the Radcliffe Camera building) is essential for fans. Tolkien spent a great deal of time there (a number of his manuscripts are now kept in the library), but for Tolkien the building was exactly how he envisaged **Sauron's temple to Morgoth** in Númenor would look.

Finally, Tolkien's final resting place is beside his wife Edith at the Wolvercote cemetery in Oxford, their simple headstones including their Elvish names: Lúthien (**Edith**) and Beren (**Tolkien**).

HIGHLIGHTS The Bodleian Library is a must. Although Tolkien's manuscripts aren't open to the public, it is worth a visit if you want to know how Tolkien thought Sauron's temple should look. It's also worth touring the university grounds to soak up the atmosphere which helped to inspire Tolkien.

PRACTICALITIES Oxford is proud of its place in Tolkien history. Tolkien's Oxford at http://users.ox.ac.uk/~tolksoc/TolkiensOxford is particularly good, and the Oxford Tolkien Society site at http://users.ox.ac.uk/~tolksoc is worth a visit to understand Tolkien's impact on the university itself. For general information about the city head to www.visitoxford.org.

✦ Ribble Valley ✦

The Ribble Valley in Lancashire already lays claim to inspiring Arthur Conan Doyle's *The Hound Of The Baskervilles*. Now the local council has set its sights on competing with Sarehole as England's most important location for Middle-earth enthusiasts. It is known that a great deal of *The Lord Of The Rings* was written here. So was Hobbiton really the Lancashire village of Hurst Green? Was the Old Forest not Moseley Bog but Mitton Wood? Follow the map of **Clitheroe**'s fields, their argument goes, and you can trace Frodo's journey across the Shire.

Tolkien described the elf home of Lothlórien as "the fairest of all the dwellings... There are no trees like the trees of that land. For in the autumn their leaves fall not, but turn to gold." Anyone who has visited the area could be forgiven for thinking he was simply describing the Forest of Bowland, with its green pastures and lush forestland. But there are plenty of more specific sites in the Ribble Valley. So many, in fact, that the local council has now organised its own Tolkien Trail.

High on its list of sites is Stonyhurst College, which opened its Tolkien Library in 2002 (www.tolkienlibrary.com) and is the real reason for all this controversial talk. The author and his immediate family visited the college and walked in the surrounding area on a regular basis during the 1940s, when Tolkien was busy working on his masterpiece. Two of Tolkien's sons were based at Stonyhurst: Michael, who taught Classics there, and John, who had been evacuated to the nearby Jesuit seminary of St Mary's Hall from the English College in Mussolini's Rome (where he was studying for the priesthood).

When visiting John, the family would stay at the New Lodge within Stonyhurst's grounds. Tolkien was so fond of the grounds that he would paint the views from New Lodge, the scene of the garden from the kitchen window eventually cropping up as the view from Tom Bombadil's garden in chapter seven of the first book. Michael's house also features on the Tolkien Trail, but it is a relatively nondescript building, especially when compared to other considerably more exciting sites further on.

Is it Ribble Valley or Middle-earth?

The Shireburn Arms in Hurst Green is the start of the trail. It was frequented by Tolkien in the 1940s, and doubtless helped him to decide that a hobbit's favourite drink would be ale. In Tolkien's day the crossing point on the Ribble was a ferry, and this is said to have become the Bucklebury Ferry which Frodo takes to enter the Old Forest. Near the ferry is Hacking Hall, which is believed to be Brandy Hall in the book. Behind it is the dark Mitton Wood – the start of the Old Forest. A map of the converging Ribble, Hodder and Calder rivers also bears a striking resemblance to Tolkien's map of the Brandywine, Withywindle and Shirebourn rivers.

Then there's Pendle Hill, a huge, steep hill that rises above the Forest of Bowland, and infamous long before Tolkien arrived. In 1612 two of the

South Woodham Ferrers

Students nicking street signs is nothing new, but it's not what you would expect from grown men and women. Yet the Essex town of South Woodham Ferrers keeps having to replace stolen signs on one housing estate because no fewer than 25 streets have names inspired by The Lord Of The Rings.

The local council has tried to shift attention away from the estates desirable signs, saying: "The reason why the estates roads were named like this has nothing to do with Tolkien." What it does admit is that when the estate was built in the 1980s and a set of names was needed, "someone mentioned The Lord Of The Rings and it was considered a good idea." Nothing to do with Tolkien at all then...

The two main roads are Gandalf's Ride and Celeborn Street, the latter originally set to be called Gollum's Reach. For Tolkien completists, the other street names in full are:

Arwen Grove
Bree Hill
Buckland Gate
Bucklebury Heath
Butterbur Chase
Bywater Road
Elrond's Rest
Galadriel Spring
Gladden Fields
Goldberry Mead
Great Smials
Hobbiton Hill
Lórien Gardens
Meriadoc Drive
Rivendell Vale
Rohan Court
Shirebourn Vale
The Withywindle
Thorins Gate
Took Drive
Treebeard Copse
Westmarch
White Tree Court

hill's residents were accused of witchcraft, and in 1652 a lay preacher called George Fox had a vision there which helped to shape the Quaker movement. If you can climb to the top you get tremendous views for miles around, but for Tolkienites the significance of Pendle lies in its being the inspiration for the Misty Mountains.

HIGHLIGHTS Stonyhurst College is worthy of a visit even without its Tolkien Library. The 16th-century manor house was built by Richard Shireburn (what a coincidence!) and is one of the largest and most beautiful buildings in

Lancashire. It is only open to visitors during summer months, however: for more information call +44 (0)1254 826 345 or see www.stonyhurst.ac.uk.

Tolkien also persuaded his son Michael to plant a copse in the garden adjoining his residence at Woodfields (where Stonyhurst owned several houses for its teachers), along the road to Hodder Bridge.

PRACTICALITIES The Ribble Valley Tourist Board has produced a guide called In The Footsteps Of JRR Tolkien, available to anyone free of charge. Go to www.ribblevalley.gov.uk for more information. You can also arrange to go on one of their guided walks of Tolkien sites for £10, or a package of DIY walks is available from the Clitheroe Tourist Information Centre for £1.50 (call +44 (0)1200 425 566 and ask for Journey Through The Centre Of The Kingdom). For information on the best way to get to Clitheroe, call Traveline in the UK on 0870 608 2608. Anyone wishing to stay at Tolkien's favourite watering hole, the Shireburn Arms (he was also reported to visit the nearby Bayley Arms and The Punchbowl), should go to www.shireburn-hotel.co.uk.

✦ Bournemouth ✦

"Tolkien is not exactly attractive to the young these days," opinioned a far-sighted spokesman for tourism in Bournemouth. "We're much more likely to promote the fact that footballer Jamie Redknapp comes from Bournemouth." To be fair to the said official, he was speaking in 2001, before the release of the first of *The Lord Of The Rings* film; these days the local council is much keener to promote its Tolkien heritage.

Tolkien's wife Edith favoured the town, speaking particularly highly of her stays at the Miramar Hotel, so when Tolkien retired from Oxford University in 1968 the couple bought a bungalow at 19 Lakeside Road in Branksome Park. But Tolkien never warmed to the seaside resort as his wife had, and on her death in 1971 he returned to Oxford to seek refuge in the more stimulating atmosphere of the university. It was in Bournemouth, however, that Tolkien died on 2 September 1973, while visiting Dr and Mrs Tolhurst, who had become firm friends of the Tolkiens during their brief stay in the town.

Today Tolkien's home can be seen from a seaside walk which begins at Branksome Chine [a Dorset word for ravine] car park before climbing through the Branksome Chine Gardens and passing the author's former home (which he called Woodridings). It's a route which, we're assured by one local website, "Tolkien must have walked dozens of times."

Aragorn had always liked the great outdoors. Just as well really

HIGHLIGHTS The Branksome Chine walk not only offers an insight into the final years of Tolkien's life but, even without such heritage, is a beautiful ramble. A step-by-step guide to the walk is available from the Dorset Mag website at www.dorsetmag.co.uk/walks/issue075-c0.phtml.

PRACTICALITIES The Miramar Hotel was used by the Tolkiens to entertain any friends visiting from Oxford. It is still open today (www.miramar-bournemouth.com) but makes no claim to have any Tolkien connections.

✦ New Zealand ✦

If you've taken the recent film adaptations to your heart as much as the books, the selection of exotic filming locations over the following pages should be of interest. Each one holds a specific importance in terms of how director Peter Jackson brought Tolkien's vision to the silver screen.

North Island

✦ Hinuera Valley ✦

This is where the Hobbiton set was created. It's a spectacular, wide, low valley through which the **Waikato** river – the longest in New Zealand at 354km – flowed, until volcanic eruptions millions of years ago caused it to change course. The village was constructed – and all plants and trees planted – a year before filming; the resulting weathering made it look as if it had been the hobbits' home for centuries.

HIGHLIGHTS You can visit the set of Hobbiton, but only via an official tour. Book at Matamata Information Office or visit www.hobbitontours.com. The area is also an environmentalist's Mecca: the changes in the course of the Waikato and the debris from centuries of volcanic activity have meant the river has followed several different routes, creating some of New Zealand's most important wetlands. Waitomo, to the west of Hinuera Valley, is famous for its underground network of caves festooned with glow-worms; organised trips cover just about all ability levels.

PRACTICALITIES Hinuera Valley is located near Matamata, a small town on North Island about 200km south-east of Auckland, just inland from the Bay of Plenty. The town offers plenty of homestays – essentially bed and breakfast – which offer good value for money and a homely atmosphere (www.cottagestays.co.nz). Some of the Matamata homestay owners will even lay on free transport to the organised Hobbiton tours (www.matamata-info.co.nz/accommodation.htm).

✦ The Taupo Region ✦

Mordor, the stronghold of evil where Frodo must go to destroy the Ring, was created in **Tongariro National Park**, New Zealand's first, and the world's fourth, national park. All scenes involving the Dark Lord Sauron were filmed in the **Taupo** region. To respect Maori beliefs, Peter Jackson came to a careful agreement with the tribal elders about using their sacred **Ruapehu volcano** to represent Mount Doom. Cinematic effects (the top of Ruapehu was heavily disguised with erupting lava) combined with the use of neighbouring **Mount Ngauruhoe** achieved the desired effect, with sulphuric pools and hot springs adding to the dark atmosphere.

This national park doubled as Mordor – but don't let that put you off going there...

HIGHLIGHTS At the heart of the region is Lake Taupo, which occupies 619sq km in a series of volcanic craters that, in their day, were seriously destructive. The last big blast was more than 1,800 years ago but it left much of North Island under a metre of pumice and ash (the red skies were noted in Chinese and Roman literature of the time). The lake is famous for its trout fishing, there's an interesting 150km drive around the edge, or you can visit one of the many villages on its shores. In the Wairakei National Thermal Valley, north of Lake Taupo, is the world's only geothermal prawn farm, and north of Taupo itself (which sits at the origin of the Waikato River) there are great areas of boiling mud, steam and geysers, courtesy of an underlying thermal belt. For walkers, the Tongariro Northern Circuit Great Walk includes the day-long Tongariro Crossing, said to be the best day hike in New Zealand.

PRACTICALITIES Lying at the centre of the North Island, Taupo is about 370km from Wellington, at the southernmost tip of the island, and 280km from Auckland to the north-west. For accommodation check out www.jasons.co.nz/destinations/taupo.

✦ The Kapiti Coast ✦

The countryside near **Otaki**, north of Wellington along the **Kapiti** Coast, became the East Road from Hobbiton to Rivendell.

HIGHLIGHTS **The Kapiti Coast, some 30km from Paekakariki up to Otaki, acts as Wellington's weekend getaway area. At the** Nga Manu **nature reserve you can learn about the New Zealand species recovery programme and see native flora and fauna, or try a quad-bike tour of its 18,000 acres. Trips to** Kapiti Island, **5km offshore, are also available (see www.kapitimarinecharter.co.nz). The island only allows 50 visitors per day therefore slots get booked well in advance, especially weekends between December and January. Don't expect to see exotic mammals on the island; they've all been removed as part of an attempt to boost the island's bird life (www.nzbirds.com) and floral species.**

PRACTICALITIES **The Kapiti Coast is on the south-western side of North Island. Just 40 minutes' drive from Wellington, it has a relaxing atmosphere far removed from the capital. International flights to Wellington are limited, so an internal flight from Auckland or Christchurch is probably your best bet. For accommodation in Wellington go to www.kapiti.org.nz.**

✦ Upper Hutt ✦

Upper Hutt provided the backdrop to Rivendell, the house of Elrond and the home of Arwen where the Council considered what to do with the Ring. Although most of Rivendell was computer-generated, some scenes involving Isengard and the Great River Anduin were filmed around the **Hutt River**, just north of **Upper Hutt** in a village called **Kaitoke**. (During the filming here, both Orlando Bloom – Legolas – and Viggo Mortensen – Aragorn – were swept out of their boats.)

HIGHLIGHTS **Upper Hutt is an attractive town at the top of the Hutt Valley, with peaceful riversides and bush. There are countless things to do, but trips should include a journey to one of the wave pools in the area –** H2Oxtream **has a rapid-river ride, water slide and lane swimming. For historians there is** Golder Cottage, **a pioneer's cottage built in 1876 (family members lived there until 1985) and now a time capsule of the past. Akatarawa Forest is home to the 25-acre** Staglands Wildlife Park **(www.staglands.co.nz), which has walk-through aviaries and enclosures housing native and exotic wildlife.**

PRACTICALITIES **Upper Hutt is a 30-minute drive from Wellington on North Island. Cheap, comfortable accommodation can be found at many motels in the area; www.jasons.co.nz/destinations/upperhutt is a good place to start.**

✦ Lower Hutt ✦

All scenes involving Minas Tirith, Isengard, Minas Morgul and Helm's Deep (a stronghold in the mountains where some of the Rohirrim sought refuge) were shot in **Lower Hutt**. The climactic battle of *The Two Towers* – the most spectacular of all *The Lord Of The Rings* sets – was also shot here. Filming, which was all done at night, took several weeks.

HIGHLIGHTS The Hutt River winds its way through the centre of Lower Hutt before ending up in Wellington harbour, so there are a host of river-based activities – such as rafting, kayaking and fishing – on tap, and there are attractive beaches at Days Bay and Eastbourne. For the historically inclined, the Petone Settlers Museum provides an insight into the heritage of the residents of Hutt City, including fascinating stories of migration and settlement. The Dowse Art Museum focuses on contemporary art, with changing national and international exhibitions (entry is free). At the edge of the Hutt Valley, dividing it from the Wairarapa Plains, is the Rimutaka Forest Park, which takes in most of the most southerly range of the North Island mountains that run unbroken from Wellington to East Cape. The mainly beech forest includes the Catchpool Valley recreational area, which is good for walking, swimming and barbecues; there is also a visitor centre.

PRACTICALITIES **Lower Hutt is 15km north-east of Wellington. For an insight into what's going on in Hutt City (including a comprehensive listing of accommodation), see www.huttcity.govt.nz/tourism.**

✦ Wellington ✦

New Zealand's capital changed its name to Middle-earth for the film's opening, but then it had good reason – it was the base for the production of *The Lord Of The Rings*. It was here that the studio scenes were recorded, including some of the Fangorn forest and Helm's Deep interiors. (For the Helm's Deep battle three sets were built, two of them in a quarry just outside **Wellington**.) Bree (shot at nearby **Fort Dorset**), the Shire, Moria

Canterbury, New Zealand – perfect for skiing as long as you mind the sheep

and Weathertop all benefited from post-production work done in **Wellington**. The city was also used for a fair amount of location filming: **Mount Victoria**, on the outskirts of the city, is one of the city's locations that appears in the movies.

Wellington is home to director Peter Jackson's Weta Workshop effects company and **Te Papa**, the national museum of New Zealand, which was given exclusive rights by New Line Cinema to create *The Lord Of The Rings* touring exhibition. The exhibition – featuring props, costumes, insights into the film's computer wizardry and a raft of interactive elements – had its inaugural run at Te Papa, before heading off on a world tour set to take in many major cities, their first stop London.

HIGHLIGHTS **Choose anything from** The Botanical Gardens **(www.wbg.co.nz), reached by a cable car from the heart of the city, to the** Te Papa **museum, where you can do a virtual bungee jump or a spot of virtual wind surfing, (see www.tepapa.govt.nz for more details). Wellington was also the birthplace of** Katherine Mansfield**, and the writer's childhood home has been meticulously restored. Just 2km from the city centre, the relatively new** Karori Wildlife Sanctuary **is implementing an epic, multi-million-dollar plan to restore purely native flora and fauna to its 253-hectare valley, as an extension of the project under way on Kapiti Island. Guided tours last between one and three hours, and cost around $15. And from the top of** Mount Victoria **there are 360-degree panoramic views of the city and the surrounding landscape.**

PRACTICALITIES **Carriers including British Airways, Qantas and Air New Zealand all fly direct to Wellington. The airport is also a busy domestic hub for internal flights. Accommodation in the city – or just outside – is extensive (see www.wellingtonnz.com/new_zealand_accommodation.html for more information).**

South Island

✦ Canterbury ✦

Canterbury – one of New Zealand's few flat regions – was the location for Edoras, the home of Théoden and the fortress-city where the Riders of Rohan had their base. Later, in *The Two Towers*, it fell under Saruman's spell, due to the manipulations of his sinister spy, Wormtongue. With a steep hill in the middle of a vast expansive plain, bordered by impassable mountains of rock and ice, this awe-inspiring location was a perfect location for Edoras, the set of which took 11 months to build.

HIGHLIGHTS The vast Canterbury plain, which stretches from the coast in the east to the Southern Alps in the west, is home to Christchurch, the country's third largest city. Otherwise, it's primarily agricultural and livestock farming terrain, though the coastal town of Kaikoura – situated on a rocky peninsula, in the shadow of permanently snow-capped mountains – is one of the few places in the world where you can see whales all year round. It's also home to arguably New Zealand's best ski fields (more than ten ski areas lie within a two-and-a-half-hour drive of Christchurch), offering everything from snowboarding to heli-skiing.

PRACTICALITIES To help you get as much as possible out of a trip to Canterbury, www.christchurchnz.net suggests a variety of touring routes; the same site also has details of accommodation across the region.

✦ Nelson ✦

Mount Owen (where the Dimrill Dale hillside was filmed) and Mount Olympus (the setting for the Eregion hills and the rough country south of Rivendell) are both found in the Kahurangi National Park – one of three national parks in the Nelson region.

HIGHLIGHTS Nelson – originally called Whakatu (which means "the standing place") by the Maoris – got its first influx of European settlers in 1840. In 1858 it was renamed after Admiral Nelson, and became New Zealand's second city by royal charter from Queen Victoria. To see the city in style, you could hire a limousine (www.executivelimousines.co.nz) or, for the more adventurous, there are heli-tours of the area (www.tasmanhelicopters.co.nz). There are also full-day and half-day wine and champagne tours which also give you the chance to learn the history of the region at the same time as enjoying a few tastings.

The Kahurangi National Park (for which Motueka, Takaka, Karamea and Murchison are the gateway towns) has more than 570km of tracks, the most famous of which is the Heaphy Track, a four-to-five-day walk from the Aorere Valley, crossing the northern West Coast and Karamea en route. Its 451,000 hectares of glaciated mountain ranges and rich forest are home to

Hobbiton: all amenities are within easy walking distance

an exceptional variety of native plants and wildlife. Its remote, wild rivers are suitable for experienced kayakers only, but commercial rafting tours are also available. And where Kahurangi's caves – some of the deepest in the world – are concerned, experience is a must.

PRACTICALITIES Nelson is tucked into Tasman Bay on the north-west of South Island. There are direct flights, but they're pretty expensive: most people choose to fly to Christchurch and drive the 420km or take an internal flight (Nelson regional airport is New Zealand's fourth busiest, with flights from Christchurch, Auckland and Wellington). If you're coming from North Island there are ferry crossings from Wellington to Picton, which is about 50km from Nelson.

✦ Takaka ✦

Takaka Hill, in the very north of South Island, became Chetwood Forest, which featured early on in *The Fellowship Of The Ring*, as the hobbits and Strider fled Bree with the Black Riders in hot pursuit.

The realm of the beauteous pointy-eared one, aka Galadriel, Lady of the Wood

HIGHLIGHTS: Rocky headlands and forest-rimmed bays are the distinguishing features of the famously laid-back Golden Bay region. Its fine, sandy beaches are big in the world of water sports – windsurfing, kayaking and boat cruises are particularly popular. The main town, Takaka (which boasts a big craft and café scene), lies on the western edge of the Abel Tasman National Park, home to fur seals, penguins, dolphins and sea birds. The wetlands and bird sanctuary of Farewell Spit are also within easy reach, and 8km north-west of Takaka you'll find Waikoropupu Springs (usually called just 'Pupu'), reputed to be the largest freshwater springs in the world.

PRACTICALITIES Takaka, which lies towards the most northerly tip of South Island, is a couple of hours' drive from Nelson. The town offers the usual mixture of motels, homestays and backpacker accommodation – try www.nelsonnz.com/golden/#Takaka for details.

✦ Queenstown ✦

On the shores of Lake Wakatipu, surrounded by mountains, **Queenstown** was used to create Lothlórien, home to Galadriel, Lady of the Wood – a part which Cate Blanchett took because she said she'd "always wanted pointy ears". Arwen's most dramatic scene – when, with Frodo on her horse, she was confronted by the Black Riders at the Ford of Bruinen in *The Fellowship Of The Ring* – was filmed in nearby **Arrowtown**.

HIGHLIGHTS There are safari tours of The Lord Of The Rings sights offering a range of half-day or full-day tours: www.nomadsafaris.co.nz/rings.html has more information. Queenstown is also the place to try jet-boating. The Hamilton Jetboat was invented by Bill Hamilton in the 1960s to get around the shallow rivers of the Canterbury plain at speeds of up to 80km per hour; jet-boating is now a staple of the deep Shotover River and the shallow, twisting Dart River at nearby Glenorchy. During winter Coronet Peak, Cardrona and The Remarkables (best seen from the mountain road up to Arrowtown) are popular with skiers, and there is also an annual winter festival – visit www.winterfestival.co.nz for more information about all the snow-based activities and cultural events. Arrowtown initially sprung up following the discovery of gold in the Arrow River in 1862. There are now guided tours which include your very own chance to pan for gold, and explain much of the history behind the Chinese Settlement – a series of mud-walled huts – in the town.

Getting Around New Zealand
THE BEST WAYS TO GET TO, AND AROUND, NEW ZEALAND

Most international flights go to Auckland International Airport, which lies about 15km south of Auckland. Air New Zealand, Qantas and a few other local airlines provide internal flights between cities.

There are good rail links between Auckland and Wellington on North Island, and between Christchurch and Picton or Greymouth on South Island. The bus services on each island connect the major cities with smaller towns, and you can buy a travel pass that allows you to combine several different modes of transport.

Car ferries sail between the North and South Islands, but be warned: if you hire a car on one island, you won't be able to transport it to the other. Most rental companies, however, will arrange a second car for you to pick up at the opposite ferry terminal if you would like to visit both islands.

Wherever you're coming from or going to in New Zealand, it's worth planning your trip in advance to get the best deals.

PRACTICALITIES **Queenstown** is in the south-west of South Island, about 480km from Christchurch: there are good rail links if you don't want to drive all the way. Queenstown is one of New Zealand's most popular towns, and its compact town centre – less than a square mile – means that all amenities are within easy walking distance. Camping around the area is popular, but the town has accommodation to suit every taste and budget (www.queenstown-nz.co.nz/accommodation.asp).

✦ Tarras And Wanaka ✦

When the film crew arrived on the banks of the Clutha River, near the town of **Tarras**, it was in helicopters. They were searching for an area of land with great plains, no houses or fences, and with snow-capped mountains in the distance. The area around Tarras and **Wanaka** (some 25km away) fitted the bill exactly, and no major construction was needed to provide the backdrop to the search for Frodo and the attacks on the Fellowship, plus many scenes featuring the Black Riders.

HIGHLIGHTS Wanaka, combining spectacular surroundings with a real sense of adventure, is regarded by many as the next Queenstown (albeit in a more refined way). Puzzling World, with its maze and its collection of buildings, will test your sense of time and spatial awareness, and every other year the Warbirds Over Wanaka airshow draws thousands to see the spectacle of Spitfires and other planes from different eras. Other activities include boating, skiing, walking, fishing and hunting. About 40km north-west of Wanaka, at the heart of the Te Wahipounamu South West New Zealand World Heritage Area, is the impressive Mount Aspiring National Park, with Mount Aspiring itself the crowning glory of some 13 peaks (to say nothing of 100-odd glaciers).

PRACTICALITIES Tarras and Wanaka are about 400km from Christchurch. Visit www.nzhealth.net.nz/nzitinery/wanaka-chch.html for more details about the scenic routes. Details of the many budget hostels in the area are at www.backpack.co.nz.

✦ Twizel ✦

The spectacular opening scenes of *The Two Towers* were shot just outside Twizel, a mountain town in the **Aortaki National Park**. Nearby **Ben Ohau** station became the plains of Rohan, where Aragorn, Legolas and Gimli pursue the orcs, and the Rohan villages were also situated here before they were destroyed by Saruman's armies. Extensive scenes set in Rohan were filmed in the town of **Twizel** itself; the Battle of Pelennor Fields in the third film, *The Return Of The King*, was shot on a vast, grassy field next to this remote South Island town.

HIGHLIGHTS Situated in the middle of the Mackenzie Basin, Twizel was only built in 1968 as a support town to a hydro-electricity project. It was due to be demolished before its residents won a campaign to take it over. A pleasant new town with good facilities, Twizel enjoys warm summers and cold winters, making it ideal for ice skating; it's also a base for skiing in the region. Lake Ohau nearby is good for fishing and the area is famous for its walking trails. Mackenzie Country and Mount Cook (New Zealand's highest mountain) National Park provide a variety of outdoor activities in a rugged landscape.

PRACTICALITIES Twizel is a comfortable four-hour drive (with a break) from Christchurch, or three hours if you're coming north from Queenstown.

Accommodation ranges from camping to homestays to modern hotels: visit www.twizel.com for more information.

✦ Te Anau ✦

Te Anau is the gateway town to the Fiordland National Park. With more than 400 inches of rainfall a year in some parts, the park has both dense, moss-covered rainforest and marshes, making it perfect for the Dead Marshes in *The Two Towers*. The Marshes were the site of a battle of old, and a watery burial ground for many, and they proved a major barrier for Frodo and Sam in their quest to reach Mordor.

HIGHLIGHTS Lake Te Anau is the largest on South Island, covering some 530sq km. Along the western shoreline are the Te Anau-au caves – massive limestone caverns lit by glow-worms, deep inside the Murchison Mountains. They can be reached by a scenic cruise across the lake.

PRACTICALITIES Te Anau is 650km from Christchurch, but if you don't want to drive the entire way, an internal flight from Christchurch to Queenstown (170km from Te Anau), followed by a drive along the Great Southern Route, has proven a popular alternative. Head to www.nzhealth.net.nz/nzitinery/southcoast.html for more details. There are a number of good bed and breakfasts in the Fiordland National Park; for more information, visit www.fiordland.org.nz.

✦ Milford Sound ✦

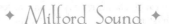

Numerous areas around Milford Sound, also in the Fiordland National Park, became Amon Hen, Nen Hithoel and Fangorn Forest (home to the talking trees in *The Two Towers*, named after the oldest surviving ent, who is also the guardian of the forest). The logistics of clambering up and down from their talking tree, Treebeard, in *The Two Towers* were such that Billy Boyd – Pippin – and Dominic Monaghan – Merry – were forced to have their meals on their lofty perch. This could have been something of a hindrance, but in between takes the pair using their time to write a screenplay of their own.

HIGHLIGHTS In addition to its Lord Of The Rings connection, Milford Sound is famous for its sheer peaks and crashing waterfalls. Day cruises allow

Even the European alps never looked quite as spectacular as this...

visitors to see some of the spectacular scenery, but remember to book in advance: the number of different trips is mind-boggling but just about all of them are very popular. Milford Sound is also home to a rare black coral reef system which you can learn about at Harrison Cove. With the fjord surrounded by towering cliffs and snow-capped mountains it's hard to know where to start, but the Mitre Peak, the photographic focal point, is as good a place as any. Then there's the Milford Track, a four-day trek that explores the region's rainforest and crystal clear streams; it also offers visitors with astounding views from the top of Mackinnon Pass and takes in Sutherland Falls, justly famed as New Zealand's highest waterfall, measuring an impressive 580m.

PRACTICALITIES Milford Sound is on the western edge of South Island, approximately 285km from Queenstown and 765km from Christchurch. The accommodation available in the area is surprisingly limited, though – the no-frills Milford Sound Lodge essentially the only option for those planning overnight stop.

✦ Southern South Island ✦

The **Southern Alps**, situated across central and Southern South Island, were used extensively during the filming of *The Lord Of The Rings*. The dramatic peaks and glacier-carved lakes and rivers closely resembled how director **Peter Jackson** imagined Middle-earth to be. They would not have come too high on **Sean Bean's** wishlist of locations, however: the actor's fear of helicopter flights was such that in order to reach the film set he would generally spend a couple of hours clambering up to it through the snow – in full Boromir costume – rather than clamber aboard the chopper.

HIGHLIGHTS The south of **South Island** contains two **National Parks**, **Fiordland** and **Mount Aspiring**, which offer some of New Zealand's most rugged landscape and thrill-seeking activities such as rafting, bungee-jumping, heli-skiing or speedboat rides. Also worth a trip is Dunedin, the focal point of the Otago region – it's famous for its colourful gold-mining history and is rich in Scottish heritage and architecture (Dunedin was the old Scottish name for Edinburgh).

PRACTICALITIES An internal flight to Queenstown gets you straight into the heart of Southern South Island. Once there, the choice of accommodation is almost endless, ranging from luxury hotels to camping grounds; check out www.southisland.co.nz or www.accommodationz.co.nz for details.

THE LORD OF THE RINGS

THE TWO TOWERS

EPHEMERA

**EVERYTHING YOU NEED TO COMPLETE
YOUR LORD OF THE RINGS COLLECTION**

New Line Cinema's official promotional poster for The Two Towers

"Well here comes Christmas! That astonishing
thing that no 'commercialism' can in fact
defile... unless you let it"
Tolkien in a letter to his son Michael, December 1962

What would Tolkien have made of it? This nether world of Middle-earth ephemera where the Witch King of Angmar is a child's piggy bank that shrieks every time a coin is deposited; where the watcher in the water, the nameless creature from the noisome pool at the gates of Khazad-dûm, becomes a water feature for your garden; where Aragorn, heir to the throne of Gondor, is a 12in bobble-head doll, part of a set that includes Frodo, Gandalf, Legolas and Gimli.

Tolkien would have been perplexed, of course, but it's here all the same: the films have spawned a huge business in *The Lord Of The Rings* merchandise. What, not so very long ago, was a respectful and tasteful cottage industry run by pipe-smoking enthusiasts with a weakness for made-up languages is now a brand with global reach: it is books and DVDs, baseball caps and badges, pillowcases and towels, fridge magnets and pointy plastic ears. It's hobbitmania!

If you had enough dedication and/or disposable income (or, failing that, parents with a disposable income) you could wake up in the morning, your head turning on your Lord Of The Rings pillowcase, gaze up at the posters of Aragorn and friends on your bedroom wall, before picking up your Lord Of The Rings pewter goblet to sip your morning cuppa and peer out over the garden specially designed (by David Fountain and singer-cum-gardening celebrity Kim Wilde) at your request to resemble Bilbo Baggins's front garden (they did it for the Royal Horticultural Society show in Chelsea last year, so surely they could design one for you). Then you could put on your gold ring, with the slogan "One Ring to rule them all, One Ring to find them" engraved on the outside in red Elvish characters.

Over breakfast (during which you take a refreshing swig of orange juice from a Gimli figural mug) you could re-read a few pages of The Hobbit, then scramble upstairs to change into your *Lord Of The Rings* T-shirt, put on your 'Frodo Lives!' baseball cap, pick up a plastic replica of **Sting** – Frodo's sword, not the rock singer – and leave the house ready, willing and able to do battle with any passing ringwraiths. Of course, those fans with grander ambitions might want to don their Gandalf child's costume (or, for girls, an Arwen costume).

After meeting your mates, you might want to compare souvenirs – that kid from across the road dressed up as the Witch King has somehow acquired a complete set of The Lord Of The Rings stamps, issued to honour the films (and the movies' settings) by the New Zealand government.

Feeling inadequately souvenired, you might stomp home, turn on the computer – the desktop covered with The Lord Of The Rings wallpaper – and email a friend in Australia your next move in the game of The Lord Of The Rings chess you've been playing thanks to the magic of the Internet. After telling your opponent of your move, you actually move the hero knight – represented by a white **Aragorn** figure – to the right square.

You then log on to *The Lord Of The Rings* news site to catch up with the latest on the new movie, before running downstairs, while the living room's quiet, to load the DVD of *The Fellowship Of The Ring*, packed with loads of fantastic extras as it is, into *The Lord Of The Rings* DVD player, and try on a pair of 3D wireless Lord Of The Rings glasses, designed to make watching the movies even more spectacular than it already is.

You relax afterwards by puffing on your **hobbit pipe** – or pretending to if you're under 16 – before starting a 160-piece 3D Gandalf sculpture puzzle – equivalent to a 1,000-piece jigsaw in terms of complexity – and then, after a couple of hours rejigging all the pieces, try unsuccessfully to explain the intricate nuances of The Lord Of The Rings trading-card game to dear old Dad. Giving up, you challenge him instead to a *Lord Of The Rings* game of Risk – apparently he used to play it at university when he was a member of the student branch of the Labour party – and after trouncing him, you go up the wooden hill to Bedfordshire. Adjusting the pillow so it's more comfortable, you imagine that you are Aragorn, about to go hunting some orcs, and, content, you drift off into dreams of Middle-earth.

What follows is a **Shadowfax** gallop through what is available for collectors in *The Lord Of The Rings*-land, aimed at the expensive and interesting, but with advice for those disposed towards cheap and tacky.

✦ 14 Ways To Start Your ✦
Lord Of The Rings Collection

1 ✦ Live In Tolkien's House ✦

This is not easy. Nor, according to the scanty recent evidence, is it cheap. The last time a house that JRR Tolkien lived in came up for sale was just a couple of years ago. It wasn't particularly special: a seven-bedroom, Grade II listed, Oxford town house lacking certain amenities (like central heating and a kitchen). Tolkien never owned it either: he'd only rented it for six months way back in 1918, when Bilbo Baggins was not yet a twinkle in Belladonna Took's eye. But it still sold for **£745,000** – fifty grand over the asking price – not bad for a house needing an estimated £200,000 of renovation.

In one of his letters now in the British Library's archive, Tolkien criticises "Hoopers, Snoopers, Goopers, press-gangs, phone-bugs, and transatlantic lion hunters and gargoyle-fanciers." It would be interesting to know how he would have described people prepared to pay three-quarters of a million pounds to live in his house. It didn't even go to a fan, which probably tells you more about house prices in southern England than about people who name their homes Bag End.

2 ✦ Buy First Editions ✦

The Hobbit, first published in 1937, is now rarer than dragon droppings in first-edition form. One, a family copy and signed by Tolkien, sold recently at auction for £40,000, but that was a special case. A more typical price for a decent condition copy, if you can find one, is **£20,000**.

The Lord Of The Rings is a later work (1954-55) and had a bigger initial print run, so there are more first editions out there. Which is not to say they're plentiful or cheap. A near-fine set will cost you £7,500 and a pristine set will swipe £25,000 from your credit card. The average asking price is around £12,500, and all the authorities agree that you should be very, very careful about the authenticity of signed copies.

The Ten Most Expensive Lord Of The Rings Items On eBay

Whether you've got thousands or just a few pence, there's something on eBay for every fan. This lot may not be there when you visit, but there's likely to be something similar (prices relate to bidding at the time).

1. The Lord Of The Rings, UK first edition (1954), $15,000
There's speculation these leather-bound gems could double in price over the coming years.

2. The Lord Of The Rings, signed by JRR Tolkien, $7,750
Bound "in full Red Morocco", no less, which means an awful lot in the book-binding world.

3. Seven-foot tall carved Lord Of The Rings wizard, $2,500
Apparently carved by one of Oregon's most notable carvers – and the globe lights from the inside. Nice.

4. The Lord Of The Rings, first edition, $1,525
Published by Allen & Unwin in 1954 and 1955, and predicted to shoot up in value.

5. Complete Lord Of The Rings eight-sword set, $1,245.85
Scant description when we visited. The seller obviously hopes the use of three exclamation marks gets their sales message across.

6. Complete Lord Of The Rings nine-sword set, $1,200
Speaking of exclamation marks, "these are not MINIATURES!!!" says the seller. OK, we believe you.

7. Huge Lord Of The Rings action-figure collection, $1,000
Aside from Twilight Frodo, this collection has everything. Maybe.

8. The Lord Of The Rings toys, from Toybiz, $999
Includes all the Fellowship and Two Towers basic figures, apart from that elusive Twilight Frodo.

9. Artist proof of a balrog statue, $900
Artist proof apparently means one of the first 60 produced.

10. Balrog statue, $900
Mint condition and allegedly one of the most rare and sought after items from Weta/Sideshow.

Prices plummet for later impressions. For under £500 there are plenty of old but cared-for copies, and special limited-edition box sets from the more recent past. If it's just the reading you're after, you can always pop down to WHSmith and get them all in paperback for rather less than the price of a Lord Of The Rings magic flip cube ($59.95 plus p&p).

If you're looking for something rarer, how about this? Unbound page proofs of the first US edition with corrections written by the American editor in accordance with Tolkien's hand corrections of the British proof copy. Many of the amendments are pretty obscure stuff – the precise shape of runes incorporated into body copy, for example – but the big note of interest is the revision to the book's key line. "One Ring to bring them all and in the shadow bind them" is changed to "… in the *darkness* bind them".

The tortuous process by which a mistake elsewhere in the US edition allowed an unauthorised paperback to be printed in America in the 1960s, making Tolkien a household name in the process, is something we'll come on to shortly. But these page proofs, housed in 'custom folding chemises and slipcase' are the vital paperwork behind the tale. They were recently sold at a snip, for only £34,000.

3 ✦ Find Special Editions ✦

Having sold over **50 million** copies in nearly 50 years, *The Lord Of The Rings* regularly tops polls to find the most influential book of the 20th century. During that time, the books have been published in many formats. Your only problem is deciding which one(s) to buy.

Type "The Lord Of The Rings" into the search engine at *Amazon.com* and it'll respond with a staggering 350-plus items. These include books on Tolkien's poems, maps and places, complete guides to – and treasuries of facts about – his work, and audio CDs (abridged or unabridged, single narrator or full-cast dramatisations). There's academic criticism (*Return Of The Heroes: The Lord Of The Rings, Star Wars, Harry Potter And Social Conflict*, by Hal GP Colebatch – "available for digital download now!"; or *Celebrating Middle-earth: The Lord Of The Rings As A Defense Of Western Civilization* by Joseph Pearce, et al); satire (Private Eye's *Lord Gnome Of The Rings*), and earnest tomes on its spiritual themes, myths and magic. There's a Lord Of The Rings Oracle, with cards or runic rings (apparently the landscapes represent archetypal scenarios through which we all pass at some point in our lives). There's even a **Lord Of The Rings tarot.**

Buried among all this paraphernalia (surely as much of a tree-killer as Saruman ever was) are the countless reprints of the books themselves – singly or in one compendium, hard or paperback, boxed or unboxed, with or without *The Hobbit,* and with or without new movie artwork. If you're looking for something a bit special, perhaps as a gift, here are three of the best.

Possibly most suitable for (and easily digestible by) younger readers is the seven-volume millennium edition of paperback books, presented in a black presentation box (Collins, around £17.50). A HarperCollins hardback version for grown-ups – if you can find it – comes with a CD of Tolkien reading excerpts.

Into comic books? The prize-winning single-volume edition of the trilogy, first published in 1992 to mark the 100th anniversary of the birth of Tolkien, includes 50 colour paintings (created especially for the book) by London-born illustrator **Alan Lee**, now 'conceptual designer' for the movies. The 2002 reprint (HarperCollins) will cost you around £35 for the single volume, or around £52.50 for the three-book edition.

Finally, and just about as up-market as you can get, there's the deluxe leatherbound hardback edition set in a cloth-bound slipcase (HarperCollins, 2001). Printed on Bible paper with an ornate gold-leaf edging, it has Christopher Tolkien's maps of Middle-earth and Gondor as end papers (there is also a matching companion volume of *The Silmarillion* too.) However, be prepared to part with up to £100 for each volume, and place it well out of reach of any young sticky fingers.

THE LORD OF THE RINGS IS AVAILABLE IN A MULTITUDE OF EDITIONS. YOUR ONLY PROBLEM IS DECIDING WHICH TO BUY

Fancy a cheap collectible with a whiff of the illegal? When US publishers Houghton Mifflin bought the American rights to *The Lord Of The Rings,* they imported pages printed in England to be bound in the US. Unfortunately they imported too many copies enabling the copyright to be challenged. In 1966 Ace Books rushed out a pirate paperback version of the trilogy, saying that Tolkien had no rights to royalties under copyright law. Ballantine Books – innovative publishers of paperbacks – responded by getting Tolkien to 'revise' his books just enough to create a 'new' edition and give it his exclusive approval. Ace eventually had to withdraw their books which, somewhat

Ten Cheaper Items On eBay

1. The Lord Of The Rings Official One Ring, $2.50
We won't say they're ten a penny, but we lost count of the One Ring lots listed. This features the Elvish script inside and outside.

2. The Lord Of The Rings original soundtrack, $1.30
What's described as the "animation/human flick" made in 1978.

3. The Lord Of The Rings Merry and Pippin pencil case, $1
A tin pencil case with inner tray, from a pet- and smoke-free environment, which presumably ups its value.

4. Rare Lord Of The Rings Wormtongue bookmark, $1
It's rare and limited edition and won't be available much longer – and it's got a tassle.

5. German stickers, $1.99
A mint-condition set of foil iridescent holographic orc stickers from the German store BSB. Who could want more?

6. Sean Bean as Boromir magnet, £2
The seller admits that the photo they have taken of the magnet looks 'bad' on the screen. It's much better than it appears.

7. The Lord Of The Rings: The Two Towers mug set, $2
Limited-edition production decal mugs with heat-sensitive design that cleverly reveals runes.

8. The Lord Of The Rings official first day cover, $2.25
Postmarked with the Eye of Sauron, and there's no telling what the value might be one day, says the seller.

9. Uruk-hai paint set, $2.25
Ten detailed uruk-hai warriors to lovingly paint – and you get the paints and paintbrush.

10. Nine Burger King figures, $2.50
A meat-free way to secure a fairly comprehensive set of BK figures.

ironically, have now become Tolkien and Lord Of The Rings collectibles. Expect to pay around $10 each but be warned: these books were printed on very poor quality paper.

Once you've finished the trilogy itself, you can move on to *The Complete History Of Middle-earth*, edited by Tolkien's son Christopher, and published by HarperCollins. This monumental work comprises 12 books in three hardback volumes and presents more than 5,000 pages of alternate versions of events in **The Silmarillion** and **The Lord Of The Rings**, unpublished fragments, rare maps and illustrations, and a full account of the writing of *The Lord Of The Rings*. Although this set is £150, it is actually a snip at only 3p per page.

Then there are the whole raft of movie books and guides, official guides, photo guides, calendars, planners, visual companions and the like that the films have spawned. When it comes to check-out tills, it would seem that **Tolkien** is indeed the lord of the rings. See page 259 for a few examples of *The Lord Of The Rings*-related books you can buy.

4 ✦ Search For Tolkien Artifacts ✦

If the attraction of film-related merchandise has started to fade, there's always the world of **Tolkien** memorabilia. Items associated with the man himself have always sold well, and the renewed interest in the books following Peter Jackson's films has pushed prices higher, but there isn't much of it about.

The **Tolkien Society**'s archives hold an exceptional range of photographs and personal items. **The British Library** also has several of Tolkien's letters, notes and manuscripts, but it's unlikely that they're up for sale.

A better bet are signed copies of the books, but you'll need several thousand pounds and a working knowledge of London auction houses. Unlike modern authors, **Tolkien** signed comparatively few copies, and most that were signed were given as presents, so they come with fairly hefty price tags.

A first edition of *The Hobbit* with Tolkien's dedication "Aunt Jane from JRRT with love, October 6th 1937" sold for over £40,000 at auction in July 2002, and Sotheby's sold a specially-bound set of *The Lord Of The Rings* for £32,450 the year before.

A collection of proof copies, first editions and letters belonging to Tolkien's friend George Sayer sold for £58,000 to an anonymous telephone bidder, with a six-page letter written by Tolkien to Sayer after the funeral of CS Lewis selling for £7,000. But even without Tolkien's signature, first editions fetch high prices. *The Lord Of The Rings* books have changed hands for anything between £1,600 and £17,000.

5 ✦ Find The Ring Of Power ✦

Let's be clear about this. There is no One Ring. There are millions of them. You can get one anywhere, for just about any price, of almost any material that can be made ring-shaped and will take an impression of Elvish script. Unfortunately, none of them have the power to make you invisible, it's doubtful they'll remain cool to the touch after being in fire and they certainly won't prolong your life.

That said, if you're into Tolkien collectables it's the prop you must have. Simple, ubiquitous and, if you get carried away, really quite expensive. Prices vary across a number of US-based Internet sources, but around £530 should buy you a handmade 22-carat gold ring, available in finger sizes 5 to 13, individually hand-polished and with "Elvish runes engraved by artist David Bedali in a choice of black, red or plain colouring". You could hardly ask for more. It's apparently very popular as a wedding ring in places like Iowa.

The same firm offers a cheaper ring, in 10-carat gold, for about £300, and if you're not bothered about getting one that fits and prefer to keep it on a chain in Frodo-approved fashion, then you can get a 14-carat ring from a different source for under £200. You have to provide the chain yourself, but the ring comes in a "handsome black cardboard box" and

with a "certificate of authenticity", whatever that means. Signed by Gollum perhaps. If you keep looking through the various Tolkien store websites long enough, you'll find gold-plated rings for around £25.

New Zealand-based jeweller Jens Hansen may not have Gollum's approval but it does have director Peter Jackson's, who called upon the company to produce the trilogy's 'One Ring'. In actual fact, by the end of shooting over forty One Rings had been produced to fit different cast members. For

Ten Random Items On eBay

I. Arwen's blood-red gown, $450
The makers admit they're unlicensed, but it's as close to the original as possible and "exquisite enough for weddings."

2. The Lord Of The Rings mythic and magic chess set, $41
Each piece holds its own Swarkovski crystal – but check the shipping, as this sparkling line-up weighs in at 3kg.

3. The Two Towers poster, signed, $265.22
Signed by no less than 20 members of the cast at premiéres and after-parties – no tears or creases, says the seller.

4. The Lord Of The Rings, signed by Liv Tyler, £30
As signed by the lovely Liv, which considerably ups the book's value.

5. Uruk-hai scimitar, $68
From United Cutlery and authentically 'battle-worn' with corrosion, rust and tarnish to simulate the original movie prop.

6. The official movie ringwraith costume, $99.99
Made of a unique fabric that lets you see through it even though it covers your face – handy.

7. 18 Lot Vintage, $49.99
If you struggle with Tolkien's plot, you'll be pleased that this includes that sixth-former's friend, Cole's Notes On The Lord Of The Rings.

8. The Lord Of The Rings flying jacket, $40.59
A genuine ex-competition prize that can't be bought in a shop, apparently, and they've been known to fetch £100.

9. The Fellowship Of The Ring movie script, $105.58
Signed by various cast members including Elijah Wood and Sir Ian McKellen.

10. Pippin autocard, $53.20
Apparently rare and authentic autograph card from The Two Towers, which is kindly shipped in bubble wrap for extra protection.

your own replica 'one ring' go to *www.jenshansen.com*.

If the thought of wearing the dread creation of Mordor on your hand day and night doesn't do it for you, then look around for others in the rings of power line. These include the rings of Elrond, Galadriel, Gandalf, Aragorn and the **Witch King of Angmar**. You can get the whole lot in a gift set for about £70. Should cover most eventualities.

6 ✦ Own A Rings Chess Set ✦

A chess set seems an obvious *Lord Of The Rings* spin-off – white versus black, good versus evil. But it's not as simple as that. Is Gandalf a king or a bishop? Are the hobbits just pawns? If the point of the game is to protect your king, shouldn't that be Frodo? Where does Aragorn fit into this? And whatever happened to **Tom Bombadil**?

The Royal Selangor chess set (£450) with pieces made from pewter (good) and Florentine bronze (evil) does its best to surmount these challenges, but takes a couple of liberties. **Treebeards** versus **Smaugs** for the knights is just plain wrong: Smaug failed to emerge from the splashdown phase nearly 80 years before the main *Lord Of The Rings* action began, and whoever heard of vegetable knights?

If money is no object and taste not an insurmountable problem then you should go for the shot glass *Lord Of The Rings* chess set. "Sculpted," it says, "with exquisite detail by Dr Graeme J Anthony of Australia" this is a drink-yourself-into-oblivion chess set, lacking only bottles of light and dark liqueurs for an intensive evening's struggle between good and evil. It's officially licensed by Tolkien Enterprises, includes a 22in board, and will give you no change at all from £750.

Chess sets go back a long way in *The Lord Of The Rings* memorabilia and a number of different sets have been issued. A 1991 Danbury Mint set recently came up on auction with the bidding starting at £450. Easier on the pocket is an official licensed set, priced at around £25.

7 ✦ Wear Gandalf's Gear ✦

We're assuming here that you have sufficient bed linen and blankets to fashion Gandalf's main garments in the shade of your choice. (Is white the new grey?) What you need now are the essential accessories, which at a bare minimum means the staff, the sword, the hat and the pipe.

The staff is the hardest to find and the most expensive. If you can track one down (eBay is a good place to start) then expect to pay no less than £300 and possibly a fair bit more. It seems to have fallen off the list of official *The Lord Of The Rings* products available from the usual sources. Alternatively, you can make your own with a large stick and a strategically placed light bulb.

The sword, **Glamdring**, is rather easier to locate. United Cutlery has produced a range of *The Lord Of The Rings* weapons (see 'Own Your Own Sword' on page 256), including Gandalf's blade. Made of tempered stainless steel with a 36in blade and engraved in Elvish with words to the effect that the sword was forged for **Turgon**, the king of **Gondolin**, it's a precise replica of Ian McKellen's sidearm. Prices range considerably. One British source (*www.otherlandtoys.co.uk*) quotes £249, but a similar figure in US dollars (try *www.newlineshop.com*) seems to be the general going rate. If that seems a bit much, you can always get a one-fifth scale model for around £35.

The pointy hat can be obtained from a number of Tolkien store sites; usual asking price is around £25. The inordinately long-stemmed pipe costs a little over £60, tobacco not included.

There are various other costumes and accessories to be had, ranging from hobbit outfits for kids to Legolas wigs and plastic hobbit ears. You can even get a one-size adult Gandalf costume made from finest polyester for around £50. If you're prepared to suspend disbelief and imagine that a shapeless white dress will really turn you into **Arwen**, that's also available for around £50, from *www.lordoftherings.net*.

8 ✦ Wear The Jewellery ✦

Necklaces, brooches, earrings, pendants, rings – they're all out there, available at a click of the mouse to anyone with a sufficiently resilient credit card. Priciest is probably the **Éowyn** earrings and necklace set, "crafted in 14-carat gold" and costing the best part of £400. For a little bit less you can supplement your **Arwen** dress with earrings (£75) and pendant (£60) from a limitless selection of elven-inspired, generally leaf-shaped jewellery. Prices start around £35. All are available from the official websites *www.lordoftherings.net* and *www.newlineshop.com*, and a host of worldwide, officially affiliated websites.

9 ✦ Play The Recordings ✦

The Lord Of The Rings has inspired some very famous musicians, including **Marc Bolan** and **Robert Plant** (see page 286). It's also inspired some not-so-famous musicians, and over the years Middle-earth has grown accustomed to the well-intentioned wibblings of a thousand bedroom synthesizers. And it's all just a mouse click away.

Texan philosophy professor Gene Hargrove (*www.oldforestsounds.com*) has created *The Music Of Middle-earth*, a two-volume series based on the songs and chants in the book. *Volume One: A Musical Journey From The Shire To Rivendell* and *Volume Two: A Musical Journey From Khazad-dûm To Gondor* are both synth-based albums, but there's a separate songbook if you fancy creating your own arrangements.

According to Alan Horvath's site, *www.alanhorvath.com*, the acoustic folk rocker's early work on a planned three-album masterpiece *The Rings Project* attracted some interest from David Bowie and the producers of Peter Jackson's films. It never went any further, but the first album, celebrating "*The Lord Of The Rings* in narration and song" and featuring Alan on guitar, dulcimer, octave mandolin and autoharp, can be ordered online.

An organisation which rejoices in the name of Metrognome Studios is selling 1,000 copies of a limited-edition *Lord Of The Rings*-based album called *One Ring* on its site *www.metrognome.demon.co.uk*, but it's the creation of the MP3 format that has given the genre a whole new lease of life. The entire output of The Poetic Fellowship, a group of Czech musicians whose songs are based on the Tolkien universe, can be downloaded from its website *http://poetspol.web4u.cz*.

The **Brobdingnagian Bards** released their tribute song Tolkien (The Hobbit And The Lord Of The Rings) directly onto MP3.com, and it is currently the most popular Celtic title on the site. It has inspired them to release an album, Memories Of Middle-earth, which is a largely instrumental album including the memorably-titled The Psychopathic, Chronic, Schizophrenic Gollum Blues.

'We are Hobbit and we're here to make you feel two-feet tall,' observes *www.hobbitcd.com* cryptically. Home to fantasy-rockers Hobbit, the site provides details of the band's album *Rockin' The Shire*. A mix of Tolkien influences and AOR, the track listing happily omits the easily-misconstrued woodburning tribute **Faggots In The Fire**.

10 ✦ Own Your Own Sword ✦

So what do you want then? Aragorn's sword? Legolas's bow? Gimli's axe? Gandalf's power? Like Frodo you can have them all; unlike Frodo you will have to pay for them. These three alone will set you back

a minimum of £500.

The United Cutlery collection has Aragorn's Ranger blade; Sting (with and without scabbard); Narsil, the sword of Elendil in both complete and 'shards' form; plus the swords of Arwen and the Witch King of Angmar, and a uruk-hai scimitar.

On the US sites most of these are available for around $250 (say, £150), but UK and European sources are distinctly more expensive. The dearest of the lot is the **six-foot Legolas longbow**, which costs $369.99 and doesn't even come with a quiverful of arrows. **Gimli's axe** is the cheapest at $199.

It's worth looking around the auction sites, though. We saw one gift set incorporating nearly all the available swords, ready to go for $1,500. Again, as in the case of Glamdring, there are one-fifth scale models for most of the weapons, priced between £30 and £40.

11 ✦ Buy Autographed Posters ✦

A full set of signatures from the nine members of the Fellowship will take some hunting around, but it can be done. One Internet source offers autographed film posters that start at around £50 for **John Rhys-Davies** (Gimli) and range up to about £100 for **Viggo Mortensen** (Aragorn) and **Ian McKellen** (Gandalf). Interestingly, it's the signature of Christopher Lee (Saruman) that seems to attract the highest prices (£100-plus).

If you want to go the whole hog and add the autographs of other leading members of the cast, such as **Cate Blanchett** (Galadriel), **Liv Tyler** (Arwen), **Brad Dourif** (Gríma Wormtongue) and **Bernard Hill** (Théoden), you can soon rack up a bill that runs into four figures without a decimal point in sight.

The Lord Of The Rings Coins
THE LORD OF THE RINGS AS CASH IN YOUR HAND, LITERALLY

The profitability in The Lord Of The Rings is old news today. However, Tolkien may have been surprised to discover that when it comes to his trilogy, his words "All that is gold does not glitter" couldn't be more wrong.

Coinciding perfectly (marketing heads should be proud) with the release of the third and final film The Return Of The King, Britain's Royal Mint has produced a set of The Lord Of The Rings-inspired coins that can be used as legal tender in New Zealand. Denominations ranging from NZ$0.50 to NZ$10 are available, although experts don't expect many fans will be able to part with the latest edition to their memorabilia collection.

New Zealand's prime minister, Helen Clark, struck the first coin at the Royal Mint in Wales. The gold and silver coins, which feature characters and scenes from the three films, will hold a special place in the heart of Tolkienites in the home of Peter Jackson's movies. But the collection is also available in the UK from the Royal Mint and specialist coin dealers.

12 ✦ Collect Figurines And Statues ✦

Most of what you can find on the market today is spun-off from the films, but if you look hard enough you might stumble across something older and rarer. Royal Doulton produced a set of 12 china Lord Of The Rings figurines way back in the mists of time (1979-81 to be precise), and a good set of these will leave a **£2,000** hole in your pocket.

Even the more recent movie merchandise could give your bank manager cause for concern. How about a limited-edition balrog statue for £500? Or a watcher in the water with "authentic wet finish and animated legs" for £180?

Life-size cardboard 'stand-ups' of the main characters are also widely available, at a rather more reasonable £25 upwards. Some of them even talk. You can get Gollum hissing "My preciousss", for example.

Then there's the bewildering range of toys and dolls, some of which you'll find in your local Woolworths. There's a 12in Treebeard, for example, which comes with removable Merry and Pippin figures riding on his shoulders – an absolute bargain for £50. Apparently. But our favourite has to be the Sauron figure (£30 including postage and packaging). It features light-up eyes and says things like "There is no life but the void" and "Build me an army worthy of Mordor." You've got to have one.

Games Workshop meanwhile offer a huge selection of *The Lord Of The Rings*-inspired figures for you to paint yourself. The figures can then be used to recreate battles from the film using the character figures and dice. For more information on *The Lord Of The Rings* wargaming and figures available to buy from the site, head to *www.gamesworkshop.com*.

13 ✦ Collect Stamps ✦

Everything from football to aspirin has graced a postage stamp, so why not Tolkien and The Lord Of The Rings? In Britain in 1992 we celebrated Tolkien's centenary with a commemoration pack of £6's worth of stamps. You can also buy a collection of New Zealand stamps to coincide with Peter Jackson's trilogy. At the time of going to press, a set for *The Return Of The King* movie had yet to be released, but it's worth seeking out all three. Head to *www.lordoftheringsshop.com* for more details. Even more exciting are the British Royal Mail's plans to release a set in 2004 featuring original artwork by the author himself.

14 ✦ And If All Else Fails... ✦

Correct us if we're wrong, but we don't remember Gandalf looking at his watch and telling the Fellowship that they'd better get a move on if they wanted to be through the Mines of Moria in time for tea. However, you can get *The Lord Of The Rings* timepieces: the standard Middle-earth watch costs £60 and an Eye of Sauron one retails for around £80.

Equally inauthentic is the Middle-earth pinball game that Atari®

produced in 1977. The bidding on an Internet auction site started at $450. If you have young kids and a decent-sized garden you might want to invest £400 on a Lord Of The Rings bouncy castle from Inflatables-R-Us of Oklahoma that bears no resemblance whatsoever to **Minas Tirith**. And there's probably no way you can do without a matching pair of *The Lord Of The Rings* pewter goblets at roughly £85.

◇ ⊰≫≷≪⊱ ◇

✦ Books ✦

Tolkien Guides

THE COMPLETE GUIDE TO MIDDLE-EARTH
Robert Foster, HarperCollins
Sauron to Saruman; Gollum to Gandalf; Riders of Rohan to the Fangorn Forest; Robert Foster's Complete Guide does just what it says on the cover. Don't even consider a trip to Middle-earth without it.

TOLKIEN: THE ILLUSTRATED ENCYCLOPEDIA
David Day, Mitchell Beazley
From the evolution of Middle-earth to the genealogy of Tolkien's myriad characters and creatures, this encylopaedia is a useful resource for both casual followers of *The Lord Of The Rings* trilogy and those with a more avid interest in all things Tolkien.

THE PEOPLE'S GUIDE TO JRR TOLKIEN
Erica Challis, Open Road Publishing
This guide, created by the writers of *TheOneRing.net* website, covers a range of topics, from why people become so immersed in the writings of Tolkien to the things that inspired the man himself. It also addresses many of the FAQs asked about Middle-earth in a range of articles, some new, some taken from the site.

THE LORD OF THE RINGS LOCATION GUIDEBOOK
Ian Brodie, HarperCollins
Detailed GPS (Global Positioning System) references to the locations used in the filming of *The Lord Of The Rings* trilogy, photographs (including stills from the movies), a foreword by Peter Jackson, explanations of both Maori mythology and Elvish lore and practical travelling tips all combine to make this a gripping guide for anyone planning a trip to Middle-earth.

HOBBITS, ELVES AND WIZARDS – THE WONDERS AND WORLDS OF JRR TOLKIEN'S THE LORD OF THE RINGS
Michael N Stanton, Palgrave for St Martin's Press
Part guide, part criticism, *Hobbits, Elves And Wizards* delves into many of the issues and characters that crop up in *The Lord Of The Rings*, creating a book with appeal for both the new Tolkien reader and those already well-steeped in the subject.

THE ROAD TO MIDDLE-EARTH: HOW JRR TOLKIEN CREATED A NEW MYTHOLOGY
Tom Shippey, HarperCollins
The Silmarillion and *Unfinished Tales*, as well as *The Lord Of The Rings*, are among the works covered as the spotlight falls on the poetry of language and myth.

THE HOBBIT COMPANION
David Day, Friedman/Fairfax Publishing
The premise is a simple one: that all of Tolkien's writing stems from the word 'hobbit' and words associated with it. With that as a start point, David Day explores the hidden meanings, the intriguing secrets and the key characters of the worlds created in *The Hobbit* and *The Lord Of The Rings*. The book is made all the more compelling thanks to Lidia Postma's illustrations.

THE TOLKIEN COMPANION
David Day, Mandarin
David Day's at it again, this time with an A-Z of the plants, places, events and creatures that, together, make Middle-earth and the Undying Lands the places they are.

THE COMPLETE TOLKIEN COMPANION
JEA Tyler, Pan

You guessed it: a trip through the legends, history, languages and people of Middle-earth with facts, dates, insights into the Elvish writing systems and maps. It even includes events in *The Silmarillion*, the book which set things up nicely for *The Lord Of The Rings*.

Biographies Of JRR

TOLKIEN: A BIOGRAPHY
Humphrey Carpenter, Allen & Unwin

With pretty much unrestricted access to Tolkien's papers, Humphrey Carpenter has produced what is widely regarded as the definitive biography of JRR Tolkien. Tolkien is portrayed here as a philologist first and foremost, and then as a man who uncovered, rather than created, the peoples, languages and adventures of Middle-earth.

TOLKIEN: MAN AND MYTH – A LITERARY LIFE
Joseph Pearce, HarperCollins

In contrast to Humphrey Carpenter's biography, Joseph Pearce takes Tolkien's view of life and his deep-seated faith as a central axis, with the epic tales of Middle-earth taken as a leap into reality rather than an escape from it. It also looks at his influence on other storytellers such as CS Lewis, and his involvement with the Inklings, the writers' group of which he was a key member.

TOLKIEN: A BIOGRAPHY
Michael White, Abacus

In this able biography by Michael White – briefly a hired keyboard player with 1980s pop-combo The Thompson Twins, one-time journalist and science lecturer at d'Overbroeck's College, Oxford – JRR Tolkien is made more accessible without excessive 'dumbing down'; the linguistic and the literary sources of *The Lord Of The Rings* still feature prominently. White also focuses particularly on the relationship between Tolkien and fellow Inklings member, CS Lewis.

THE LETTERS OF JRR TOLKIEN
JRR Tolkien, Humphrey Carpenter (editor), HarperCollins

Having sifted through the mountains of correspondence that Tolkien generated during his life, Carpenter, with the help of Tolkien's son Christopher, has collated those letters that give the greatest insight into both the academic (including the ways in which Middle-earth evolved) and the family man.

'Inside Tolkien'

JRR TOLKIEN: AUTHOR OF THE CENTURY
Tom Shippey, HarperCollins

Shippey, having taught the same Old English syllabus at Oxford as JRR Tolkien himself, is perfectly placed to delve into the author's sources and origins. Here he provides a compelling – and highly readable (no mean feat given the intricacies of Middle-earth) – explanation of Tolkien's enduring appeal.

MEDITATIONS ON MIDDLE-EARTH
Karen Haber, Earthlight

Despite causing barely a ripple in the literary world on its initial release, the impact of Tolkien's essential fantasy has finally been recognised. Fantasy authors such as Ursula Le Guin and Raymond E Feist offer their thoughts about the author and the impact of his most famous work.

DEFENDING MIDDLE-EARTH: TOLKIEN, MYTH AND MODERNITY
Patrick Curry, HarperCollins

A life-long fan of Tolkien's work, Curry defends his hero against those who see his writings as purely reactionary and escapist, highlighting the book's links to today's society.

A TOLKIEN TREASURY
JRR Tolkien, Alida Baker, WH Auden, Edmund Wilson, Courage Books

Collated articles and commentary on Tolkien's life and works, including a critical essay written by WH Auden and Tolkien's reply to it. Lots of differing viewpoints of *The Lord Of The Rings* and *The Hobbit* are represented here, among the beautiful illustrations, poetry and even recipes that are included – so even the oldest Tolkien reader can discover new ways to look at his work.

JRR TOLKIEN: MYTH, MORALITY AND RELIGION
Richard L Purtill, Ignatius Press
Something of a defence of Tolkien in the face of flak from the critics – like Tolkien, Purtill was both a staunch Catholic and an academic – this book merits having a look at for the way in which it not only explains **Tolkien's moral views** but also goes on to demonstrate how Tolkien has used myth in his works to convey them.

Maps

JOURNEYS OF FRODO – AN ATLAS OF JRR TOLKIEN'S THE LORD OF THE RINGS
Barbara Strachey, HarperCollins
Strachey, a fan of *The Lord Of The Rings* since it first appeared, makes it possible to track **Frodo** and the story's other main characters with 51 maps based on the detailed descriptions and the original maps in *The Lord Of The Rings*, combined with Tolkien's own illustrations.

THE ATLAS OF MIDDLE-EARTH
Karen Wynn Fonstad, Houghton Mifflin
All the battles, cities and territories of Middle-earth introduced in *The Lord Of The Rings*; the routes taken by Frodo and company throughout their epic journeys; and even the history, climate, population and languages of the land created by Tolkien.

MAPS OF MIDDLE-EARTH
Brian Sibley & John Howe, HarperCollins
Four individual maps from the conceptual artist who worked alongside Alan Lee on the motion picture trilogy, included together with a fascinating book detailing the stories behind the maps by noted Tolkien scholar, Brian Sibley.

Miscellaneous

BORED OF THE RINGS
The Harvard Lampoon (Henry N Beard and Douglas C Kenney), Gollancz
As parodies go, they don't get much better than this. Characters, locations, plot twists – all will be pretty familiar from Tolkien's original but all have been on the receiving end of the wit and wisdom the co-founders of America's leading satirical institution, National Lampoon.

THE TOLKIEN QUIZ BOOK
Andrew Murray, HarperCollins
A chance to prove how much you do – or, more likely, don't – know about *The Lord Of The Rings*. Some 1,200 questions based on the works of Tolkien, split into 100 categories, ranging from easy to fiendishly difficult.

Film Books

THE LORD OF THE RINGS – THE MAKING OF THE MOVIE TRILOGY
Brian Sibley, HarperCollins

The official inside story about the making of Peter Jackson's epic goes into the intricacies of film-making, includes some 300 photographs (many not published anywhere else before) and features exclusive interviews with the film's cast and crew (everyone from Jackson through to the people who make the wigs). Lavishly illustrated and with a foreword by Sir Ian McKellen, it is a fitting celebration of the films.

THE LORD OF THE RINGS: THE FELLOWSHIP OF THE RING – INSIDER'S GUIDE
Brian Sibley, HarperCollins
Essentially an adaptation of Brian Sibley's official guide to the trilogy aimed at a younger audience, but it doubles up as a handy pocket-sized guide to the stories behind the making of the films.

THE LORD OF THE RINGS – THE ART OF THE FELLOWSHIP OF THE RING
THE LORD OF THE RINGS – THE ART OF THE TWO TOWERS
Gary Russell, HarperCollins

While many of the blockbuster movies of recent years have been accompanied by 'art' books, those produced for *The Lord Of The Rings* show the way these books should be done, with faithful re-interpretation of the different scenes, the creatures, the weaponry and even the clothing in the detailed artwork, as well as plenty of illustrations charting the creative development of the movies.

THE LORD OF THE RINGS: THE FELLOWSHIP OF THE RING – VISUAL COMPANION
THE LORD OF THE RINGS: THE TWO TOWERS – VISUAL COMPANION

Jude Fisher, HarperCollins

Big, glossy and with smart details (such as a fold-out map of Middle-earth), the Visual Companion books offer yet another way into the movies. Given the detail of the shots you can feel as though you're actually inside the cold, black metal interior of Isengard, while the individuality of the hobbits is plain to see. And there's plenty of insight and information in the text too.

THE LORD OF THE RINGS: THE FELLOWSHIP OF THE RING – PHOTO GUIDE
THE LORD OF THE RINGS: THE TWO TOWERS – PHOTO GUIDE
Alison Sage, Collins

The Photo Guides each include a vast number of shots from the the motion picture trilogy (more than 100 photos in the case of *The Two Towers*), some previously unseen. And while these guides are billed as children's books, the way in which the photographs follow through the stories makes the books' appeal much wider.

✦ Fan Clubs ✦

Once upon a time being a member of a fan club guaranteed you a key ring, a certificate and maybe the odd letter from your hero, although it was more likely from their press dogsbody. All good things come to those who wait however, and at www.lotrfanclub.com is a fan club finally worthy of dedicated, if occasionally obsessive, fans.

It was created in 2001 to coincide with the release of the first of Peter Jackson's films, and Jackson has taken it upon himself to champion the fan-club members' cause and give them what they deserve. Members have exclusive access to the official movie magazine to accompany the films, discounts at the online store and access to a fan-mail forwarding service linked directly to the cast. As if this weren't far better than getting a stinky old key ring, Jackson has included the names of all members in the credits to the DVD versions of the films. Thus Elijah Wood's name will appear twice on the credits, once as Frodo Baggins and once as a fan-club member, the actor being so enamoured by the dedication of *The Lord Of The Rings* fans that he became the first member of the club.

If your name in lights and the wealth of information offered on the site still hasn't satisfied your capacious appetite, below are links to just a few of the hundreds of Tolkien-inspired fan clubs on the World Wide Web.

Tolkien Society
www.tolkiensociety.org

Official Fan Club
www.lotrfanclub.com

The One Ring
www.theonering.net

Planet Tolkien
www.planet-tolkien.com

Ring Bearer
www.ringbearer.org

Official Peter Jackson Fan Club
http://tbhl.theonering.net/index.shtml

A Hobbits Tale
www.warofthering.net/ahobbitstale/
ahobbitstale.htm

Corner Of Viggo
www.frostyland.com/Viggo/
viggo.index.shtml

Official Ian McKellen Site
www.mckellen.com

Full Bloom
www.full-bloom.net/main.shtml

Sam & Frodo
http://just-an-illusion.com/~samfrodo

Sean Astin
www.seanastin.com

Billy Boyd Official Website
www.billyboyd.net

Christopher Lee
http://gothlupin.tripod.com/vlee.html

Aussie Cate Blanchett
www.geocities.com/Hollywood/
Land/9730/

Adventures of Ian Holm
http://IanHolm.homestead.com/
FanPage.html

Lovely Liv Tyler
www.lovelylivtyler.com

✦ Shelob's World Wide Web ✦

Tap the words "The Lord Of The Rings" into the Google search engine and it will reply with 2.59 million entries. If you were to spend eight hours of every working day, 48 weeks a year, taking an average of five minutes to look at each site, it would take you 112 years to get to the end of the list. And you thought the book was long.

The extent to which this colossal number is inflated by sites dedicated to swooning appreciations of the looks and long blond hair of Orlando Bloom cannot be precisely calculated in the average life span. But the sites listed below and the links they provide will keep you in front of your screen for long enough.

http://film.guardian.co.uk/lordoftherings

Reviews, news, features, quizzes, interviews and a myriad of links make this an excellent place to start, but Tolkien devotees should realise that not everybody in *Guardian*-land has succumbed to hobbitmania.

www.newlineshop.com and www.lordoftherings.net

The official websites for *The Lord Of The Rings* film merchandise, behind-the-scenes exclusives and downloads.

www.noblecollection.com

Regal-looking site offering fans everything from ornate chess sets to *The Lord Of The Rings*-inspired jewellery. Arwen's Evenstar pendant will set you back a mere $95, whilst Elrond's headdress, perfect as an unusual wedding tiara, is only $195. Not that we're saying he wears girly jewellery.

www.starstore.com

Another store site carrying most of the usual *The Lord Of The Rings* merchandise but with a particularly good selection of posters, especially if Legolas and Aragorn are your thing.

www.sideshowtoy.com

The very latest addition to this memorabilia site was a bronze statue of Gandalf the Grey, with only 36 available. Surely that alone is enough to have your mouth-watering in anticipation of what else they sell?

www.addall.com

American rare-book site with an excellent search engine for hunting down old and first-edition books.

www.tolkientown.com

The world's largest Tolkien store with *Lord Of The Rings* merchandise handily split into categories for quick browsing. Prices are pretty competitive, too.

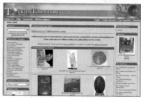

www.ea.com

As the official *Lord Of The Rings* interactive games licensee, EA offers the chance to buy games, read reviews and download screensavers.

http://lordoftherings.shadowdark.org

Another all-purpose link site with sections that include collectables, biographies, fan sites, music and scholarly studies.

www.unitedcutlery.com

Although you can't buy any of the swords featured directly from the website, avid fans will find the making of *The Lord Of The Rings* weaponry worth the visit alone.

www.CollectTolkien.com

As good a place as any on the Web to start your search for *The Lord Of The Rings* memorabilia. However, while it's refreshingly different to find a dedicated 'humour' section in a Tolkien website, it would help if it was funnier.

www.thelordoftherings.com

Not an officially approved site, but thoroughly respectful all the same, with news, film reviews and links to collectables and academia.

www.lordoftheringsshop.com

This self-proclaimed *Lord Of The Rings* fanatics shop offers a wide range of movie merchandise, including swords, action figures and clothing.

www.decipher.com

Slick official movie magazine website, perfect for fans of *The Lord Of The Rings* roleplaying games and trading cards.

www.gamesworkshop.com

Comprehensive website with news, reviews and an online shop from which to buy your *Lord Of The Rings* figures and games.

http://tolkien.slimy.com/essays

If you ever wanted to know the truth about balrogs or Tom Bombadil, you could do worse than spend a day or two at this site.

www.TheOneRing.net

Good source for movie news and rumours, with a heavy bias towards Orlando Bloom.

www.tolkienonline.com

Huge site, not always easy to follow, with all the latest movie-related gossip and links to places you might not expect.

www.tolkien-movies.com

Recognised by the *Wall Street Journal* as a leading source of *The Lord Of The Rings* film news, pictures and rumours.

www.Ringzone.net

Good source for *The Lord Of The Rings* artwork with an impressive choice of professional and fan-made images, plus downloadable spoof trailers.

http://flyingmoose.org/tolksarc/tolksarc.htm

Dedicated to taking the mick out of Tolkien's work, containing, among other things, the spoof summaries of the three volumes of *The Lord Of The Rings* that fooled *The Sunday Times*. Probably the only place on the Web where you can find William Shakespeare's little-known work, *The Tragedie Of Frodo Baggins*.

http://ww2.greentrust.org:8383/bagend.htm

The online source for constructing an environment-friendly hole-in-the-hill house inspired by Bag End.

www.zovakware.com/tests/lordoftherings.htm

On the bizarre side: a questionnaire where you can discover which of the main characters of *The Lord Of The Rings* you have most in common with.

www.coldal.org/quotes.htm

Collection of quotes from the books, with MP3 sound files.

www.nationalgeographic.com/ngbeyond

Explore the parallels between the imaginary world of Middle-earth and our own, courtesy of the world's largest non-profit educational organisation.

www.quintessentialwebsites.com/lordoftherings/home

Excerpts from the books, plus pictures and scenes from the films and downloadable scripts.

www.houghtonmifflinbooks.com/features/lordoftheringstrilogy

Good site for books by and about Tolkien from Houghton Mifflin, the exclusive US publisher of illustrated *The Lord Of The Rings* books.

www.waroftthering.net

Large site with potted biographies and tons of background information on the main *Lord Of The Rings* characters, plus an immense photo gallery.

http://home.nyu.edu/~amw243/diaries/

The secret diaries of main *Lord Of The Rings* characters in sub-Bridget Jones style. Sample entry by Aragorn: "Met up with hobbits. Walked 40 miles. Skinned a squirrel and ate it. Still not king."

www.itzalist.com/sci/ancient-elvish-language-guide.html

The National Elf Service? The essential guide to speaking the Elvish tongue, with discussions of elven philosophy, among other things.

www.glyphweb.com/arda

Encyclopedia of Arda, or an interactive guide to Tolkien's work. Offers more information on the fauna of Middle-earth than most people could possibly want.

www.marvel.com/toybiz

A Middle-earth sword with "realistic slashing and clashing sound effects" and an uruk-hai crossbow are among the treats on offer here.

www.hasbro.com

Use the search engine to find everything from Middle-earth editions of board games like Trivial Pursuit and Risk to chess sets and jigsaws.

www.tolkien.co.uk

Last but not least, the official Tolkien site, including a Tolkien biography and interviews with the great man himself, recent Tolkien and *The Lord Of The Rings*-related book releases, a diary of up-coming events and a quiz.

THE CONTEXT

A GUIDE TO THE SIMPLY IMMENSE IMPACT
OF THE LORD OF THE RINGS

Even four hobbits with disturbingly hairy feet aren't a match for a ringwraith

"In Moscow, people remembered Tolkien when they made barricades from trolley buses, just like hobbits with country wains, and Moscow members of the Tolkien Society spent fearful nights near the White House holding a defence, as Gandalf stood saying 'You shall not pass'"

Maria Kamenkovich, on how Tolkien inspired Muscovites to foil the attempted Communist coup in Russia in 1991

JRR Tolkien once stated that, "Being a cult figure in one's own lifetime I am afraid is not at all pleasant. However, I do not feel that it tends to puff one up; in my case at any rate it makes me feel extremely small and inadequate. But even the nose of a very modest idol cannot remain entirely untickled by the sweet smell of incense." And, like Dr Frankenstein, he must have been more than a little surprised by what became of his creation, once referring to his fandom as "my deplorable cultus". His books had, by the 1960s, begun to enchant America's academia, with the result that treatises with such titles as A Parametric Analysis Of Antithetical Conflict And Irony In JRR Tolkien's Lord Of The Rings, were produced on a – for him – all too regular basis. Yet even more bizarre manifestations of his influence began to appear almost daily. Students at **Warwick University** renamed the ring road around their campus Tolkien Road, a Frodo Society was formed in northern Borneo and a Vietnamese dancer in Saigon was seen with the lidless eye of Sauron on his shield. The author's work was suddenly taken up in ways that passed the author's own understanding. It's been the same ever since. Tolkien's work refuses to be pigeonholed or labelled and his influence pops up in some very surprising places indeed.

✦ The Environmental Activist ✦

"I cordially dislike allegory in all its manifestations," JRR Tolkien once stated. But legions of academics and experts weren't about to let that inconvenient fact get in the way of a good theory. And, having been claimed by everyone from pagans to Catholics, Tolkien's straightforward battle between the forces of good and evil has most recently been

Gardeners' Question Time

HOW GANDALF INSPIRED A MYSTICAL COMMUNE IN SWINGING CHELSEA

Americans aren't the only ones to read too much into Tolkien's compositions – 1960s London also saw a commune of flower-power devotees embracing the book's mysticism. A shop, a magazine and a community, Gandalf's Garden was originally based in Chelsea (before relocating to Norfolk, that other spiritual capital) and offered new ideas and practical advice aimed towards a better, more spiritually sound life.

Horticulture, hippy-style

Founded by Muz Murray, the group focused on free spirits within London; but the word quickly spread throughout Britain, the magazine becoming a bible for those who couldn't visit their spiritual base at the World's End, Chelsea. Printed on suitably psychedelic paper with equally abrasive-on-the-eye ink, the magazine was an instant cult success. Band reviews became a regular feature, with such oddly titled acts as Junior's Eyes, Soft Machine, The Third Ear Band and Quintessence all receiving the Gandalf treatment.

But the magazine was most noted for its ability to seek out the unusual in British society. They were among the first to openly discuss the mystical Glastonbury Zodiac (signs of the zodiac carved into the Somerset landscape). The Aetherius Society's theories on the link between mankind and UFOs, and Aleister Crowley also fell within its remit, as did much tamer features on Atlantis and the Hari Krishna movement.

Occasionally, however, they went too far, an article in issue five on trepanning failing to sit well with most readers, despite a disclaimer urging readers not to try it at home. The response to the feature goes some way to explaining why the magazine only lasted six issues.

Since its demise, Gandalf's children have gone their separate ways. Murray is now a mantra, meditation and massage teacher in the south of France. Other former devotees now range from a Shaman guide in the Peruvian jungle to a chiropractor and a photographer.

adopted by the environmental lobby. The idea of Tolkien as a prototype green activist dates back to the late 1960s and early 1970s. The fantasy world that The Lord Of The Rings described, with its sunlit appeal to timeless rural values, was a whole lot simpler and more attractive than the very real and more complicated one of Nixon, Kissinger and Vietnam. The hippy counter-culture adopted the trilogy as an unofficial set text, and its popularity continued with the environmental movement that followed on from the hippy era.

Faced with a sea of long-haired demonstrators proclaiming Gandalf's surprise candidacy for president of the United States, a bewildered Tolkien observed: "Art moves them and they don't know what they've been moved by and they get quite drunk on it. Many young Americans are involved in the stories in a way that I'm not." But you don't need a pointy hat and a cloak to find an environmental message in his work. In 1972 David McTaggart, sailing into a French nuclear-testing area in an act which led directly to the founding of Greenpeace, noted in his journal: "I had been reading *The Lord Of The Rings*. I could not avoid thinking of parallels between our own little fellowship and the long journey of the hobbits into the volcano-haunted land of Mordor."

ONE ACADEMIC HAS CLAIMED THAT, WERE HE ALIVE TODAY, TOLKIEN WOULD HAVE BEEN A MEMBER OF THE COUNTRYSIDE ALLIANCE

It's certainly not stretching credulity too far to see the war between the hobbits' peaceful Shire and the destructive forces of Mordor as a dramatisation of the conflict between rural life and the Industrial Revolution that was being played out as Tolkien was born. "I was born in 1892 and lived for my early years in 'the Shire' in a pre-mechanical age," Tolkien once said. "I like gardens, trees and unmechanised farmlands." He later added that the Shire in his books "is a 'parody'… of rural England, in much the same sense as are its inhabitants: they go together and are meant to. After all, the book is English."

But 'the Shire' was always under threat. Sarehole Mill in Warwickshire (where Tolkien spent much of his early life and which became the mill at Hobbiton) was menaced by the sprawling industry of nearby Birmingham, and would certainly have been affected by pollution in the same way that the hobbits' world is contaminated by the smoggy Isengard. So when war starts in Middle-earth, the lines of conflict are clearly drawn. While the Fellowship relies on Gandalf's ancient magic,

Sauron's army relies on machinery, built by industry whose fires are fed by trees torn from the Fangorn Forest – much like the ancient Forest of Arden that disappeared as the city of Birmingham grew and spread.

Writer James Surowiecki has noted of the film that, "At Helm's Deep, the men and elves get by purely on quickness of wit and strength of arm, while the orcs deploy all manner of newfangled technology – explosives, catapults, siege ladders. The victory of men is a victory of the heart over the machine." The turning point of *The Two Towers* comes when Treebeard, chief of the tree people (or ents), leads an uprising against the orcs that ends in the destruction of Isengard.

Similarly, in Literature And The Environment, Dr Bridget Keenan enthuses that "the green and pleasant land that is the hobbits' Shire is threatened by what can only be described as Sauron's earth-destroying military-industrial complex. When the very trees begin marching to exact revenge on the Dark Lord, Tolkien's eco-politics are hard to miss."

Certainly, while Tolkien would probably have raised at least a quizzical eyebrow at the idea of a 'military-industrial complex', when it came to man versus nature he was definitely on the side of nature. "The savage sound of the electric saw is never silent wherever trees are still found growing," he wrote. "Every tree has its enemy, few have an advocate. In all my works I take the part of trees against all their enemies."

Tolkien had better reason than most to take that stance. After completing his degree at Oxford and joining the Lancashire Fusiliers as an officer, he saw the horror and terror of industrial warfare at first hand, during the Battle of the Somme in 1916. Within two years the war had been responsible for the death of all but one of his closest friends. Even Tolkien, for all his dislike of allegory and his impatience with the idea that his books might have had some deeper meaning, once wrote that "an author cannot remain wholly unaffected by his experience."

> TOLKIEN INITIALLY REFUSED TO HAVE A TV OR FRIDGE IN THE HOUSE, AND WAS INEXPLICABLY WARY OF TAPE RECORDERS

It's even possible that the Dead Marshes of Mordor, full of the submerged slain from a "great battle long ago... fought on the plain for days and months," are the Middle-earth equivalent of the muddy slaughterhouse of the Somme. Whether or not this was the case, Tolkien did start work on what became The Silmarillion, creating a world where nature would eventually triumph over machine, shortly after he was invalided home from World War I with trench fever.

Some commentators have even suggested that Tolkien could be the patron saint of direct action. Halfway through World War II he wrote a letter to his son **Christopher** in which he outlined his growing belief in anarchy and praised "the growing habit of disgruntled men of dynamiting factories and power stations." While one academic has claimed that, were he alive today, Tolkien would have been a member of the Countryside Alliance, a more interesting observation – on one of the many Internet messageboards – is that Tolkien was influenced by **Sir Arthur Tansley**, a pioneering British ecologist who invented the term 'ecosystem'. (That would, of course, make Middle-earth the first fully realised fantasy ecosystem.)

It can be hard to separate Tolkien the ecologist from Tolkien the anti-modernist or Tolkien the neo-Luddite. Apparently he initially refused to have a television or a fridge in his house, held the internal-combustion engine in utter contempt and was inexplicably wary of tape recorders. It's difficult to say how much of this concern was the product of environmentalism rather than a knee-jerk reaction against change. But ultimately it doesn't really matter.

The Lord Of The Rings might not be complicated allegory, and the Ring almost certainly was not intended as a metaphor for the atom bomb. But, whether it was intentional or not, there is an environmental message in the trilogy that offers one explanation for the books' resurgent popularity. In the words of **Lev Grossman** writing in Time magazine: "A darker, more pessimistic attitude toward technology and the future has taken hold… The future just isn't what it used to be – and the past seems to be gaining on us."

✦ The Hackers' Hero ✦

While one group of Tolkien readers were heading for San Francisco with flowers in their hair, another group were heading for the computer research laboratories of **Stanford** and **UCLA** with their pens in their top pockets. Staring at streams of computer code might not have been as much fun as partying and tripping out with the beautiful people, but it produced the Internet and email, and created a world where to know *The Lord Of The Rings* is – and this is only a very slight overstatement – to be the lord of the hackers.

Writing in the *Village Voice*, journalist **Julian Dibbell** described *The Lord*

Tolkien The Marxist

STRANGE BUT TRUE – JRR TOLKIEN WAS A FAN OF THE MARX BROTHERS

The idea that JRR Tolkien liked the movies of the Marx brothers appears, at first glance, to be just another of those urban myths that seem to pollute so many parts of cyberspace these days.

Yet the story is confirmed by Humphrey Carpenter, Tolkien's biographer who met him several times – once to discuss a college plan to stage an opera based on The Hobbit and once, over a pub lunch, to discuss plans for him to read his children's book Farmer Giles Of Ham on Radio Oxford.

As Carpenter would recall later when discussing his biography, "He hopped conversationally around a range of surprising topics – I particularly remember him praising the Marx Brothers."

As Tolkien didn't own a television at the time, the assumption must be that if he did watch such classics of comedy as A Night At The Opera (1935) and A Day At The Races (1937) he probably did so at a cinema in Oxford, where he lived from 1925 until 1967. His own pranks, too, had a certain Marxian madcapness about them. He once appeared at a formal party for dons clad in an Icelandic sheepskin hearthrug and white face paint and, in the 1930s, told the audience at one of his lectures that leprechauns really did exist, pulling a four-inch green shoe out of his pocket.

In later life, Carpenter notes, Tolkien took great delight in offering inattentive shopkeepers his false teeth in a handful of loose change. "I have," he noted once, "a very simple sense of humour, which even my appreciative critics find tiresome." It was proof that Tolkien wasn't at all self-important or pretentious and it was just the kind of remark Groucho Marx might have made.

Certainly, Groucho was no stranger to the literati, becoming a pen pal of TS Eliot – the two would have dinner in London in the 1960s after the poet had written to Groucho asking for a signed picture.

The comic never met Tolkien though, nor would he have entirely agreed with the author's famous remark that "If more of us valued food, cheer and song above hoarded gold, it would be a merrier world." Groucho certainly valued food, cheer and song, but he wasn't bad at hoarding gold either.

Tolkien's four favourite Marxists: Not a Karl, Friedrich or Vladimir among them

Of The Rings as "geek culture's defining literary creation," adding that the history of computing had been "shaped by a hacker culture that insisted some of the earliest dot-matrix printers be programmed to produce the Elvish script." Two Stanford researchers went on to write Adventure, a game that adopted Tolkien's world (see page 295).

It's unlikely that Tolkien, who resisted what he saw as the worst manifestations of the 20th century, would have given house room to a dot-matrix printer, whether it understood Elvish or not. But his fascination for creating languages had a direct appeal for the nascent community of programmers already used to systems of signs and codes that were unintelligible to the outside world (and they don't come any more unintelligible than Elvish, whose rules are set out in the appendices to The Return Of The King).

According to **Denis Howe**'s fine Free On-line Dictionary Of Computing, it's traditional for most peripherals, not just printers, to work in Elvish. The dictionary adds that Elvish is also hackerspeak for "any odd or unreadable typeface produced by a graphics device." But as Howe's

Merry and Pippin stage an early pre-Swampy demonstration of direct action

dictionary shows, the hackers have appropriated more than just Elvish. They've lifted a whole range of terms from Middle-earth, including 'Great Worm'. This was the name given by Tolkien to dragons powerful enough to destroy entire kingdoms (including Glaurung, the first of the dragons of Morgoth, and Scatha, mentioned in The Hobbit), so it was the natural choice of nickname for the program created by the hacker Robert T Morris that infected more than 6,000 computers in 1988. Ultimately, though, neither Great Worm rampaged with impunity: Glaurung was slain by Túrin, while Morris, whose mischief-making had cost companies around $96 million, went to jail.

In the Tolkien universe, 'Elder Days' are the ones described in The Silmarillion, predating the events in The Hobbit and The Lord Of The Rings. To hackers, they refer to the time before the Internet – pre-1980 according to Denis Howe. (There's also a Led Zeppelin anthology called Elder Days And Latter Days.)

Treebeard, chief of the ents and unlikely hero of The Two Towers, described Saruman as a "tree-killer" for his destruction of the Fangorn

Forest. That term is another one that makes it into the *Free On-line Dictionary Of Computing* as hackers' slang for "a person who wastes paper" – including those involved in "the production of spiffy but content-free documents."

For **Sherry Turkle**, a professor in Sociology of Science at the Massachusetts Institute of Technology, hackers' fascination with Middle-earth goes well beyond its vocabulary. In an article published in the August *New York Times*, Turkle compared the whole of Tolkien's world – "rule driven and bounded" – with a giant computer program. "One online contributor," she says, "theorises that the rings, the central metaphor and driving force of the story, are 'hardware-only' computers, with all their operating code permanently burned into their structure."

Turkle also believes that the hackers' love of Tolkien is a gender thing. "Frodo, the hero of *The Lord Of The Rings*, is part of a fellowship, although it is more properly called a fraternity," she says, "and the computer culture, by

> "THE COMPUTER CULTURE IS,
> BY AND LARGE, A WORLD BUILT BY
> ENGINEERS, BY MEN FOR MEN"

and large, is a world built by engineers for engineers, by men for men." Perhaps predictably, that's an argument that hasn't gained much support on the hackers' other favourite universe, the Internet, with Turkle being described on one message board as a "two-bit social scientist". Ouch.

Not everybody experiences a similar sense-of-humour failure when it comes to Tolkien and computing. **Paul Flaherty** from Stanford has created a homage to the Internet with a version of *The Lord Of The Rings*' opening poem that ends with the lines: "One Internet to rule them all, one Internet to find them/One Internet to bring them all and in the ether bind them/In the LANs of SRI where the Shadows lie." (SRI is the acronym for Stanford Research Institute and a LAN is a telecoms term for Local Area Network).

It's hard to know quite what Tolkien would have made of it all. He helped compile the first edition of the *Oxford English Dictionary*, and it's partly thanks to him that we know the meanings of a whole range of words including waggle, wampum and Walpurgis (Walpurgis being, of course, the eve of 1 May, or Walpurgis Night – the night of the witches' sabbath in Germany's Harz Mountains). Now, nearly 50 years after the last book of *The Lord Of The Rings* was published, another set of Ws, the World Wide Web, is helping to keep his legacy alive.

The Middle-earth Scene
TALES OF SWINGING LONDON, SCOTLAND AND, ER, KRAKOW

The Lord Of The Rings has had many unexpected repercussions. Few, though, were as odd as the emergence of a club called Middle Earth in the geographical heart of the Swinging Sixties.

43 King Street, Covent Garden, London had been called the Electric Garden, and a band called John's Children, starring a certain Marc Bolan, played there disastrously. Two name changes later, Bolan's group became Tyrannosaurus Rex and the Electric Garden became the Middle Earth club. The joint was, to use 1940s vernacular, jumping. As Bolan later recalled: "They asked John Peel to go down there and do something for nothing and we just played. They never had any mics down there or anything. And it became sort of fashionable. After a while we were packing it with 2,000 people and we'd get about ten quid." You can buy a CD of the very first gig (Tyrannosaurus Rex: There Was A Time) from the T. Rex Action Group.

So fashionable did the Middle Earth club become that bands like Pink Floyd, The Doors, Jefferson Airplane, David Bowie and Soft Machine played there. Pink Floyd (then with Syd Barrett in their line-up) and Soft Machine had both been synonymous with the UFO club, the swingingest venue in London before the Middle Earth club stole the limelight.

The UFO had been a tripper's paradise in the unlikely surroundings of a dance hall on Tottenham Court Road. Now the Middle Earth club was bigger and bolder, and reigned over by two DJs: Peel and Jeff Dexter (who would later discover America – the group that is). It also had the advantage that when its stoned denizens left the club after dawn, they could pick up some fruit and veg from the local market.

David Bowie also played there in the summer of 1968 – as part of a trio called Feathers, with his then girlfriend Hermione Farthingale and

Vintage Tyrannosaurus Rex

bass-player John Hutchinson, but the group split within six months.

Inevitably, the club's notoriety led to a police drug raid, while financial pressures, and the fickleness of fashion, hastened the demise of what some regard as the last true underground club in 1960s London. By 1969 the underground had gone overground, with long hair and LSD sweeping the suburbs.

In a completely unrelated venture, there was also a short-lived Scottish hippy record label called Middle Earth. Only one of its acts ever made the charts – Tam White, who reached No.36 in 1976 with What In The World's Come Over You (on Mickie Most's RAK label). By then he'd become a very unhip MOR crooner.

But the spirit is still with us. A club called Middle Earth, a cellar "transformed into a magical grotto" – say the owners – has recently opened in the Polish city of Krakow. And back in Chalk Farm, London (the original club's second home), Jungle Records has started a new label called Middle Earth in honour of the club.

Could Telegram Sam have been Marc's ode to Sam Gamgee?

✦ A Musicians' Muso ✦

Rock festivals, like Glastonbury, weren't regular events on the calendar when Bilbo Baggins staged his eleventy-first birthday party in Hobbiton. So the music that reverberated through the Shire sounded more like traditional English folk music. If Baggins restaged his party today, he'd have plenty of music inspired by his creator to rock the Shire.

When JRR Tolkien was writing *The Lord Of The Rings* it's entirely possible that strange, otherworldly music animated his imagination, for, like all his work, the book is full of songs and poetry. It's less likely that Tolkien could have foreseen how many bands and musicians would be inspired to set events in his books to music of their own. From T. Rex to Led Zeppelin, long-suffering Middle-earth has heard it all.

To 1970s prog rockers, Tolkien wasn't so much an influence as another member of the band, albeit one given to smoking a pipe and with an unusual fondness for tweed. Tolkien's world inadvertently gave prog-rock bands a way of cloaking pompous bombast and portentous lyrics in mystic otherness. Among the first to work this out was Led Zeppelin.

Vocalist Robert Plant had been plying his trade in a band called Hobbstweedle, a suitably faux-rustic name for a band inspired by Tolkien's books, when he met guitarist Jimmy Page. Both Page and Plant had read *The Lord Of The Rings*, and reportedly spent some time writing Tolkien-themed songs. It took a while, though, before any of them appeared on Led Zeppelin's albums.

> ONE TYPE OF MUSICIAN TOOK TOLKIEN'S STATEMENT "I AM FOND OF MUSHROOMS OUT OF A FIELD" AS A RECOMMENDATION

There is a reference to "the darkest depths of Mordor" and "Gollum and the evil one" in Ramble On from *Led Zeppelin II*, but it's *Led Zeppelin IV* that scores highest on the old rock hobbitometer. Misty Mountain Hop sounds suspiciously like a reference to the Misty Mountains near Rivendell, and The Battle Of Evermore (where the "drums will shake the castle wall" and the "ringwraiths ride in black") is widely seen – among many fans on the Internet, at least – to refer to the climactic battle in *The Return Of The King*.

Plant denies that Stairway To Heaven, also on *Led Zeppelin IV*, has anything to do with Middle-earth, but Over The Hills And Far Away on

Leonard Nimoy sang of vulcans and hobbits, and inspired dodgy 1960s album artwork

the follow-up album, *Houses Of The Holy*, borrows its title, if not its lyrics, from a poem by Tolkien. Of less certain provenance is No Quarter, from the same album. Some argue that it's about Aragorn's attempts to reach Gondor; others suggest that it was simply written by the band after a fruitless search for a hotel room.

Still in the world of Tolkien-inspired prog rock, in 1972 Swedish keyboard-player Bo Hansson (who had played with Jimi Hendrix) released an album of instrumentals, *Lord Of The Rings*. This gave us the evocative De Svarta Ryttarna Och Flykten Från Vadstället (The Black Riders And Flight To The Ford) and the equally memorable Rohans Horn Och Slaget Vid Peleonnors Slätter (The Horns Of Rohan And The Battle Of The Pelennor Fields). The first of four solo concept albums, it is uncharitably described by one reviewer on *Amazon.com* as "1970s cheesy, porn, synth music," but was a fair-sized hit at the time. Haunting and evocative, it still has its fans and is arguably one of the better unofficial soundtracks.

But perhaps the most notable was cult American singer/songwriter **Tom Rapp** (operating under the name Pearls Before Swine). Showing

Led Zeppelin score pretty highly on the prog-rock hobbitometer

considerably more subtlety than the prog rockers, he set the trilogy's opening poem to music on Ring Thing, the closing track to his 1968 psychedelic-folk album *Balaklava* on the avant-garde ESP label. Dark, spartan and with the sound of ancient instruments (swinehorn, anyone?) droning eerily in the background, it's certainly one of the most tasteful **Tolkien** adaptations and well worth seeking out.

The Lord Of The Rings has also proved particularly popular with the type of musicians who took the author's statement "I am fond of mushrooms out of a field" as something of a recommendation. Not least of these was a certain Marc Bolan, who could often sound as though he'd nibbled one fungus too many.

Bolan was pretty obviously a big fan of both *The Hobbit* and *The Lord Of The Rings*, and apparently spent some time living with a wizard in France. History doesn't reveal whether his name was Gandalf, but when Bolan released his first single in 1965 it was called The Wizard and referred to a wizard with "silver sunlight in his eyes" who "turned and melted in the sky." Two years later Bolan formed T. Rex with **Steve Peregrin Took**, another Tolkien buff who had actually taken his name from *The Lord Of The Rings*.

Gandalf lent his name to another band from the 1960s whose self-titled album has a cover design featuring lettering from a packet of Spangles above a face that owes more to a bad trip than **Sir Ian McKellen**. There's no obvious Tolkien influence on this amiable piece of psychedelia beyond the name, but Gandalf deserve a place in history as – well, the first of many bands who called themselves Gandalf. Gandalf The Grey were responsible for such timeless classics as The Grey Wizard Am I (which starts off "Down from the Shire and Hobbiton Hills…") and My Elven Home. **Finnish death-metal** band Gandalf have given the world two albums – *Deadly Fairytales* and the sensitively titled but presumably pretty accurate *Rock Hell*. In stark contrast, with *The Good Thief Tips His Hat*, Gandalf Murphy & The Slambovian Circus Of Dreams lean much more towards **country blues**.

The most prolific Gandalf of all is Austrian **new-age** instrumentalist **Heinz Strobl**, who has released several albums under the alias. The first was 1980's *Journey To An Imaginary Land*; the last was *Visions 2001*, an eclectic 'best of' which brings together floaty and ethereal music directly influenced by Tolkien's books with floaty and ethereal music influenced by something else in a single, well, floaty and ethereal compilation.

Gandalf isn't the only character's name to have been borrowed from

Tolkien's world. Aylesbury's latter-day pomp rockers Marillion were originally called Silmarillion after the prequel to *The Lord Of The Rings*, but then shortened their name to avoid legal action over copyright from the Tolkien Estate. Not to be deterred so easily were two lots of Bilbo Baggins (the first, a 1970s troupe of **Bay City Rollers** wannabes, the second a 1990s electronica act), and Borris Baggins, a garage band from New Zealand responsible for such numbers as Borris Baggins Has The Wrong Change and Bolshevik Baggins.

If the idea of a Bolshevik Baggins sounds odd, it's nowhere near as bizarre as the metal bands inspired by Middle-earth. Finnish group Battelore cite Tolkien as an influence and German goth rockers Blind Guardian have released *Nightfall In Middle-earth*, a mammoth 22-track tribute to *The Silmarillion*. And right at the very bottom of the food chain (in every sense) are the **death-metal bands**.

Tolkien himself appeared on a posthumous album of his own in 1975, pithily titled *JRR Tolkien Reads And Sings His Lord Of The Rings: The Two Towers And The Return Of The King*. It was based on recordings of sizeable chunks from each book that Tolkien had made in 1952 (after he had tried out the tape recorder by reciting the Lord's Prayer into it in Gothic from memory). **Christopher Tolkien** followed suit in 1977 with a recording of part of *The Silmarillion*.

More ambitious is the work of The Tolkien Ensemble, a group of musicians from the Royal Danish Academy of Music committed to making "the world's first, complete musical interpretation of the poems and songs from *The Lord Of The Rings*." They're currently on their third album, *Dawn In Rivendell*, which uses **Christopher Lee** – Saruman in the films – as the narrator. Of all the music inspired by *The Lord Of The Rings* it's probably the most faithful to the spirit of the original work, with one possible exception: **Howard Shore**'s Oscar-winning soundtrack for Peter Jackson's film of *The Fellowship Of The Ring*, a commercially successful and artistically credible complement to the film.

That's a great deal more than can be said for the song which brought Tolkien-influenced music to its nadir some 30 years ago – Leonard Nimoy's **The Ballad Of Bilbo Baggins**. Recorded in 1968, the year that revolution spilled on to the streets of Prague and Paris, the 'humorous' video finds Leonard 'Mr Spock' Nimoy on a beach in California sporting a Beatle fringe, a deranged grin and something that could well be a blue velvet car coat. As Nimoy relates a, shall we say, condensed version of Bilbo's story to a jaunty beat, he's surrounded by a group of prancing female dancers with similarly fixed smiles. With all the menacing cheerfulness of a cult, they chant "Bilbo! Bilbo! Bilbo Baggins!" and later re-appear wearing stick-on vulcan ears. The video can be found – but only if you're as brave as Frodo Baggins – on the Internet at http://www.tolkiencollector.com/bilbobal.htm and is worth watching for the scene where the entire troupe attempts to recreate key events in *The Hobbit* from behind a sand dune.

Tolkien remained silent on the relative merits of the efforts of Led Zeppelin and T. Rex, but it's testament to the power of the world he created that, more than 50 years later, musicians are still finding inspiration in it. As late as 2002, Rick Wakeman – captain of a fleet of mellotrons, sometime member of Yes and creator of several keyboard-based concept albums (including one with the heroically uncommercial title *The Six Wives Of Henry VIII*) – released *A Tribute To The Lord Of The Rings*. If its title left any room for doubt, the names of the ten tracks did not, ranging as they did from Shire and Lothlórien to Helm's Deep.

> RUMOUR HAS IT THE BEATLES WANTED TO ADAPT THE LORD OF THE RINGS BUT TOLKIEN TURNED THEM DOWN

Donald Swann, half of the British musical comedy duo Flanders & Swann (best known for The Hippopotamus – "Mud, mud, glorious mud…") composed a cycle of seven songs from the trilogy, with Elvish calligraphy by Tolkien himself. These can now be found, with an eighth bonus song, in *The Road Goes Ever On* (HarperCollins), complete with a free CD of the cycle sung by Swann and Covent Garden baritone William Elvin (the name is just coincidence).

Even The Beatles wanted to adapt *The Lord Of The Rings*. That idea was apparently quashed by Tolkien himself, which is probably just as well – Middle-earth might have survived everything from psychedelia to death metal, but finding a part for Ringo Starr (Bilbo Baggins? Sam Gamgee?) would be too much. Peter Jackson recalled recently: "It was something John [Lennon] was driving, and JRR Tolkien still had the film rights at that stage, but he didn't like the idea of The Beatles doing it so he killed it."

George Harrison, apparently, was head of the queue to play Gandalf, with Lennon fancying himself as grasping Gollum and McCartney, inevitably, hoping to bring his cherubic sex appeal to the role of Frodo Baggins. (For a rundown of even more obscure Tolkien-inspired sounds that you can add to your collection, turn to page 255.)

Lord Of The Games

MEET THE FELLOWSHIP OF COMPUTER GAMERS

Tolkien may have begun his trilogy around the time the world was struggling to understand how the moving pictures got into the box in their living rooms, yet he managed to write a book which lends itself well to more than one kind of screen.

Often movie tie-in computer games are below par, released at speed to coincide with initial hype and guaranteed to sell regardless of whether or not Batman looks like he's being operated by strings. But even before the computer-boffin versions of Gandalf have performed their wizardry, the battles, adventures and bizarre creatures which inhabit Middle-earth ensure The Lord Of The Rings games comprise what every computer game should: excitement and mystery.

With this in mind it's no surprise there are a wealth of The Lord Of The Rings titles. Vivendi produced the official games tie-in for The Fellowship Of The

Ring, but disappointing reviews by fans who didn't appreciate story revisions to suit the role-playing game format led Electronic Arts (EA) to take over. Their Two Towers and The Return Of The King titles for all platforms have been better received. With The Two Towers coming in at 120 levels, Datel Direct's Cheat CD is worth its £7.99 cover price if you're in need of a boost.

Vivendi are now concentrating on The Lord Of The Rings strategy games, recently releasing The Treason Of Isengard and The War Of The Ring. Designed to compete with EA titles (both are aimed at children aged 11+), each title has good graphics and is capable of holding the attention span of any teenager or regressive adult.

For ages three and above, Sierra Entertainment has released The Hobbit on most formats. Combining role-playing and puzzle-solving, the graphics are bright and playful, with no scary orcs to terrify the children.

✦ The Game Developer ✦

"AS YOU WALKED, NEW DISTANCES OPENED OUT; SO THAT YOU
NOW HAD DOUBLE, TREBLE AND QUADRUPLE DISTANCES, DOUBLY,
TREBLY AND QUADRUPLY ENCHANTING. YOU COULD GO ON AND ON,
AND HAVE A WHOLE COUNTRY IN A GARDEN"

JRR TOLKIEN, LEAF BY NIGGLE

For a brief period during the early 1980s the sentences, "You are in a comfortable, tunnel-like hall. To the east there is a round green door," were probably two of the most widely read in the English language. Middle-earth had just entered into a blissful union with the personal computer boom and these were the immortal lines that announced the opening of The Hobbit: the computer game.

Today, when your average washing machine has more processing power than that offered by Sinclair's ZX Spectrum 20-odd years ago, the appeal of ye olde text-based adventures can be hard to fathom. It took an age to load; the dragon on the opening screen looked like an angry cat vomiting custard, and the graphics were limited to bad line drawings in wildly inappropriate colours. (Was that really a campfire or a burning turd? Was that a doorway or another bit of wall?) There was also much frantic pecking at the keyboard, trying to type "run from dragon" before said dragon devoured their character in a single gulp. But that was as advanced as it got in those days, so it didn't really matter. The game sold millions and is widely seen as a classic of its kind.

But it wasn't the first 'classic' game to be inspired by the Tolkien universe and to become a worldwide phenomenon. Some 25 years earlier, Dungeons & Dragons had taken the role-playing world by storm. And that too had to cast a glance back over its shoulders to pin down its origins. According to the brief history of Dungeons & Dragons published on the site Places To Go, People To Be, the first formalised rules for wargames – and the idea that figures could represent individual units – were introduced by sci-fi author HG Wells in his book Little Wars in 1915.

Taking this a step further, the concept that figures could represent individual people was introduced by two gamers with a passion for medieval warfare, Gary Gygax and David Arneson. The pair, who also had more than a passing interest in Tolkien, adapted an existing game Gygax had co-created called Chainmail, and their creation was given the unwieldy subtitle **Rules For Fantastic Medieval Wargames Campaigns, Playable With Paper And Pencil And Miniature Figures.** This classic pen-and-paper game was finally published under the vastly more engaging (not to mention marketable) name Dungeons & Dragons.

"There is no question we were influenced by Tolkien," Gygax once said in an interview. "I loved The Hobbit. I read it myself and then read it three or four times aloud to my children. Just about all the players were huge **Tolkien** fans. It became apparent to me that the more of Tolkien's creatures I put in there, the more people would enjoy playing fantasy." The more interest copyright lawyers would take in it too – Gygax was forced to change the name of the hobbits that appeared in the first edition to 'halflings'. Such is the influence of Gygax and Tolkien that *GameSpy.com* listed them jointly in its ranking of the 30 most influential people in gaming, noting: "Tolkien didn't invent the fantasy genre; rather, he created the modern, popular version of fantasy folklore with *The Hobbit* and *The Lord Of The Rings*, drawing upon common mythology throughout Western culture (and more than a little pulp fiction à la Edgar Rice Burroughs).

> "THE ROLE OF FANTASY IS TO PROVIDE A SECONDARY WORLD WHICH YOUR MIND CAN ENTER"

It's a testament to Tolkien's influence that when you say 'role-playing game in a fantasy world', what you really mean is wizards, orcs, swords, spells and epic quests in a Tolkienesque setting."

Not everybody has had to be as coy as Gygax with his halflings. Sensibly recognising that a generous cash sum produces an official licence enabling you to wield roughly the same amount of power as Gandalf, **Iron Crown Enterprises** bought the rights to produce its own range of role-playing games under the umbrella Middle-earth Role Playing (usually abbreviated to MERP by those in the know).

A rival, the more prosaically named **Lord Of The Rings**, was released by Decipher last year, while Games Workshop sells its own strategy battlegame series, also named **Lord Of The Rings**, which uses imagery from the movies (just in case anyone was still under the impression that The Lord Of The Rings was a jewellery superstore just off the M25). A range of miniatures designed to supplement the figures that come with the Games Workshop game is also available from, you guessed it, Games Workshop.

While Gygax and Arneson were experimenting with fantasy wargames, computer technicians at UCLA and Stanford were busy inventing the

Internet – or rather ARPAnet, a primitive prototype that linked together computers on the two campuses. William Crowther, a programmer involved in the ARPAnet project, was also interested in Dungeons & Dragons and started to write a primitive, text-only game called Adventure that was distributed across the network and refined by another programmer called Don Woods. Set in a world of caves that was peopled by trolls, it might not have been based directly on *The Lord Of The Rings* but it wasn't too dissimilar.

Other public domain games have appeared with a more explicit Tolkien influence, including Moria – named after the Mines of Moria – and Angband – named after the Pits of Angband – which gave rise to a customised version called Zangband, reportedly peopled by everyone from Santa Claus to Barney the Dinosaur. As Adventure and its many spin-offs developed, several users could play simultaneously over a network, creating a genre known as Multi-User Dungeon (MUD for short), with a complex vocabulary of its own that would have gladdened Tolkien's heart. There are thousands of different MUDs in existence and although some are based around science-fiction themes, many more include fantasy elements that will instantly ring a bell to anyone familiar with *The Lord Of The Rings*.

Home computing has obviously moved on in gigantic leaps since a generation risked its sanity and its eyesight blinking at *The Hobbit* on the garish ZX Spectrum screen. Fans of the Tolkien universe who want to act out the events in the books no longer need to make do with two sentences of text and a line drawing, with games like Tomb Raider now offering the challenge of solving puzzles as well as arcade action in living, breathing 3D. And a new single game promises to combine the role-playing elements of Dungeons & Dragons, the puzzles of Adventure and the multi-user element of an MUD, all wrapped up in ultra-real graphics. Due out in 2004, The Lord Of The Rings: Middle-earth Online is an MMORPG – a massive multiplayer online role-playing game.

Played online and paid for by subscription, this is arguably the most ambitious attempt ever at a virtual rendering of the Tolkien universe. It's intriguing to wonder what Tolkien the technophobe would have thought of it all, but then you realise that he had in fact predicted it when he said that the role of fantasy is to provide "a secondary world which your mind can enter." And in his short story Leaf By Niggle, his hero gets to "paint the only truly beautiful picture in the world" and gets to walk around inside it, in an eerie nod towards such concepts as virtual reality. You might expect this from a prophetic, futuristic sci-fi writer like Aldous Huxley, but JRR Tolkien is the last author you expect to read coming over all JG Ballard. So maybe Tolkien would just have lit his pipe, picked a character and logged on. In Elvish, of course.

✦ The Religion Of Middle-earth ✦
"I NEITHER PREACH NOR TEACH" JRR TOLKIEN

There have been many attempts to characterise The Lord Of The Rings as a religious, specifically Christian, text. Yet such an attempt, ultimately, is to misread Tolkien's intentions. One reason so many people have read so many meanings into The Lord Of The Rings is that, as novelist Orson Scott Card says, "Tolkien, like most storytellers in most societies throughout history, values stories as stories, not essays in disguise. Tolkien does not want you to read his stories decoding as you go. He wants you to immerse yourself in the tale... he does not want you to start wondering if this is some sort of undoing of the Christ myth or an analogy to the way the authority-loving patriarch destroys its male children."

This is not to deny the book has many elements we can recognise as Christian. Indeed, one of the author's own letters described The Lord Of The Rings as "a fundamentally Catholic work". Tolkien's friendship with CS Lewis, author of the allegorical Narnia series of novels in which the lion Aslan is an obvious Christ figure, has led many to believe that the books are Christian works.

Yet Tolkien himself protested, at times, against that very interpretation, writing to WH Auden that, "I don't feel under any obligation to make my story fit with formalised Christian theology, though I actually intended it to be consonant with Christian thought and belief." And, reacting to complaints about the trilogy's alleged moral stance, he wrote in 1971: "I cannot understand how I should be labelled 'a believer in moral didacticism'. It is in any case the exact opposite of my procedure in *The Lord Of The Rings*." In this same letter Tolkien also avows that he never intended to preach or teach.

The books do grapple with religious issues (the contest between good and evil, the nature of evil), use religious metaphors (the journey undertaken by Frodo and his allies owes an obvious debt to the character's journey of self-discovery in John Bunyan's *Pilgrim's Progress*), and draw on Christian values, such as pity and forgiveness: Frodo asserts, at one point, that the orcs were not originally evil.

There are also Christlike figures – like the resurrected Gandalf the White – although none are as obvious as Lewis's Aslan/Christ in Narnia. Saruman, the good 'king' turned bad, can be interpreted as the good angel gone rotten, Lucifer. Gollum's 'fall' is sometimes seen as symbolising man's expulsion from the Garden of Eden. Some critics have pointed to the obvious symbolism of calling the third book The Return Of The King, a title proposed by the publisher – Tolkien originally wanted it called The War Of The Ring. The significant dates of the Christian calendar have a part to play (although it has been suggested the use of dates is coincidental): the day darkness passes and Sauron's realm crumbles is 25 March, traditionally the date of the Crucifixion, Good Friday and the day of Christ's conception – being nine months before the 25th December. And Christmas Day is the day the Fellowship set out from Rivendell.

Tolkien's Catholicism probably influenced him when he wrote the book. But not, perhaps, in the obvious way some critics have suggested. As he wrote in a letter in 1956: "Actually I am a Christian, and indeed a Roman Catholic, so that I do not expect 'history' to be anything but a 'long defeat' – though it contains (and in a legend may contain more clearly and movingly) some samples or glimpses of final victory." Such pessimism gives *The Lord Of The Rings* much of its power. The sense for much of *The Lord Of The Rings* is rather of the fragility of heroism, the power of temptation, the likelihood of betrayal and the impressive array of resources the forces of evil have at their command.

Yet you could equally argue that Middle-earth is a pre-Christian world in which good and evil battle in a manner that recalls the dualism of certain eastern religions like Zoroastrianism. Gandalf's resurrection may recall the Gospels, as Tolkien himself admitted, but he went on to add, "it is not really the same thing at all" as Christ's resurrection. As Patrick Curry points out in his book **Defending Middle-earth**, Gandalf is actually described in terms which are reminiscent of the Old English god Wodan (Odin in Norse). Curry goes on to detail the pagan roots of many other characters, too many for comfort if you would like to see The Lord Of The Rings in a purely Christian context.

If Tolkien really planned for the trilogy to be a "fundamentally Catholic" work, some things are conspicuously absent. The hobbits, for all their rural Englishness, are not particularly pious – they worship at no churches and seem to tend no tombstones or burying grounds. The dwarves do have tombstones but seem to believe in a form of reincarnation, rather than any great divine force.

As Tom Shippey says in his book JRR Tolkien: Author Of The Century, "Middle-earth is a sort of limbo, in which the characters, like unbaptised innocents or the pagan philosophers of Dante, are neither heathen nor Christian but something in between." And Frodo, ultimately, leads himself into temptation but is delivered by evil.

In short, Tolkien's blend of mythology (pagan and Christian), religion and linguistics, and the power of his imagination, has created a novel which is far too mysterious and elusive to be categorised simply as being wholly or predominantly or even, with apologies to the man himself, "fundamentally Catholic".

✦ The Politics Of Tolkien ✦

"MY POLITICAL OPINIONS LEAN MORE AND MORE TO ANARCHY (PHILOSOPHICALLY UNDERSTOOD, MEANING ABOLITION OF CONTROL, NOT WHISKERED MEN WITH BOMBS)" JRR TOLKIEN

"TOUCHING YOUR CAP TO THE SQUIRE MAY BE DAMN BAD FOR THE SQUIRE BUT IT'S DAMN GOOD FOR YOU" JRR TOLKIEN

Anarchist, conservative, ecologist, even fascist: all terms used to describe either Tolkien personally or his political creed as expressed in books like The Lord Of The Rings. The ferocity of the debate may surprise some who probably see The Hobbit and The Lord Of The Rings as essentially apolitical novels. But Tolkien's fiction has been taken up in many surprising ways. In Communist eastern Europe, his novels were regarded as underground texts – the Black Riders who came at night reminding some of the dreaded knock on the door from the secret police.

They were officially disapproved of by the Communist authorities (and owning the books is still regarded as subversive by the regime in Kazakhstan, which finds Tolkien's eco-friendly passages inflammatory) because they didn't advance the "socialist realist" view that mankind's history was a 'scientific' progress towards a Marxist classless utopia.

Circulated as samizdats – clandestinely printed tracts – Tolkien's novels seemed not to offer escapism (a charge routinely levelled at the books in the West) but an oblique commentary on the horrors and absurdities of Communist society. In the West, the idea of a land whose prosperity depends on mass slavery seemed a fantastic conceit. In the USSR, where millions were imprisoned by the Gulag and thousands died on such grandiose, yet pointless, projects as the **White Sea Canal**, the horrific vision of Mordor as an authoritarian slave-based economy was painfully pertinent. So, in the summer of 1991, when a handful of generals and Communist hardliners tried to stage a coup, members of Moscow's Tolkien Society were among those who thronged around the Parliament building, the **White House**, in Moscow with **Boris Yeltsin**.

Russian writer Maria Kamenkovich takes up the story: "It is important to note that the first complete translation [of *The Lord Of The Rings*] officially went on sale only a few days before Moscow members of the **Tolkien Society** spent all those fearful thunderstorms and rainy nights near the White House holding a defence... many people remembered Tolkien when they made barricades from trolley buses (just like hobbits from country wains)." It doesn't do to get too carried away here – the coup didn't fail because of the example set by *The Lord Of The Rings* or the opposition of a sizeable corps of members of the Tolkien Society. But as Kamenkovich says, "Tolkien never meant to describe any real events either in the past or the future, but he certainly added something to earthly events."

The obvious place to start in the controversy over the politics of *The Lord Of The Rings* is with the author. As his biographer Humphrey Carpenter puts it, "in one sense he was an old-fashioned conservative, in modern jargon right-wing, in that he honoured his monarch and his country and did not believe in the rule of the people because he believed in the end his fellow man would not benefit from it."

He also, as the quote at the start of this discussion about doffing your cap to the squire suggests, thought each member of society should know his or her station in life. Yet he was not personally snobbish, and he also claimed to believe in a kind of anarchy, or absence of control, which hardly fits with the rigid authoritarianism of the archetypal right-wing dictatorship. The Shire is not without its paternalism, but it is largely free of official authority figures – the Mayor's main job is to preside over banquets. It's also worth noting that when Tolkien's king does accede to the throne, he does so only with the people's approval.

Those who have sought to portray Tolkien (or his fiction) as fascist or racist have often struggled to come up with convincing evidence that he held those views in his life. He loathed Adolf Hitler for "ruining, perverting, misapplying and making for ever accursed, that noble northern spirit, a supreme contribution to Europe which I have ever loved and tried to present in its true light."

And, in 1938, when a German publisher asked him to declare his **Aryan** ancestry so that one of his books could be translated into German, he declared: "I do not regard the (probable) absence of Jewish blood as necessarily honourable; and I have many Jewish friends and should regret giving any colour to the notion that I subscribe to the wholly pernicious and unscientific race-doctrine."

He protested against the use of the word Nordic in relation to his book, as it smacked of the daft and dangerous theories of Hitler, "that ruddy little ignoramus". In 1944, he complained about a local newspaper article suggesting Germans should, as a race, be exterminated.

Fascism, as it developed in the 1930s and 1940s, also made something of a cult out of technological progress. Yet Tolkien's critics on the left who have often implied fascism in the *The Lord Of The Rings* have also accused him of offering an escapist, nostalgic vision of an idealised way of rural English life which never actually existed. Certainly it would be a radical critic who found evidence in The Lord Of The Rings that Tolkien was as impressed by the galvanising power of technology as Hitler or Mussolini were.

The charge of fascism against Tolkien personally or against the books is hard to substantiate – unless you are simply using "fascist" as a pejorative term, without worrying about literal or ideological accuracy.

The charge of racism is built, largely, on the incidence in the books of "swart, slant-eyed" villains who often come from the south, rather than the north (from where the tall heroes come) and the frequency with which black is a colour of terror and/or evil. Yet the use of black and white is not as clear or consistent as Tolkien's critics like to suggest – evil Saruman's sign is a **white** hand, whereas Aragorn's standard is mainly **black**. And black, as Patrick Curry points out, is associated with darkness and night, not race. As Jenny Turner says in her excellent essay 'Reasons For Liking Tolkien' in the *London Review Of Books* (you can find it at *www.lrb.co.uk/v23/n22/turn03_.html*), "those fears, those resentments, that kind of paranoia, were not a driving force in Tolkien's personality – he just wasn't much of a blame-it-all-on-the-other-bloke."

There is some justice in Andrew O'Hehir's comment on *Salon.com* that the orcs are "a northern European's paranoid caricature of races he has

Trolley-bus barricades in Moscow in the August 1991 coup were inspired by the hobbits

dimly heard about", though even he finally concludes Tolkien was "not a racist or an anti-Semite." Many critics of the book's racism focus on the clear division of good and bad tribes at the start of the book, yet, as the novel progresses, such simplicity disappears. Race does not, as critics allege, determine behaviour to the exclusion of all else. Evil infects the blond riders of Rohan, and even the hobbits themselves who, it's not often noted, seem brown-skinned rather than white. There are also interracial friendships (Gimli and Legolas) and marriages (Aragorn and Arwen).

Tolkien didn't warn readers against any racial interpretation of his work – he may not have seen any need to – but neither did he build into *The Lord Of The Rings* any intellectual framework which would justify racism. He may have drawn on some of the same mythological roots as Hitler's favourite composer, Richard Wagner, but that doesn't mean he shared the world view of the composer or the dictator.

In 1969 the critic **Catherine Stimpson** accused Tolkien of class snobbery. As we have seen, he certainly believed in classes but this isn't the same as saying he's a snob about social class. The true heroes of *The Lord Of The Rings* are hobbits, Tolkien's interpretation of the rural people he knew in his day and the characters he most identified with. If Stimpson were right, the baddies would usually sound like characters from *EastEnders*, when actually the most obviously working-class accent belongs to the peasant hero (some would say the true hero) Sam Gamgee, while many of the villains, Smaug and Saruman to name two, speak the Queen's English.

✦ And Finally... ✦

"IT MUST BE EMPHASISED THAT THIS PROCESS OF INVENTION WAS/IS A PRIVATE ENTERPRISE UNDERTAKEN TO GIVE PLEASURE TO MYSELF BY GIVING EXPRESSION TO MY LINGUISTIC 'AESTHETIC' OR TASTE AND ITS FLUCTUATIONS" **JRR TOLKIEN**

JRR Tolkien deliberately didn't make life easy for his readers, admirers or critics. He created a fictional universe realised in immense detail and with great clarity, backed this up with the usual apparatus of an academic scholar – fiendishly detailed and annotated appendices and the like, which seemed, as much as the books themselves, to be a life's work for the author – and then left us with a work which seems to **defy definitive interpretation** but allows almost anyone – greens, hippies, hackers, Christian theologians, computer-game inventors, progressive-rock musicians of the 1970s, Russian dissidents in the Communist era – to find in it what they will.

The author himself might, if he were still alive, regard all this controversy as proof that he had, in some sense, succeeded. The fact that we are still arguing about the symbolism, the colours and the subtexts of The Lord Of The Rings is in itself a mark of the book's greatness.

What Tolkien loved most in literature was something Shippey calls "glamour – that shimmer of suggestion that never became clear sight but always hints at something deeper further on." He admired this quality especially in **Beowulf**, what Turner in the *London Review Of Books* calls a "broken text" he translated and proceeded to study for much of his life.

In *The Lord Of The Rings* he has deliberately produced his own broken text, full of fragmented layers which suggest age, depth and mystery and textual variants. And he would probably be very cheered to find that so many of us are scrambling around among the fragments he left us. More than half a century since it was first published, Tolkien's "private enterprise" still holds millions in its thrall.

"All dead and all rotten, elves
and men and orcses"

Gollum